Making the grade

A study programme for adult students

(£7.95)   £5⁼

Making the grade

A study programme for adult students

Volume II   *Thinking and writing*

Bill Jones and **Roy Johnson**

Manchester University Press
Manchester and New York
Distributed exclusively in the USA and Canada by St. Martin's Press

Published by Manchester University Press
Oxford Road, Manchester M13 9PL, UK
and Room 400, 175 Fifth Avenue,
New York, NY 10010, USA

Distributed exclusively in the USA and Canada
by St. Martin's Press, Inc.,
175 Fifth Avenue, New York, NY 10010, USA

British Library cataloguing in publication data
Jones, Bill
    Making the grade : a study programme for adult students.
    Vol. 2. Thinking and writing
    1. English language. Composition
    I. Title II. Johnson, Roy
    808.042

Library of Congress cataloging in publication data
Jones, Bill, 1946–
    Making the grade : a study programme for adult students / Bill
    Jones and Roy Johnson.
        p. cm.
    Contents: v. 1. Reading and learning — v. 2. Thinking and
    writing.
        ISBN 0-7190-3177-X (v. 1). — ISBN 0-7190-3178-8 (pbk. : v. 1). —
    ISBN 0-7190-3179-6 (v. 2). — ISBN 0-7190-3180-X (pbk. : v. 2)
        1. Study, Method of.   2. Reading (Adult education)   3. English
    language—Rhetoric—Study and teaching.   4. Distance education.
    I. Johnson, Roy, 1939– . II. Title.
    LC5225.M47J66   1990
    374—dc20   89-77465

ISBN 0 7190 3179 6 *hardback*
       0 7190 3180 X *paperback*

Photoset in Linotron Palatino
Northern Phototypesetting Co Ltd, Bolton

Printed in Great Britain
by Dotesios Limited, Trowbridge

Contents

Introduction

Sophocles wrote that 'A man, though wise, should never be ashamed of learning more and must unbend his mind' (*Antigone*). We assume most readers of Volume II will have already worked through Volume I and, although 'wise', are keen to 'unbend their minds' in order to learn more.

Volume I was concerned with
● **orientation:** helping you to feel at ease with the adult student role
● **verbal communication:** in small groups and other situations in which you might be called upon to make a presentation
● **assimilating information and ideas:** through active listening, reading and note-taking

Volume II takes the study process squarely into the area of written work but it also plays considerable attention to *clear thinking* – This is dealt with directly in Chapter 4 but Chapter 1 on understanding the question and Chapters 2 and 3 on essay planning are also relevant to this issue. To write clearly and produce good logical structures for your essays you need to think clearly. The first three chapters have a second major objective: to develop your skills in *writing*. Detailed elements of writing are addressed in Chapter 5 on grammar and punctuation and Chapter 6 on sentences and paragraphs. The short Chapter 7 is designed for revision purposes to pull your thoughts together on the organisation, thinking and writing processes required in the production of high-quality written work.

Chapter 8 concentrates upon the appreciation of written style. This is not an essential requirement of good essay-writing but we feel that those people who are highly sensitive to and take pleasure in words and their nuances of meaning are those who most often produce the highest quality work.

Chapter 9 tries to demystify examinations; occasions where written ability has to be complemented by good organisation, excellent preparation and the correct mental attitude. Volume II concludes with Chapter 10 on opportunities for employment, further education and the key question of access into the higher education system.

1 *Understanding the question*

By nature all men are alike, but by education widely different   *Chinese proverb*

Contents

Introduction

Many students, when faced with an essay or examination question, either feel bewildered, or fail to read it carefully because they fear the task before them. Others spot one or two words which they recognise and start writing immediately – only to find some time afterwards that they have not answered the question properly. *Failure to answer the question* is far and away the most common failing in student essays and yet, as Chapter 9 in Volume I illustrated, it is the most important single essay requirement. This problem is so important that we have devoted a whole chapter to it. This will help you to read questions closely and carefully, then arrive at an understanding of what is required. The essence of this understanding lies in a careful consideration of *exactly what it is you have been asked to do*. You will have to pay very close attention to the terms used in the question and to any instructions contained within it. The questions, for example, may ask you to comment on a proposition, prove a case, analyse a statement, or compare and contrast two elements of a topic. In all cases your success will start from a clear understanding of what the question is *about*, and what its *instruction* to you is.

Very often a question will contain some principal idea or concept which it is asking you to discuss, but many students confuse this with the notion that questions contain hidden meanings which have been concealed in order to trick or trap them in some way. This chapter will help you to understand what these principal ideas or concepts are, and perhaps dispel the impression that questions are set as some kind of fiendishly tricky puzzle designed to baffle and frustrate you.

We might begin this process straight away by considering the *purpose* of the question.

What are questions for?   **1**

This may seem a somewhat ridiculous question itself! Obviously essay and examination questions are meant as a test of some kind. But careful consideration of their purpose by the student may help to clear away some of the mystery and fears which surround them.

---

15 minutes   Write down as many reasons you can think of why an essay or examination question is posed. What is its purpose?   **STOP**

Many answers to the question are possible, depending on the subject you are studying, but you might have listed some of the following (which are given along with some typical questions).   *Discussion*

- to prove that you know the facts of a topic ('What were the causes of the Russian Revolution?')
- to show that you can discuss an opinion (' "Children should be seen and not heard." Is this still true today?')
- to demonstrate that you can argue a case, especially an apparently difficult one ('Defend the right to tell lies')
- to give you an opportunity to present your own opinions or ideas ('How would you solve the problems of mass unemployment?')
- to show that you can evaluate the validity of a case or statement ('Lord Acton claimed that "Power tends to corrupt and absolute power corrupts absolutely." How far is this true?')
- to show that you can make an analysis ('Examine the significance of Iago's role in *Othello*')

Many variations of these answers are possible, but what they all have in common is that they indicate the question is designed to *give students an opportunity* to show what they can do: that they can make a case, argue with a proposition, or show that they have successfully absorbed a body of knowledge. The purpose then is not to trick you or expose ignorance or incompetence but quite the reverse.

Think of it from the tutor's point of view. They have no reason to be sadistic or deceitful. Their job is to pass on knowledge and teach skills, then make some check that the student is learning. The essay or examination question is just one way of doing this. It may be true that some tutors set questions which are lengthy or complex, but if you become used to the basic principles of understanding and answering the questions you will be less worried or thrown off course by these complexities.

So, stage one in this process is to take *a positive attitude* towards the question. Regard it as your chance to show what you know and can do. Remember that most questions will be set on the subject you will have been studying and your task will be to relate your knowledge to the question. In order to do this, you will need to uncover or understand the principal issue, idea, or concept which the question is asking you to discuss. This brings us to stage two.

2 *The principal issue or concept*

Let's take our imaginary questions as examples to work with. These were the six questions.
(a) 'What were the causes of the Russian Revolution?
(b) 'Defend the right to tell lies.'
(c) ' "Children should be seen but not heard." Is this still true today?'
(d) 'How would you solve the problem of mass unemployment?'
(e) 'Lord Acton claimed that "Power tends to corrupt and absolute power corrupts absolutely." How far is this true?'
(f) 'Examine the significance of Iago's role in *Othello*.'
Make a few rough notes on what you think is the essential purpose of each question. What is it asking you to do? What is the *essence* of the question? What main issue is it asking you to deal with? What would you need to do in order to produce a satisfactory answer?

You do not need to know anything about the subjects they deal with. Just try to think through what you would *need* to know and demonstrate. The questions are roughly in increasing order of complexity or difficulty.

30 minutes   **STOP**

Here are my own observations. Compare them with your own to *Discussion*
see if you are on the right lines. Don't worry about any minor
differences.

(a) 'What were the causes of the Russian Revolution?'
    Obviously this is a straightforward question to do with the
    study of history. There might be slight differences of opinion
    regarding the relative importance of the many causes, but
    you are being asked to show that you know what they are.
    They might be: corruption in the Czarist regime, Russian
    losses in the First World War, the rising dissatisfactions of
    the proletariat, the strength of the revolutionary Bolshevik
    Party, and so on. You would discuss each of these 'causes' in
    turn and show how they contributed to the revolution. The
    purpose of such a question is to give you an opportunity to
    show that you have absorbed a body of knowledge

(b) 'Defend the right to tell lies.'
    The subject here is philosophical. This question is asking you
    to use your imagination and look at things from an unusual
    point of view. Most people believe that lying is always
    wrong, but you are being asked to think of circumstances in
    which it would be preferable to telling the truth. If, for
    example, someone was dying from an incurable disease, the
    doctor could argue that a lie giving them false hope is a more
    merciful treatment than the truth. Obviously these involve
    exceptional circumstances, and you may have to stray
    beyond what you yourself regard as desirable. This is not
    important (remember you can always say 'Some people
    would argue that . . .'). The important thing is that you
    make out a case – that is, you give examples and draw up
    some general statement, with all the necessary limitations,
    which defends the right.

(c) ' "Children should be seen and not heard." Is this still true
    today?'
    This gives you a Victorian notion of child-rearing to discuss
    and do what you will with. You would obviously need to
    consider what the original statement meant and implied –
    strict control of children, the deferment of expressing their
    wishes until they become adult, and so on. Then you are
    being asked to say if such attitudes are appropriate today.
    Perhaps we now have different ideas about children and
    their need for free expression. On the other hand, more
    traditionally minded people could argue that tolerance and
    individual liberties have gone too far, and might well be
    moderated by some return to older values of the kind
    suggested by the statement. Alternatively, you might wish

5

to argue for some mixture of the two. The principal issue here then is the set of attitudes expressed in the statement. You would need to show that you understood what they implied and then consider them in the light of contemporary society and your own personal beliefs.

(d) 'How would you solve the problems of mass unemployment?'

Obviously a difficult question and equally, not one for which there is a 'correct' answer. You would need to show that you could intelligently discuss the central economic and political issues which surround this question. And although you are being asked for 'your' solution, you would be wrong to put forward, extreme, or impractical suggestions. It would be far better to show that you appreciate the links between government policies, industrial decline, financing, and the conflict between capital and labour – rather than come up with some fanciful 'solution'. Your answer would depend upon your subject – political, science, economics, economic history – but the main issues here are the factors affecting unemployment. You are being asked to show that you can discuss them rather than come up with a possible solution to the problem.

(e) 'Lord Acton claimed that "Power tends to corrupt and absolute power corrupts absolutely." How far is this true?'

This question is similar to the last two in that you are being given a proposition to which you are being invited to respond. You need to be clear, first of all, what 'power', 'corrupt' and 'absolutely' mean in this context, and you would be well advised to give sympathetic consideration to such a famous statement, even if you went on to disagree with it. The main issue is clearly the effect which power has on the character of its holder. You would need to consider several examples (Nero, Napoleon, Hitler), no matter what line you took in your answer. Again, the question doesn't ask you to come up with a yes or no answer. It asks *'how far'* the proposition is true. So relatively subtle discrimination is required. You may need to say that certain *kinds* of power (political, economic) corrupt more than others – or do so in special circumstances.

(f) 'Examine the significance of Iago's role in *Othello*.'

This topic is particular to the study of literature, but even if you haven't read *Othello* you can probably guess that the question is asking you to demonstrate and evaluate ('examine') Iago's connections with the other characters and the action of the play. You would need to show that you could single out this one character and show his relative importance to the fundamental subject and themes of the play. You would need to focus your attention onto Iago whilst at the

6

same time discussing his relation to the rest of the play's substance. This question is asking you to make an analysis of one thing (the character, Iago) in relation to a larger, more complex one (*Othello*, the play as a whole).

I hope you have grasped the basic idea. Try to approach every question with a common-sense appraisal of what it wants. A question such as ' "God is dead." Discuss,' does not require an account of Christ's descent from the cross, or his ascent into heaven: it is obviously inviting you to consider the proposition that religious belief has, in general, declined.

So stage two, understanding the key issue or the idea behind the question, should prevent you from going wildly astray. It will help you to focus your attention on what is required. And if you are not quite sure, you can bring into play the analysis of key terms which we will call stage three.

But before that there are three further suggestions we can make to help you understand the question – two dos and one don't.
1 DO – write down the question.
2 DO – paraphrase the question.
3 DON'T – rely too much on dictionary definitions.

1 *Write down the question* – and check that you have done so accurately. You may think that this is an unnecessary suggestion, but many students discover that their essays go badly wrong because they have not read the question properly (see Section 5). Write the question at the head of the paper on which you will make your notes and on your outline plan (see Chapters 2 and 3) and *always* write it down at the head of your essay.
Even missing the odd 'small' word out of an essay question can make all the difference. For instance, if the question reads:
' "Sex and violence shown on television are not the cause of declining standards in public behaviour." Refute this view.'
and you were to write down:
"Sex and violence shown on television are the cause of declining standards in public behaviour." Refute this view.'
you would be answering exactly the opposite to the question set. Another sloppy habit which some students adopt (which almost always costs them marks) is to just write down an abbreviated form of the question:
'Sex and violence on TV.'
In doing this they lose the precision of the full question which is asking for a refutation of one particular opinion about their effect.

At the risk of being boring, I am going to emphasise this point one last time.
WRITE DOWN THE QUESTION CLEARLY AND ACCURATELY AS SOON AS YOU BEGIN TO CONSIDER IT. WRITE IT ON YOUR NOTES FOR THE ESSAY, ON YOUR PLAN, ON YOUR DRAFT ESSAY, AND ON THE FINAL ESSAY ITSELF.
Some students write it in large letters on a card which they place in front of them on their desk *throughout* the period of essay-writing – you might try this yourself.

2 *Paraphrase the question* – that is, 'translate' it into your own words to demonstrate that you understand it. In offering this suggestion we are conscious that students working alone will have no way of checking if their paraphrase is accurate or not. If it is at all possible you should check it with somebody else, preferably a tutor. But if this is not possible remember that your paraphrase should aim to retain all the accuracy and precision of the original, not to lose any of its sense or subtleties, and to represent its spirit or purpose.
Thus, to take one of our earlier examples,
　　'Defend the right to tell lies'
is *not* well paraphrased thus:
　　'Is lying a good thing?'

Why is the above not a good paraphrase?

STOP **5 minutes**

Discussion There are two good reasons why this is *not* a good paraphrase. First, it creates an open-ended question – 'Is it a good thing, or is it not?' and (this is the other side of the same coin), it removes the specific instruction of the original which asks you to *defend* one particular view on lying. Second, it removes the important qualifier of the *right* to lie (that is, *if necessary* – not as a general practice).
A much better paraphrase would be
'When is lying justified?'
or 'Give arguments for the justification of lying in certain circumstances.'
And don't imagine that a one-for-one replacement of the words will be sufficient if the spirit of the question is lost. To go back to the example I have just mentioned, ' "God is Dead." Discuss' cannot be paraphrased thus:
' "Our Heavenly Father has died." Discuss'
without being slightly ridiculous. You *must* make the effort to imagine what the question really wants to discuss. Thus:

' "The Spirit of Christianity is no longer alive." Discuss', is
much better (if longer).

3 *Don't rely upon dictionary definitions*
   Many students try to solve the problems of 'interpretation' by
   resorting to 'dictionary definitions' of key terms. This is one of
   the rare cases where use of a dictionary is *not* necessarily a good
   idea. If the dictionary is small it will only give a simplistic
   explanation of the key term, and if it is a large one it will
   probably include several subtly different meanings for the term
   – from amongst which the student still has the problem of
   choosing. Most students who resort to this measure give the
   impression that they are hoping the 'definition' will save them
   having to do the work of thinking about the question.
   Here is a typical example:
       'It is often said that too much of our life is taken up with
       education. Do you agree?'
The student reaches for his dictionary and notes that 'education'
means 'the process of nourishing or rearing' and might well begin
to write an essay on looking after children.
Alternatively, he might find 'a process by which we learn' and
feel quite baffled when applying this to the question – since most
people would presumably think it a good thing that we *learn*
throughout our lives. How *could* there be too much time spent
learning?!
In both these cases the student has been either naive or perverse –
or both – since from a straightforward, common-sense reading of
the question it should be plain that you are being asked about
schooling and academic training. And even if you are forced to
look up one of the key terms, do not include the result of your
search in the essay. Nothing looks quite so amateurish (in the
worst sense) and ponderous as an essay which begins 'The dictionary definition of "education" is . . .'.

But for a fuller understanding of the question it may be necessary
to go into more detail concerning the terms in which it is
expressed. The two most important aspects of this will be covered
in the next two sections. These are the *key terms* in the question
and the *instructions* which are commonly attached to them.

Key terms   3

Essay and examination questions often come in the form of a
statement followed by an instruction:

' "Socialism offers the chance of a more just society than capitalism." Discuss.'
or sometimes the two are blended together into one sentence:
'Discuss the idea that socialism offers the chance of a more just society than capitalism.'
Whatever form they take, they can usually be boiled down to these essentials – a *statement* and an *instruction*. The instruction here is 'Discuss.' In our earlier examples:
'Defend the right to tell lies.'
'Examine the significance of Iago's role in *Othello*.'
the instruction words were 'Defend' and 'Examine'. We will be dealing with these terms in a moment (Section 4).
What we will examine first are the key terms – that is, the most important elements in the statement which it is essential that you understand and deal with in your answer.

In our statement
'Socialism offers the chance of a more just society than capitalism'
which do you think are the key terms?
No more than a few moments thought should be necessary to realise that 'socialism' and 'capitalism' are the most obviously key terms here. It would not be possible to answer this question unless you understood quite clearly what was meant by them.
Here are three more simple examples. You don't need to know anything about the subject. Just identify the key terms.
(a) 'In what sense is Dr Aziz the hero of *A Passage to India*?'
(b) 'To what extent was Clement Atlee a successful politican?'
(c) 'Computers will revolutionise society in years to come.' Discuss.

STOP **5 minutes**

Discussion (a) 'Hero' is a key term here. You would need to know what was meant: most significant character? character who performs most important actions? character to whom most happens? 'Hero' is a literary concept, and you would need to be quite clear about its meaning.
(b) 'Successful politician' is the key term here. Is a successful politician someone who manages to implement important measures of policy which benefit the country? Or someone who survives the struggles of political life and lives to be well known? Your essay would depend upon which of these concepts (or some other) you believed in. And the 'key' element might be further reduced to 'successful'. After all, we know he was a politician: but in whose terms was he successful – his own? the country's? his party's?

10

(c)   'Revolutionise society' is the key term here. And if we accept that 'society' means people and their organisations in general this leaves 'revolutionise' as the centrally key term. It could mean that: Computers will cause things to be done in new ways. They will bring about such radical changes that society will break apart.

Again your response to the question will depend upon your understanding of this term.

You might have noticed that these questions often include other elements which are not quite so important as the key terms but which might affect your answers to the questions. For instance, to go back to our example:

'Discuss the idea that socialism offers the chance of a more just society than capitalism.'

'Offers the chance' and 'more just society' seem to be parts of the statement which *qualify* its main elements (the key terms). 'Offers the chance' qualifies 'socialism' by saying that it won't or can't guarantee a more just society, but that the possibilities will be greater than under capitalism. And similarly 'more just society' qualifies 'capitalism' by suggesting that under it there exist injustices in society.

In our other examples the phrase 'in what sense' and 'to what extent' are qualifying phrases. They are an indication that there may not be hard and fast answers to the question, but that it is a matter of degree or personal judgement.

Now here is a more complex example from the study of literature which combines statement, instruction, key terms, *and* qualifying statements:

' "Human beings at odds with their society or their environment." To what extent is this a dominant theme in the twentieth-century novel?'

See if you can identify first of all (a) the statement and instruction, then (b) the key terms and qualifying statements in this question. You do not need to be a student of literature to complete the exercise. Just identify the four different parts.

---

10 minutes   **STOP**

(a)   The statement is obviously that contained within quotation   *Discussion*
marks ('Human beings . . .') – but where is the instruction?
There doesn't appear to be one. But in fact the following
question ('To what extent . . .?') carries the implication that
in answering you will *discuss* the statement. When a question
does not have an explicit instruction ('Do animals have
rights?') you can take it that you are being invited to discuss
the proposition in whatever manner you think most
appropriate.

(b) 'Human beings' and 'society' or 'environment' are the key terms in the statement, and 'at odds' is the qualifyer here. Together they create the notion which might be paraphrased (expressed in other words) as 'man in conflict with the world'. In the question that follows 'the twentieth-century novel' is obviously the subject being studied, so the key word is 'a dominant theme' and the qualifyer our old friend 'to what extent'. That is, the question is suggesting that 'man at odds with the world' crops up as an important issue (dominant theme) in many twentieth century works, and invites you to discuss to what extent this is true. You could argue that it is true, only partly true, or even untrue depending upon your own experience and opinion.

A word of warning here. Tutors who set these questions are unlikely to offer such statements for discussion unless there is some truth in them. It would be foolish to do otherwise. The student, therefore, should be cautious about taking a dismissively criticial attitude unless plenty of evidence can be offered in support of such an approach.

4 *Instructions*

We come now to those terms which are most commonly used to instruct the student in dealing with a proposition – 'discuss', 'compare', 'contrast', and suchlike. The exact meaning of these terms will vary very slightly depending upon the subject being studied, but the following will give you some idea of what they mean in general use for essay examination questions. (Adapted from Maddox, *How to Study*, Pan, pp. 119–20.)

COMPARE   Look for similarities *and* differences between two or more things.

CONTRAST   Deliberately single out and emphasise the differences between two or more things.

CRITICISE   Give your judgement about a statement or body of work; explore its implications, discussing the evidence available.

DEFINE   Set down the precise meaning of something. Take note of multiple meanings if they exist.

DESCRIBE   Give a detailed account of.

DISCUSS   Investigate and examine by argument. Explore implications. Debate the case and possibly consider alternatives.

EVALUATE   Make an appraisal of the worth of something, in the light of its truth or utility.

EXPLAIN   Make plain, account for.
ILLUSTRATE   Make clear and explicit by the use of concrete examples.
JUSTIFY   Show adequate grounds for decisions or conclusions. Answer the main objections likely to be made against them.
OUTLINE   Give the main features or general principles of a subject, omitting minor details and emphasising structure or arrangement.
RELATE   (a) Show how things are connected, how they affect each other, or
             (b) tell the story of.
REVIEW   Make a survey of, examining the subject critically.
STATE   Present in brief, clear form.
SUMMARISE   Give a concise account of the main points of a matter, omitting details and examples.
TRACE   Follow the development or history of a topic from some point of origin.

You will have to get used to seeing these terms and thinking (checking) carefully what they mean in relation to the rest of the question. And even when you have more experience, do not become blasé or inattentive. Even experienced students sometimes forget the difference between 'contrast' and 'compare'.
Now let's look at some other very common mistakes or weaknesses connected with understanding the question.

Common problems and mistakes   5

As I mentioned in my introduction, the art of understanding the question comes from paying very close attention to what is being asked, reading the terms in which it is posed as carefully as possible, and making a careful note of any instructions you are given. Conversely, most of the problems and mistakes which arise in answering questions arise from *not* doing so.
The commonest errors are
(a)   Answering the *wrong* question.
(b)   Misunderstanding the point of what is being asked for.
(c)   Failing to see the emphasis of the question.
(d)   Misreading the instructions.

You can learn valuable lessons from seeing what goes wrong. Let's inspect two or three examples to illustrate the point.

(a) **Answering the *wrong* question**

This can come about for a number of reasons. Students in a rush or being inattentive may give one quick glance at a question, then start answering it. Later on (when they get their essay back, or are half-way through an examination answer) they realise that they have *misread* the question. They may actually *not have seen* an important term in the question. Or they may have answered on a different topic from the one stated. You might think it would be difficult to answer the *wrong* question, but here's how easy it can be.

Let us say the question is

'Do you think that the Arts make any significant contribution to the economy?'

The student correctly spots that the key terms here are 'Arts' and 'economy'. Then, realising that a great deal of controversy surrounds the issue of governments subsidising the Arts with public money, he writes an essay on that topic – which turns out to be almost the opposite of what is being asked. The question concerns the Arts and their contribution *to* the economy – that is, do they *generate* wealth, *not* do they deserve to be subsidised.

On the other hand, the question could be

'Which eighteenth-century political figure do you think has had the greatest impact on European history?'

The student writes a splendid essay on Karl Marx and his influence on the development of socialism – then feels disappointed and foolish when the tutor points out that Marx lived in the *nineteenth century* not the eighteenth.

Here is another very common example:

'What is the case against banning smoking in public places?'

Another topical and controversial issue. The student knows the issues involved and produces an essay which mentions them – damage to health, inconvenience to non-smokers, the right of the individual to unpolluted airspace, and so on. But this is not what was asked for. He has not paid attention to the word 'against' in the question. The case 'against banning' (a sort of hidden double-negative) required that he discuss the arguments which *oppose* any such ban – that is, he should make the case for retaining the right to smoke in public places. The mistake is easily made.

(b) **Misunderstanding the point being asked for**

Let us say the question is:

'Discuss the importance of Newton as a mathematician and scientist.'

Again, it would not be at all unusual for a student essay to give an enthusiastic account of Newton's theories, the falling apple and gravity, his work on optics, astronomy, and his development of calculus. But if you read the question closely you will see that this is *not* what it asks for. It requires that you discuss the *importance* of his work, not that you give an account of it. What his work *was* can be taken as a starting point: your task is to say how important it was. *Very* important? If so, in relation to who else? Or *not* so important? – and so on.

(c) **Failing to see the emphasis of the question**

'Discuss the influence of Ernest Hemingway on the work of Scott Fitzgerald.'

The student has been an enthusiastic reader of Scott Fitzgerald's novels and the question *does* include the seductive phrase 'the work of Scott Fitzgerald'. He therefore produces an essay giving an extensive account of his qualities and achievement and perhaps mentions that the two writers were friends. But the question asks for the *'influence of Ernest Hemingway'* as its main subject. The essay would have to keep this emphasis in mind – even whilst discussing Fitzgerald's work. This is a fairly advanced question, but it illustrates the problem well. You must reflect in your essay the emphasis the question asks for. This mistake often occurs when enthusiasm for one topic blinds us to the fact that some similar or associated but different topic is in question. (Incidentally, it would be just as easy to make the same mistake the other way round here – writing primarily on the work of Hemingway and mentioning very much as a minor issue that it influenced Fitzgerald.)

(d) **Misreading the instructions**

No matter how clearly the question is expressed, there always seem to be some students who fail to follow its instructions.

' "An artist can produce his greatest work even under the constraints of patronage." Discuss this statement in relation to EITHER Michaelangelo or Bernini.'

Even capital letters or italics will not stop some students writing on *both* artists here, rather than just *one*, which is what the question asks for.

Always watch out for the either/or, and pay close attention to the number of examples the question asks you to deal with.

Here is a more complex example which combines both types of instruction.

'Explain the reasons why any two or more Romantic writers were led to embrace a position of EITHER political conservatism OR traditional Christian morality.'

This is not the same kind of either/or, is it? First, the question asks for *two or more* examples to be discussed. It would be a bad mistake here to be so carried away in discussing *one* example that a second or third were forgotten. And then the either/or are complementary rather than excluding choices. Your (minimum) two examples can be of 'political conservatism' or 'traditional Christian morality' – or they can both be the same.

Let us now recap on the main elements in understanding the question.

1 *The principal issue or concept behind it*

You should have some idea of the main ideas the question asks you to deal with. These will normally arise out of your study of a specific subject, but even in the case of general questions you should make an effort to 'think through' the question and be in tune with what it requests.

2 *Key terms*

You should be able to identify the most important elements in the question, which are often lodged in a particular word or expression. These contain the essence of the problem the question wants you to deal with.

3 *Instructions*

These are the formal directions on what you are to do with the question or the statement it makes. You should aim to stay within the constraint they put on you and follow their directions as closely as possible.

6   *Conclusion and summary*

Now let's go back over the topics considered in this chapter. We might seem to be making a lot of fuss over what often appears straightforward questions, but in our experience many students have difficulties at this stage of essay-writing. Questions may be brief, but understanding them can be a matter of sophisticated interpretation.

In fact that was the first point of this Chapter. Your first task on approaching a question should be an attempt to understand *sympathetically* what it is getting at. Think carefully about the topic it is addressing, and try to get an overall perspective on it.

We suggested that you might understand better what questions are getting at by asking yourself what they are *for*. The answer to this will vary according to the subject you are studying, but in general they will be asking you to demonstrate your knowledge of a topic, asking you to discuss it intelligently, or perhaps compare a number of different opinions about it. We suggested that other than view a question as a hostile 'test' you might view it as an invitation to demonstrate your ability. Trying to regard it in such a positive light may help you overcome a fear of having your ideas tested.

Next we went on to the processes of analysis which we can bring to the task of understanding a question. The most important of these is identifying the principal issue or concept behind the question. What is the central topic it is concerned with? What is it most essentially *about?* This is where the *sympathetic* understanding is necessary. Practice and experience will help you with this, but in order to acquire the experience we then suggested three detailed staged of analysis which would help 'break down' the question into its component parts.

The first of these, which we stressed very heavily, was a suggestion that you always write the question down. Even check that you have done so accurately. Understanding the question requires that you are acquainted with its terms. Another exercise which students may find useful is a paraphrase – restating the question in your own words. (You should, if you can, have a tutor check on the accuracy of your attempt.)

The next stage is a more detailed examination of the terms used in the question. There will usually be one or two examples of what we called 'key terms'. These may be to do with either the ideas or concepts within the subject, or they may be what we called 'instruction' terms. Key terms concerned with the subject will orient you to the particular topic the question wishes you to discuss. Instruction terms are those commonly used terms ('compare', 'discuss', 'contrast') which tell you how you must approach the topic under consideration – that is, what you must do *with* it.

All of this instruction so far was rather theoretical. Understanding exactly what a question is asking for is something which comes more easily with practice. But we finished the chapter by pointing to some of the most common errors in 'Understanding the question'. If you can keep these in mind during your studies, you may save yourself from one or two mistakes. But don't be too hard on yourself. Almost all of us at some time or another misread or misunderstand a question, or write a good answer but to the wrong question. If you do this, try to understand where you went wrong, and then – *learn from your mistake.* It will probably stop you from ever making it again!

Self-assessment exercises

Exercise 1
Without looking back over this chapter, list the points we have made on understanding the question.

Exercise 2
Here are some fairly straightforward questions you can use as exercises to check that you have understood what we have been

getting at in this chapter. We have stuck to general social and moral questions since at this stage we assume you are not studying any subject in particular. What you should try to identify in each case is

(a) The principal idea or concept it is asking you to discuss or deal with.

(b) The key terms in the question.

(c) Any instruction you are given.

(d) What you would need to *do* to answer the question successfully – that is, what areas you would need to cover or what issues you would need to discuss.

You might also use these questions as a convenient exercise in paraphrasing. I will be offering my own paraphrases against which you can check yours.

1 'Blood sports should be banned.' Discuss.

2 Discuss the case for and against free public transport in cities.

3 'A woman's place is in the home.' Is this still true?

4 Justify the case for retaining the death penalty.

5 'A woman should have the right to abortion on demand.' Do you agree?

6 Refute the case against euthanasia.

7 The average person watches 24 hours' television per week. Is this too much?

Exercise 3

Find as many synonyms as you can for the following words

(a) Fastidious   (e) Penury

(b) Fatuous   (f) Refuge

(c) Increment   (g) Tasty

(d) Notorious   (h) Vulgar

Planning essays 1: **2**
The 'for and against' essay

What is written without effort is in general read without pleasure *Samuel Johnson*

Contents

1 The importance of writing essays
2 Getting your points into perspective
3 The 'for and against' essay
4 Strategy II essays
5 The comparative 'for and against' essay
6 Introductions and conclusions
  Self-assessment exercises

The importance of writing essays 1

You might well be thinking that the emphasis upon essay-writing in this course is excessive.

'After all,' you might ask, 'how often are you asked to write an essay at work or in other everyday aspects of life?'

'What direct relevance', you might also ask, 'has the essay outside the closed world of education?'

The answers to these two questions are respectively 'hardly ever' and 'not much'. But don't be satisfied with this superficial treatment. Spend a few minutes thinking about this similar but wider question: 'What point is there in learning to write essays?'

---

5 minutes **STOP**

When you think about it carefully such a skill has important *direct* *Discussion* utility within the world of education and a number of very important *indirect* applications in various other walks of life.

1 It is the standard form of assessed work in education. This is true of most of the humanities and social sciences but the ability

19

to write well is a considerable advantage in science subjects too.

2 Good writing exhibits the mastery of a number of important written and intellectual skills (discussed at greater length below).

3 Essay-writing is a transferable skill; if you are good at it you will almost certainly have no difficulty in writing clear, well struc-tured reports, papers or business letters. Any good piece of analytical writing – journalism, historical writing, literary criticism – follows the same basic rules of structure, grammar and clarity.

The word 'essay' means 'an attempt': look upon essays then as 'practice' forms of writing. Almost certainly they are overused in our educational system as a means of acquiring and displaying competence in an academic subject, often at the expense of verbal and other skills, but this is not to deny the supreme usefulness of being able to write high-quality academic essays.

The required essay lengths vary considerably but they usually fall within the range of 1,000–3,000 words (4–12 A4 sized pages). Most tutors don't worry too much if you overshoot their word limit by a little but occasionally their limit is intended as a disci-pline to encourage concision and good planning. You may have noticed that I used the word 'analytical' a few sentences ago. This is because most academic writing is of this type: you are usually required to explain how and why things happen or have hap-pened, or perhaps to relate observed behaviour to different kinds of theories. The scope for the 'creative' or 'imaginative' essay which tells a story or draws upon personal experience is strictly limited in education (perhaps unfortunately so) but this is not to say that imagination or creative use of language is not relevant to essay-writing, as you will discover in Chapter 8 on written style.

The skills needed to write a good essay.   In Chapter 9 of Volume I, we saw how a good essay was supposed to read but now I want to ask you what *particular skills* are needed to produce one.

STOP   5–10 minutes

To write a good essay you need, amongst other things, to be able to:

1 Interpret the question precisely. Each question is unique and requires a tailor-made answer: in Chapter 1 you learnt and practised certain techniques to help you understand them.

2 Extract the relevant information from books, articles and other sources: Chapter 6, Volume I was designed to help you do this.

3 Have a good sense of structure. A good essay, as we all know, has a beginning, a middle and an end. The best essays give an impression of 'completeness': the very best a sense of artistic

wholeness. They have some of the qualities of a work of art. This chapter and the next will deal with structure.

4 Identify all the major aspects of a particular subject or problem. Chapter 1 dealt with this to some extent and we will return to this problem in this chapter.

5 Think clearly. Your essay must be logical and well reasoned: Chapter 4 will help you improve the quality of your thinking.

6 Be able to write good English. To write good sentences in well-structured paragraphs which lead on smoothly one from the other, all in an interesting lively style, is to be in possession of a sophisticated form of communication. Chapters 5, 6 and 8 deal with different aspects of this skill.

I hope I have established, convincingly, that essay-writing is not just a skill on its own but a bundle of them, all valuable in themselves and useful in many aspects of life outside education. Now I want to illustrate and practice the important skill of getting your points into perspective.

Getting your points into perspective   2

When planning an essay it is particularly important to separate the major points from the supporting or subsidiary ones: in other words, to see the wood from the trees. You have already encountered this problem to some extent in the chapters on note-taking and generating ideas but as this is so important I am offering a little extra practice below in the form of two exercises: one drawn from everyday life and the other from recent history.

Below are nine reasons why a particular car has a poor second-hand value. Can you organise them into suitable categories which indicate:

(a)   the major points
(b)   the secondary points
(c)   the tertiary points

1 No bulb in rear passenger side lamp
2 Uncomfortable seats
3 Body rust
4 Exposed spring in driver's seat
5 Rusted passenger door handle
6 Poor interior
7 Faulty lighting system
8 Rusted passenger door
9 Poor electronics

STOP **5 minutes**

Discussion This kind of exercise relies on individual judgement and yours may be different from mine, but according to my thinking there are three major points, each with their secondary and tertiary points. They are as follows:

$$3 \rightarrow 8 \rightarrow 5$$
$$9 \rightarrow 7 \rightarrow 1$$
$$6 \rightarrow 2 \rightarrow 4$$

Did you understand my reasoning? If not, go through the points again. If you have understood I am sorry if I appear to be labouring the point but it is quite important. If you were writing a piece on why the car had a poor second-hand value, it would make sense to divide up the points as indicated. Points 6, 2, and 4, for example, would comprise a separate section of your analysis. 'Poor interior' (point 6) is a general point covering all the faults within the inside of the car; 'uncomfortable seats' (point 2) is an important aspect of this general criticism – there could well be more, of course; and 'exposed spring in driver's seat' (point 4) in its turn is just one aspect of the second point.

Now let's try the second exercise: the principle is exactly the same but this time there are twelve points relating to the question 'Account for the formation of NATO in May 1949.'

1 The sealing-off by the USSR of Western access to West Berlin in 1948; the so-called 'Berlin Blockade'.
2 Ernest Bevin's prompt response to the American Secretary of State Marshall's speech offering aid to Western Europe.
3 The expansion of American economic influence world-wide.
4 The establishment by the USSR of a separate government in Eastern Germany.
5 Soviet expansion in Eastern Europe.
6 Statement of Truman Doctrine promising American support for countries threatened by the USSR.
7 The fleeing from Poland of politicians threatened by the Soviet-backed Polish government.
8 The determination of America to support a weakened Europe.
9 The Soviet desire to control Germany.
10 American Secretary of State Marshall's speech offering economic help to Europe.
11 The installation by the Soviet Union after the war of a government in Poland sympathetic to itself.
12 American support for Greece following British withdrawal.

Now try and sort out the points as you did in the first exercise.

15 minutes

STOP

This exercise is much more difficult, especially if you have little interest in history, and your judgement might not match with mine, but according to my thinking the points would be arranged as follows:

Discussion

$$5 \rightarrow 11 \rightarrow 7$$
$$9 \rightarrow 4 \rightarrow 1$$
$$3 \rightarrow 6 \rightarrow 12$$
$$8 \rightarrow 10 \rightarrow 2$$

If you find this difficult to follow go through the points again carefully and try to follow the reasoning which I have used.
A number of observations can be made on this exercise.

1 The points made are not an exhaustive list by any means – there are many more reasons for the formation of NATO, as I am sure you have realised.

2 The 'main points' are statements of general tendencies based upon observations of how the history of the period unfolded. 'Soviet expansion in Eastern Europe' is based upon observed behaviour not just in Poland but in Rumania, Hungary, Czechoslovakia and elsewhere. In the same way the conclusion that the USSR was seeking to control these countries is not merely based upon the fleeing Polish politicians but on a very wide range of evidence culled from several countries. The main points therefore can be seen as a series of 'conclusions' supported by various levels of argument and evidence. If we wanted to represent this diagramatically, we would end up with a pyramid.

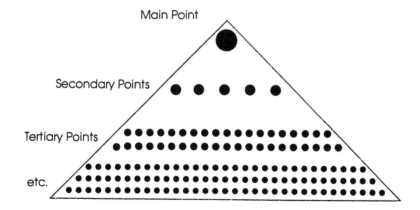

An essay written on this topic could be represented therefore as a series of pyramids, each main point being supported by the evidence beneath.

3 It has to be remembered, however, that all such reasoning from evidence is open to doubt and challenge. A Soviet historian for example, would certainly reach different conclusions from different evidence arguing in different ways. When you write an essay you are applying *your own structure* to the reality you are striving to understand. There is no final truth in this kind of exercise, merely rival versions of it. But the versions which are the most convicing are those which are based on the soundest evidence and the clearest reasoning. An ability to discern and express clearly general patterns from a complicated mass of data is one of the fundamental skills developed by academic training and is applicable to a wide range of occupations. It is also – to return to more mundane matters – central to the planning of good essays.

3 *The 'for and against' essay*

This is one of the most common kinds of essay you will encounter and a good one to start off with as the basic approach is so straightforward and the results often so rewarding. This kind of essay asks you to examine the arguments for and against a proposition and possibly to reach a conclusion. Such essays are often indicated by the instruction 'discuss', often following a quotation (genuine or otherwise). For instance – ' 'The Monarchy should be abolished.'' Discuss.' 'Consider' is sometimes another instruction requiring the same treatment as in 'Consider the view that the death penalty should be reintroduced.' But very commonly the question is straightforward: 'Would you preserve or abolish the institution of marriage?' or 'Should professional boxing be banned?'

The last title does not explicitly ask you for the 'for and against' treatment but it is heavily implied and if you wrote an essay which ignored the case *for* boxing you would probably receive a lower grade than if you had, and rightly so, because you would have neglected an important part of the problem. Just to give you some practice of planning this kind of essay try the last-mentioned one on boxing. Here is the title again: 'Should professional boxing be banned?'

Your task is to identify the points for and against the statement: don't bother with an introduction and a conclusion at this stage.

24

Again, just for the practice:
(a)   identify the key words
(b)   paraphrase the question
(c)   consider its implications
(d)   carry out the *brainstorming* or *Concept-Tree* exercise
If employing the former it's a good idea to divide up the page as shown below so that some initial division of points, for and against, is made at this early stage.

For the statement	*Against the statement*

Should professional boxing be banned?

Allow yourself 20 minutes for this exercise.

---

20 minutes   **STOP**

The key words here are 'professional' and 'banned'. A paraph-   *Discussion*
rase might be as follows. 'Should boxing for money be made illegal?' The points which I winnowed out from my brainstorming exercise were as follows (remember that to argue *for* the statement is to be *against* professional boxing!)

For the statement
1 Boxing inflicts physical damage upon the combatants, especially to the brain, and can cause death.
2 Boxing for money puts the boxers in the hands of rich promoters who cynically exploit them.
3 Boxing is one of the few remnants of the gladiatorial contests from less civilised times: it is an anachronism like bear-baiting and cock-fighting which should be ended.
4 Boxing appeals to the public's bloodlust – it reinforces the tendencies in human nature which should be curbed rather than encouraged. It brutalises the audience, glamorises violence and encourages imitation.

Against the Statement
1 Boxing gives pleasure to millions of people.
2 It is a contest of skill between highly trained sportsmen which is well supervised: fatalities are much less common in boxing than in many other sports.
3 Violence is endemic in humans and it is foolish to deny it. Boxing offers a harmless outlet for violent tendencies in the audience and helps set fair rules of combat when humans do fight – as they inevitably will.

4 Boxers participate from choice: to ban boxing would restrict their freedom and damage their livelihood.

You have probably identified similar kinds of arguments to mine. Did you find it interesting or enlightening? Try to jot down the value of this kind of exercise: why are so many essays of this kind set by tutors?

STOP   5 minutes

Discussion 1 By challenging a statement with an opposite contention the subject is opened up for close examination. The extent to which the statement can be supported by evidence is indicated and its underlying assumptions and values exposed. This approach applies a searching, critical scrutiny.

2 The approach is educational: you invariably learn something – maybe you did from the above? Most people do not think things through carefully but distribute judgements liberally on a host of issues on the basis of prejudice, misinformation, habit, and partial or no information whatsoever. If we carried out a careful dispassionate study of a number of topical issues we would probably adjust our own judgements considerably.

3 The word 'dispassionate' above is important. So many people are so convinced that a particular course of action is correct that they do not allow themselves to consider many or even any points against such a course of action. You *must* be aware of this. If a subject is controversial there *will* be a strong case for *and* against and you should open your mind to both – after all, you could be wrong and there is no shame in recognising this fact.

4 I didn't ask you to reach a judgement but after such an examination you are in a much better position to make one. The question has deliberately been phrased to be provocative, to make you think. You are not necessarily required in your conclusion to decide either *for* the statement or *against*. You may decide, for example, that boxing should not be banned but that some kind of stricter supervision is necessary, i.e. you might alight upon a position between the statement and its converse. Most judgements in practice are likely to be of this kind. 'Balanced judgements' usually recognise that contrary arguments do have some force and that most issues are too complex to allow for easy answers.

Two final points on the exercise need to be made. First, I hope you were able to muster enough points for and against to make the exercise worthwhile. In the past some students have said 'I can't do this because I know nothing about boxing at all!' Obviously it helps to know a little but it should be possible for people wholly uninterested in the sport to identify the major points. Secondly, if this were an essay set by a tutor as part of course work, you would need to read and research the topic. The point is that this kind of *prior* planning exercise enables you to find out what you *do* know and to organise such knowledge in a sensible way. Having done this you are in a better position to know what to read and you are likely to read with greater interest and understanding because you have wrestled a little with the central issues of the question – so here is a piece of golden advice: *Try to think through the question as much as you can and produce a preliminary plan before you start any serious reading*.

What you have just done on the subject of boxing is to construct the most basic of essay plans. It requires more work obviously – for example you would want to organise your points into some kind of logical order – but I hope it is recognised as the basis of a plan. The structure of any resultant essay would look like this:

Introduction
Points for the statement
Points against the statement
Conclusion

We shall call this approach, for convenience, 'Strategy I'. It is simple, direct and easily understood: all qualities which recommend themselves to writers and readers of essays alike. Here is a further exercise in using this approach. Below are a number of points all jumbled up, which provide a Strategy I answer to the question:

' "The Monarchy should be abolished." Discuss.'

Try to organise them in such a way that you end up with an Introduction, Points for the statement, Points against the statement and Conclusion (for the purposes of this exercise we will assume that all the points are main points and do not need to be grouped into secondary, tertiary points, and so forth).

' "The Monarchy should be abolished." Discuss.'

1 The Monarchy enjoys widespread popular support.
2 Heads of state should be elected.
3 The British Monarchy is one of the few of its kind left in the world.
4 The political functions of the Monarchy are now wholly meaningless.
5 On balance the case for the Monarchy outweighs the case against.
6 The honours system is absurd.
7 The term 'Monarchy' is usually used to refer to the Queen and the Royal Family.
8 The solemn ceremonies of the Monarchy enhances popular support for government and contributes towards political and social stability.

   9 The existence of the Monarchy reinforces conservative values in society.

10 The Queen is a unifying influence above parties.

11 Generally speaking most people derive pride and pleasure from the Monarchy: it would be undemocratic and unjustifiable to deny them this pleasure by abolishing it.

12 The Royal Family is a touchstone of desirable social behaviour.

13 The Queen is very experienced in politics and offers valuable advice to prime ministers.

14 The Monarchy earns money for the country through tourism and public relations visits abroad.

15 The Queen is an unjustifiably rich person who absorbs an unjustifiably large amount of public money.

STOP   **10 minutes**

Discussion   My organisation of the points was as follows:
Introduction: 3 and 7
Points for the statement: 2, 4, 6, 9 and 15.
Points against the statement: 1, 8, 10, 12, 13 and 14.
Conclusion: 5 and 11 (you may alternatively have chosen to place 11 as a point against the statement).

4 *Stragegy II essays*

Having, I hope, understood and mastered Strategy I, I now want to move on to a more sophisticated approach which I am calling Strategy II. The best way to explain it is via an illustrative exercise. The first stage is to apply the Strategy I treatment to this relatively undemanding topic (you can leave out the Introduction and Conclusion if you wish just to make it even easier).

    'Consider the advantages and disadvantages of central heating in domestic housing.'

STOP   **10 minutes**

Discussion   My points were as follows:

For

  1 The pleasantness of constant temperatures.

  2 The ability to use every room in the house.

3 The increased value of the house.
4 The ability to control the heat easily
5 The health advantage derived from a warm, comfortable environment.
6 The better value for money which central heating provides.

Against

7 Heavy installation costs.
8 High overall running costs.
9 Health risk through stuffiness and frequent transition from what may be a cold outside to a warm interior.
10 The vulnerability of the system to break down.
11 Wasted heat in rooms not used.
12 The possible unpleasantness of permanently higher temperatures.
13 Redecoration costs after installation.
14 Insulation costs.

The second stage of the exercise is as follows: try to divide up your points into matching categories so that instead of considering all the points for and then all the points against, you do a number of separate 'for and against' exercises under a number of different headings. To give you the idea I will start you off with 'comfort': under this heading you could deal with point 1 (for) and point 12 (against). Get the idea? Now try to identify some more headings.

---

15 minutes **STOP**

Finance *Discussion*
For: 3, 6. Against: 7, 8, 13 and 14.

Health
For: 5 Against: 9

Convenience
For: 4, 2. Against: 10, 11.

The disadvantage of this approach is that it is more difficult to tease out the different headings, but can you see the advantages? It is easier and neater to compare like with like: financial points with financial points, for example. Furthermore, with a complicated subject a long list of 'fors' followed by a long list 'against' is unmanageable; and perhaps by the time your reader has finished the latter the former will have been forgotten. Strategy I is suitable for shorter essays, for example in examinations, but Strategy II is better for longer course work essays on more complicated topics.

Let's try a more demanding and complex topic now. Apply Strategy II to the following title: 'Consider the arguments for and against free public transport in cities' (remember all the stages you should go through: analyse the question, brainstorm, organise the points for and against (Strategy I), organise points for and against under different analytical headings (Strategy II)).

STOP   **30 minutes**

Discussion   This topic was tackled quite successfully by a New Horizons student in October 1985. Let's see how Sid Davies handled the Strategy II approach to this particular essay question.
'Consider the arguments for and against free public transport in cities.'

1 **Introduction**
   The position as it stands. Cities strangled with cars, severe pollution, frustration, neglected road repairs, losses on under-utilised public transport systems.
2 **Environment**
   (a) **For free transport**
      (i)   Would dramatically reduce atmospheric pollution – long-term benefits for ozone layer.
      (ii) Better living conditions for people living on main routes into cities.
   (b) **Against**
      (i)   Would call for massive car parks on the periphery of the free transport zones. The congestion would there-fore move into these areas, i.e., the problem has merely been moved elsewhere.
3 **Economic**
   (a) **For free transport**
      (i)   Saving in business costs – time, fuel costs, depreci-ation of vehicles, and so forth.
      (ii) City businesses would benefit because people would flock in to shop and visit theatres (encouraging the arts) museums, exhibitions.
      (iii) There would be less wear and tear on roads, hence less maintenance costs. Rebuilding of services (old sewers, etc.) would be easier.
      (iv) Family finances would benefit – no need for second car.
   (b) **Against**
      (i)   Someone has to pay for the free transport. Ken Liv-ingstone's London scheme was criticised because London ratepayers felt they were paying the fares of foreign tourists through the rates.

(ii)   The car industry would suffer – fewer cars bought means increased unemployment.

(iii) Not everyone would benefit if not on a route into town.

(iv)   Employers could take advantage and lower wages through the excuse of lower travelling costs.

4 Health and safety

(a) For free transport

(i)   Massive saving in pain and misery (even death) through fewer accidents.

(ii) Fewer heart attacks and stress-related incidents and bad health.
      Savings in NHS cost both in direct accident costs and less definable savings through better health.

(b) Against

It is difficult to think of anything against free transport from the health point of view except:

(i)   People who would otherwise walk or cycle to work would be apt to go on free public transport and forego the life-saving exercise provided by walking/cycling.

5 National interest

(a) For free transport

(i)   Beter use of finite energy resources – oil, electricity, etc.

(ii)   Better utilisation of existing, under-used assets – railways, buses, etc.

(iii) Foreign exchange would benefit through fewer foreign cars being purchased. Also a boost would be given to our flagging bus manufacturers.

(iv)   It would give a boost to the development of rapid transport systems, new ideas (monorail) and re-introduction of past systems regrettably terminated (trams, trolley buses).

(v)   Might lead to radical solutions to other problems, e.g. acid rain, coastal pollution.

(b) Against

(i)   The cost could escalate because of the creation of monolithic transport systems which as yet, have been unable to operate efficiently.

6 Conclusion

Summary of above – more FOR than AGAINST.

What did you think of Sid's effort? My view is that it was a clear, well-organised response and would form the basis of a well-structured and illuminating essay.

Now let's try a more demanding and abstract topic (already

touched on in Chapter 9, Volume I). 'Do you think sex and violence in the media should or should not be censored?'
Remember to go through all the stages as advised, being particularly careful to identify all the important points *for* and *against*.

STOP   **30 minutes**

Discussion   ***Analysis of the question***   My paraphrase of the question was as follows: 'Do you think that portrayals of sex and violence via public methods of communication (especially broadcasting and printed matter) should be limited by law?'

My Strategy I list of points was as follows:
Case against censorship
1 *Aesthetic:* inhibits artistic talent, distorts art and denies truth.
2 *Individual judgement:* individual has the right to decide for himself whether he wants to watch, read or listen. Similarly, no one has the right to make up someone else's mind.
3 *Violence and sex as catharsis* (release of tension): portrayal of those subjects can release tension through this kind of experience at 'second hand'.
4 *Violence can deter:* certain films can show violence which reinforces opposition to it, e.g. 'A Clockwork Orange', 'All Quiet on the Western Front'.
5 *Censorship makes sex dirty:* we are too repressed about this subject and censorship sustains the harmful mystery which has surrounded it for too long.
6 *Politically dangerous:* Censorship in one area can be applied to others, e.g. political ideas.
7 *Impractical:* Who decides? How? Is it not impossible to be 'correct'? Any decision has to be arbitrary.
Case for censorship
1 *Sex is private and precious* and should not be demeaned.
2 *Sex can be offensive* to some people who should not have to see pornography displayed.
3 *Corruption is progressive:* can begin with sex and continue through until all 'decent values' are destroyed
4 *Participants can be corrupted:* especially true of children.
5 *Violence can encourage imitation:* by displaying violence – even whilst condemning it – it can be legitimised and can also encourage imitation amongst a dangerous minority.
6 *Violence is often glorified:* encourages callous attitude.

My Strategy II analysis of the question worked out as follows: As you see, I selected seven analytical headings: aesthetic, individual judgement, psychological, moral, financial, practical, comparability.

1 **Aesthetic**
For censorship
Some things are inherently unsuitable for public consumption and are harmful.
Against censorship
Artistic talents will be inhibited and expression stunted by legal restrictions.

2 **Individual judgement**
For censorship
In some situations one has no control (or insufficient control) over what one watches, reads or listens to.
Against censorship
Individuals can usually exert control over reading, TV, films, through choice – why should someone else tell us what to do?

3 **Psychological**
For censorship
Violence and sexual perversion can be imitative.
Against censorship
The catharsis of exposure to sex and violence helps release stress for some people.

4 **Moral**
For censorship
Corruption is progressive – it begins in small ways and grows. 'Participants' will suffer.
Against censorship
Censorship is more corrupting e.g. makes sex "dirty".

5 **Financial**
For censorship
Prevents exploitation of public by pornographers.
Against censorship
Regulation is expensive, curbs employment in media and *increases* role of pornographer.

6 **Practical**
For censorship
Present system works well and enjoys public support.
Against censorship
Present system arbitrary and absurd law is a mess.

7 **Comparability**
For censorship
Both sex and violence unwelcome.
Against censorship
Violence more dangerous than sex yet is disapproved of less. This essay plan needs further work and refinement but I hope you can see here a fairly sophisticated response to the question developing.

5 *The comparative 'for and against' essay*

A very common variation of the for and against essay is one which asks you for some kind of comparison. This usually calls for an adapted use of the Strategy I approach. As always the best form of explanation is an illustrative exercise. Look back to Chapter 9, Volume I and read through once again the 'good' essay entitled 'Do you agree that Capitalism is to be preferred to Socialism'? Try and find out the essay plan upon which that essay was based.

STOP **15 minutes**

Discussion The approach was quite simple, was it not? The advantages of socialism were explained, followed by the disadvantages – a Strategy I approach – and then the same treatment was applied to capitalism. It is quite possible to treat the question in a different way, of course, and write a good essay too. You might have chosen yourself to compare the advantages of both followed by the disadvantages of both, for example; my feeling though is that you might lose some clarity through such an approach because the advantages of socialism might have faded a little in the memory of the reader before the disadvantages were covered. You could also use an adapted Strategy II approach, for example, by comparing the relative merits of both philosophies under a series of headings like 'production of wealth', 'liberty', 'equality' and so forth, but such an approach is quite advanced and difficult to do justice to in the scope of a short essay.

If you have followed this chapter so far you either had a natural sense of structure before you started or you have rapidly developed one. Starting from the simple idea of 'for and against', more sophisticated approaches can be built up depending upon your ability and the topic with which you are confronted. Remember, simplicity and clarity are the watchwords: a clear approach is more likely to produce a clear result.

So far we have been dealing with the 'middle' of the essay but most good pieces of writing have effective introductions and conclusions.

6 *Introductions and conclusions*

This chapter will conclude with a brief note on introductions and conclusions. Obviously, the body of the essay is more important than either but this is certainly not to devalue their importance. Using your own experience of essay-writing plus what you have learnt so far in this course (and not forgetting your best ally, your common sense) what elements do you think could properly go into the introductions and conclusions of essays?

---

15 minutes   **STOP**

Introductions   *Discussion*
The important elements as I see them are as follows:
1 A good opening sentence. This strays a little into the unit on written style, but no matter. You must try to interest your reader from the outset and the boring convoluted opening sentence is no way of doing this. You might try an apposite quotation or a bold provocative statement: the idea is to set yourself off and to ensure that your reader stays with you.
2 Some indication that you have understood the question thoroughly. You can do this by explaining or defining any key terms which may occur in the title (your paraphrasing practice will stand you in good stead here). Try to avoid quoting dictionary definitions as this can seem dry and pedantic.
3 Some background to set the question in context. This may be historical or comparative or may discuss some of the basic assumptions underlying the question.
4 Depending on the complexity of your task it is a good idea sometimes to map out briefly the approach you are going to take; this helps your reader to understand the stages which your essay is going to pass through.

Introductions should not be too long of course: as a rule I would say no more than 10% of the whole, but you may feel in some circumstances that rather more or rather less is required.

Conclusions
Conclusions are usually briefer than introductions. I think they could include the following elements.
1 Some brief summary of the main arguments covered in the body of the essay – though be careful not to make your summary too long.
2 Possibly a re-emphasis of certain key points which you may believe to be decisive in determining the balance of the arguments.
3 A personal judgement if specifically requested by the title. If not requested you are under no compulsion to make up your mind but my feeling is that it is good practice to try to reach a judgement even if only a tentative and interim one.

4 If you can rise to the occasion a neat or memorable finishing sentence is also desirable, possibly linking up with your opening sentence.

Self-assessment exercises

Exercise 1
Without looking back over this chapter, can you list all the points we have covered in it?

Exercise 2
Plan 'for and against' essays on the following statements. For the practice and ease of doing the exercise you may like to go through all the processes worked through so far: analysing the title, brainstorming, categorising your ideas and so forth.

1 Licenses should be introduced for cats.
2 Children should not be given pocket money.
3 Education is concentrated on the young whilst it should be available to all age groups.
4 It is in no way justifiable to use animals in scientific research.
5 Poets are no use to anyone.
6 The Monarchy is more useful than the House of Lords.
7 *Coronation Street* is closer to life than *EastEnders*.
Note: Use Strategy I or Strategy II where you think it appropriate.

Exercise 3
Choose one of the essay plans you have completed for Exercise 2 and write it up into a short essay of about 1,000 words (3–4 sides of A4 paper).

Exercise 4
Construct sentences to illustrate the meanings of the following words:
Example: ramifications 'We explored the ramifications of this idea during our later discussions.'

1 abnegation   7 rabid
2 visceral   8 salubrious
3 escutcheon   9 expiation
4 otiose   10 redolent
5 prolix   11 sepulchral
6 prurient   12 vapid

Planning essays 2: Different types of essay   **3**

Most people won't realise that writing is a craft. You have to take
your apprenticeship in it like anything else.   *Katherine Ann Porter*

Contents

Introduction

So far in the discussion of essay planning we have limited our
examples to the relatively straightforward ones of arguing the
case 'for' and 'against' some topic. This concentration on what we
called Strategy I and II was designed to give you a basic grasp of
the need for shape and form in an essay plan. It is also a very
useful tool which will help you analyse arguments and present
your own case on a variety of topics. But not all the essays you
might be asked to write will fall into this pattern of a case for or
against. Depending upon the subject(s) you are going on to study
you will be presented with questions which need to be answered
in a number of different ways. The problem of answering the
question successfully then becomes more difficult because you
must find the most suitable *form* for your arguments – that is, the
best arrangement for the points of argument you wish to offer.
That is the problem this chapter will be dealing with. What we

want to illustrate are a number of the most popular *types* of questions and the different *forms* your answers to them might take. There are no absolute rights and wrongs in such matters: it is a question of finding the most suitable and logical arrangement for your answers – and doing so *at the planning stage* rather than waiting until you have actually started writing the essay.

You will perhaps remember from Chapter 1 ('Understanding the question') that typical essay questions are often posed in terms such as

'Discuss the importance of . . .'
'To what extent . . .'
'In what sense . . .'

Many students find that even if they know the *facts* surrounding the topic, they are puzzled by such questions because the way they are posed does not suggest the form which the answer might take. Typically, the student might wonder:

'Where should I *begin*?'
'In what order should I put my points of argument?'
'How can I decide which are the most important aspects of the answer?'
'How can I avoid just wandering from one point to another?'

This is the most important problem we shall be tackling in this chapter: helping you find the most appropriate approach for a range of questions; suggesting how you might give them shape and coherence; and pointing out how you can get the *best* out of the evidence you have.

But in addition we will be looking at a number of different *types* of essay (from different disciplines) which require approaches which do not fit neatly into the for/against category. In fact, many essays require that you devise a scheme or plan which will be appropriate just for that question. We will be helping you to develop the skills for this very important stage in essay-writing.

You will not however need any specialist knowledge in these different subject areas. What we will be concerned with is the organisation of ideas and points of argument. We will be concentrating on *adopting the best approach*.

Various types of essay 1

You will remember from our discussion of 'Understanding the question' in Chapter 1 that essay questions can be set for a variety of reasons. Just as a quick self-assessment exercise I am going to ask you to try and remember what reasons we gave. The original question was:

'Write down as many reasons you can think of why an essay or examination question is posed. What is its purpose?'

5–10 minutes STOP

These were the reasons we offered:
● To provide that you know the facts of a topic.
● To show that you can discuss an opinion.
● To demonstrate that you can argue a case.
● To give you an opportunity to present your own opinions or ideas.
● To show that you can evaluate the validity of a case or statement.
● To show that you can make an effective analysis.

This list probably covers the majority of essay questions you will be faced with in the study of the humanities and social sciences. But there do exist other *types* of essay. You may, for instance, be given the opportunity to be creative or entertaining, or you may have to present an essay which is a report on an experiment or a piece of investigation. What I shall offer now is a list of the various kinds of essay you may encounter, and we will work through an exercise on each one to illustrate how essay-planning needs to be taken into account.

There do not exist generally agreed terms to describe the variety of essay forms, so what I offer here are my own descriptions. It should also be apparent that some essays could fall into more than one category. You must simply get used to such complications and be prepared to be sensitive to what is being asked for.

The descriptive essay 2

This is a relatively straightforward type of essay in which you are asked to describe or give an account of something. In general this will be to check that you have absorbed and understood a body of knowledge or a topic you have been studying. No special analysis or evaluation is called for – just a comprehensive account of the phenomenon or topic.

Let's take a sample case. In a study of how Parliament works, for instance, you might be asked to 'describe the role of select committees in the legislative process'. Such a question is *not* asking you to decide if they are a good or bad thing. It is *not* asking you to make political judgements about the government of the day. What it wants is a clear description of the *role* of select committees. You might begin with an account of how they are composed, with representatives from various parties: then you could move on to say what their relationship is *to* Parliament, what their powers and responsibilities are, how and when they make their deliberations, and what happens to the reports they make. You would, of course, say *why* they are considered necessary, and you might possibly indicate (very briefly) how successful they are in executing the work they are given. In order to animate this rather dry information you might illustrate the process at work by outlining a committee's dealings with a real problem. This would give you the opportunity to point to any problems, difficulties, or limitations inherent in the system of select committees.

You can probably tell from what I am saying that the material to be covered itself suggests the order in which it might best be dealt with. Since select committees are formed from the body of Parliament itself, it seems logical to begin at that point. How the committees work would form the obvious 'middle' of the essay, with each stage of their workings being taken in turn. And the outcome of their work would make an equally logical end to the essay. This is a good example of how the *form* of an essay (the arrangement of the information) can be derived from the subject itself. There *may* be other ways of shaping the material, but whichever arrangement you choose should have some strong sense of order or logic to it. There would be no point, for instance, in switching from small details of procedure to larger issues and back again. Even though the essay is purely descriptive, to do so would give the impression that you did not have full control over your material – that you were unable to discriminate between more and less important material.

I have chosen a relatively complex example in order to cover the full range of what is possible in such an essay. The important point is that in a descriptive essay you are being asked to give a straightforward account of something. Other examples might range from 'Describe how to bake a fruit cake' to 'Give an account of the workings of a Bessemer Steel Converter'.

Now we will move on to an exercise in essay-planning based on the above discussion. To make matters easy for you I have devised a question which is very similar to the one I have just discussed. You don't need to have detailed knowledge of the subject (local government) to complete the exercise. And even if you have very little knowledge you should *try to imagine* what is required. The exercise is one of putting information in the best order – *not* in measuring how accurate or well informed it is.

What you should do is brainstorm the question and then put your topic headings into the most suitable arrangement you can. Don't forget, there is no 'right' and 'wrong' answer. You should strive for an arrangement which is coherent and logical. And don't imagine that you can necessarily achieve the best arrangement at one attempt. Be prepared to make several if necessary. Move your topics around until you have the best arrangement. Be prepared to use several pieces of paper. Try to get used to this approach to planning.
   'Describe the role of councils in local government.'

---

20 minutes   **STOP**

Sample essay plan   *Discussion*
1 Election *to* Council and its political 'balance'.
2 Composition and structure of Council Chair, Vice-Chair, Officers.
3 Council's (a) powers – local by-laws
           (b) responsibilities – education, social services, roads, cleansing.
4 Relation of council to central government
      (a) legal
      (b) financial.
5 Role of sub-committees.
6 Relation of council to full-time local government officers.

I am not suggesting that this is an ideal essay plan, but I hope you will see that at least it has a certain logic and clarity. Other topics might suggest their own plan – but the essential point which I am stressing is that they should have a coherence and order which will hold their separate parts together. In an essay 'Describe the workings of a steam engine', for instance, it would be logical to describe *first* the generation of the steam and *then* say how its energy was used/converted – rather than the other way round.

3   *The 'for and against' essay*

We covered this type of essay extensively in the last chapter, but I think that the points made there are worth reinforcing.

The prime function of a for and against type of essay, no matter what the wording of the question, is to force you to consider both 'sides' of an issue. It is testing your ability to think up and present fairly arguments you may not personally agree with. It requires that you are able to separate the arguments 'for' an issue from those 'against' it (not always as easy as it might seem). And you will be required to present those arguments as effectively as possible, using what we call Strategy I or II.

Let me briefly describe what would be required for this type of essay using the sample question 'What are the arguments for and against the banning of smoking in public places?'
There is little difficulty producing the most obvious arguments 'for':

1 Smoking interferes with rights of others to 'clean air'.
2 It endangers their health via 'secondary smoking'.
3 It is offensive to many as a smelly, dirty habit.
4 It should be regarded as offensive as spitting in public.

But non-smokers might find more difficulty in producing convincing arguments 'against':

1 The individual should have a right to do as he/she wishes.
2 The nervous strain of being prohibited from smoking could be injurious to some individuals.
3 Where does 'public' begin and end?
4 *Is* there convincing evidence health risk, especially regarding secondary smoking?

These are not comprehensive in either case. I'm sure you could think of other arguments. The point is that they should be clearly differentiated. And having drawn up your points of argument you should be prepared to think 'through' the topic in relation to any other topic you may have missed. Let me explain.

In our sample questions, let's say I decide to think about it from an economic point of view. It doesn't require much imagination to realise that *if* the overall level of cigarette consumption went down as a result of such a ban then the government would receive less money from the tax on tobacco, and we could even argue that workers in the tobacco 'industry' might lose their jobs.

Addicted smokers would be very happy to add these arguments to their 'against' column: and non-smokers would seem to be stumped! But are they? Just think – if the level of cigarette consumption does go down and there is a corresponding decline in the incidence of lung cancer then there will be fewer sufferers occupying hospital beds and thus a financial saving to government expenditure on the health service.

You can perhaps see that this approach *could* lead to these arguments being pushed even further (subsidised redeployment of redundant tobacco workers, and so on) but you must keep the question in mind and make sure arguments are firmly related to it. Don't stray too far from the central issue.

Enough on the for and against essay, but if you wish to practise making such essay plans on your own, all you need do is choose an issue around which there is some sort of moral contention or debate.
For example, consider the case for and against
(a)   vegetarianism
(b)   use of animals in scientific experiment
(c)   abortion
(d)   capital punishment

The 'compare and contrast' essay   4

This is an old favourite with many examination boards and question-setters. As you might possibly have guessed it represents one stage further on in the level of difficulty from a descriptive and a for and against essay. This is because of the two key instruction words in the title – 'compare' and 'contrast'. You are being asked to do *two* things as you were in the for and against essay, but they are probably harder to distinguish and separate. You may ask yourself: 'Which elements should I *compare* and how will I know which to *contrast*?' And *that* is the whole point! This type of question is asking you to *make* those distinctions; that is, you should sort out what the two topics might have in common (comparing one with the other), and also draw out distinctions between them to highlight any contrasts. Let's look at a practical example to illustrate what I mean.

Try to plan an answer to this essay title.

Question: 'Compare and contrast running and cycling as a means of taking exercise.'

STOP   **30 minutes**

Discussion   My first reaction here is to list what they have in common. There might be very minor differences – but these would form the basis for comment in the comparison.

Both
- take you out into fresh air
- can be done alone *or* in groups
- can be done at almost any time
- provide good exercise for the heart (but predominantly exercise the legs)
- are rhythmic and smooth activities
- can be done at your own pace
- don't require special terrain or clothing
- can be done at all ages

This list could be made much longer, as I am sure you will appreciate. But contrasts might be harder to find. These are my suggestions

(a) Running – requires virtually no apparatus, whereas Cycling requires a bicycle, and is therefore more expensive.

(b) Cycling – might be slightly more dangerous (falling off bicycle, injuries from road traffic).

(c) Running – marginally more 'convenient': can be done at any time with minimal preparation.

(d) Cycling – could leave you inconveniently 'stranded' in the event of a mechanical breakdown.

I think you will see from this last 'contrast' that I am having to scrape the barrel for ideas, but two other topics might have produced more contrasts than similarities. I hope you can see the point – that this type of essay question is both forcing you to *think* of one thing in relation to another (not just *one* topic) and it is asking you to make the distinction between what they *do* have in common and what they do *not*.

The next question is – having come up with similarities and contrasts, what *order* do we put them in? This is the same problem as that we encountered with the for and against essay.

Either You can offer all the points of comparison *first*, and then separately all those of contrast – a bit like Strategy I in the for and against essays.

or You can deal with one topic at a time and discuss points of both comparison and contrast – more like Strategy II.

In the example of running and cycling above I used Strategy I, but a slightly more sophisticated approach could be to adopt Strategy II.

Scope for variety of place and scenery –	both take you into fresh air but cycling takes you further afield – out of the city maybe – whilst running is more spatially limited.
Conditions and requirements –	neither requires special terrain or clothing *but* cycling requires apparatus and is therefore more expensive.
Convenience –	both can be done at almost any time *but* running is slightly more convenient.
Degree of dangers –	neither is particularly hazardous, *but* running seems to promote strains and cartilage damage whilst cycling has potential dangers from other road traffic.

You may well agree with me that Strategy II is likely to produce a slightly more interesting essay which will hold the reader's attention more than a long catalogue of similarities followed by one of differences.

The main point, again, is that this type of essay is testing your ability to bring out those similarities and differences and comment intelligently upon them.

The analytic essay 5

This is probably the most common variety of essay found in further and higher education, and it is based upon the supposition that you have been taught a certain body of knowledge – that is, your subject. What the essay of this type requires is that you show you are familiar with the material, and can make discriminations, analyses, and even offer judgements on a particular topic drawn from it.

A student of political history might be faced with the following question: 'Estimate, critically, the achievement of the Labour Goverment 1945–1951.'

This requires more than a *description* of what the government did; it would certainly not be enough just to give an account of legislation that was passed (which might not be quite the same thing as 'achievement'); and for/against and compare and contrast approaches are simply not appropriate for a question of this type. What is required is a thorough knowledge of the facts, perhaps of other governments as well. You would need to: compare what was achieved with what was originally intended;

consider whether ministers ran away from problems which could have been overcome; judge the impact of measures passed upon the life of the nation, and so forth. It would help considerably to be aware of what other historians had said on the subject especially if rival schools of thought existed. This is altogether a more complicated process and one which requires the co-ordination of a number of intellectual skills, but you soon become used to dealing with such problems – with practice and the ability to learn from your mistakes.

It is also perhaps worth mentioning at this point that questions of an 'evaluative' nature don't have a 'right' and 'wrong' answer; or that the tutor has one opinion on the matter – and that the student's sole task is to discover what it is. On the contrary, analysis and evaluation often involve ultimately very subjective judgements, and students will be judged not on coming to any 'correct' solution, but on the depth, perceptiveness and thoroughness of their analyses. Of course it is possible to 'go wrong' if you wander off the point, or offer some conclusions which do not logically follow from your analysis or are otherwise bizarre or eccentric. In this question on the Labour Government, it would be no use straying on to a discussion of Winston Churchill or offering merely uninformed personal views on the party's policies: the element of well-informed critical assessment must be present.

Let's move on to a practical example to give you practice at the sort of thing which is required. Brainstorm the following question, and then spend some time putting your points of argument into some logical order. (If you know nothing about the subject, you can read on into the 'Discussion' and start from my list of 'points' to make your own essay plan.)
Question: 'Analyse the reasons for the outbreak of the Second World War.'

STOP   20 minutes

Discussion   Here is the result of my own brainstorming:
(You may have other points – or the same ones put into different words.)
1 The rise of fascism in Germany, Italy and Spain.
2 Unresolved conflicts of First World War.
3 Ideological conflicts of totalitarianism and democracy.
4 Hitler's invasion of Austria, Czechoslovakia and Poland.
5 German notions of *lebensraum*, or the need of Germany to expand eastwards.
6 Rising nationalism in Europe.

7 Rearmament policies in Europe as a 'cure' for economic depression of 1930s

8 The false belief of Western leaders that Hitler could be successfully handled via conciliation rather than confrontation.

I am not suggesting that these are the only reasons, or even necessarily the most important. What I want to illustrate here is

(a) The need to identify and evaluate such points.
(b) The need (as ever) to put such points into some logical order.

Before we put them in order, therefore, there must be a certain evaluation (analysis) and to illustrate the sort of thing I mean I offer the following observations on each of the above points.

1 Reasonable claim – but take care. Each of these three forms of fascism was slightly different, and Spain remained neutral during the war.

2 Don't spend so much time on these issues that the essay goes backwards, to deal with a different question.

3 Careful distinctions should be made here. Many would argue that the Soviet Union was totalitarian – and Germany and the USSR were *allies* when the war started!

4 This seems like the strongest and least problematic argument.

5 This is very close to point 4 and ought to be absorbed into it.

6 Where is the evidence that nationalism begets war?

7 Reasonable – but at what point did this become a 'reason' for the outbreak of war?

8 Subsequent judgements by historians suggest this is accurate. My own suggestion for an essay plan is therefore as follows:

(a) Point 2   (unresolved conflicts of 1918–1939) used as a *brief* introduction.
(b) Point 1   (rise of Fascism in Germany) this would follow logically from (a).
(c)   (Hitler's imperialism) (ditto from (b).
(d) Point 3   (ideological conflicts).
(e) Point 6   (nationalism).
(f) Point 7   (rearmament policies).
(g) Point 8   This seems to me a 'strong' point on which to finish.

I am not suggesting that this is an ideal or model essay plan. What I hope you can see is that some sort of shape or logic has been given to the basic points of argument. In a topic like this it is often possible to use chronology – the actual sequence of events – as a framework on which to build your essay; but beware, *don't* become drawn into a mere recitation of the facts polished off by a conclusion which purports to 'answer' the question. Identify your key points first and *then* organise them chronologically if this seems the best way.

Another factor affecting the organisation of your points could be the various *connections* which exist between your points because they can be used to link up the different parts of your essay and give it that flowing, seamless, quality which is one of the hallmarks of a quality piece of work. For example you might think that point 5 about *lebensraum* might lead directly into point 8 about the naivety of Western leaders.

6   *The literary appreciation essay*

Many courses of study in the humanities include an element of literary appreciation, requiring that students become more sensitive to and appreciative of the subtleties and insights which literature has to offer. Many students find those glimpses into the psyche or observations of human behaviour which writers have to offer very rewarding – but then they are commonly bewildered when they are asked to write an 'appreciation' of a piece of work. Sometimes they can do little more than summarise the story, although they know that something else is required. Common responses to this sort of task are 'Where could I *start*?' or 'What do they want me to say?' Even students who are able to deal with the literary subtleties of a work are not always able to find any 'logical' order in which to put their observations. After all, if you were dealing with a novel, where would you begin – with the plot? the characters, or the story itself?'

This is another example of the essay task where you must make up your plan, and a combination of practice, common sense, and the work itself are the only things you will have to help you. Let's take the example I have just mentioned to illustrate the problem and indicate some way out of the difficulty.

You have been asked to write an appreciation of a short novel, including mention of its literary merits. Here is a list of the topics on which you might comment:

(a)   The story or plot.
(b)   The characters.
(c)   Any themes or issues it deals with.

(d) The setting.
(e) The author's style.
(f) What 'type' of novel it is (comic, serious, etc.)
(g) Its relation to other novels by the same author.
(h) Some of the key incidents.

Now there is no *necessary* order in which these must be dealt with. Your choice will depend upon what you have to say about the novel. But let me comment upon each of those possibilities indicating what factors might affect their position on your plan.

(a) The story: if recounted *very* briefly, this could form a good introduction to the essay. This would indicate your overall grasp of what the novel was *about*. To leave it until the end of your essay would not really make much sense.
(b) The characters: there is no right or wrong position for this within the body of your essay, but it would obviously not be a good idea to either start or end on this topic.
(c) Themes: this could either follow directly your outline of the story, or it could be left until after your consideration of the characters. It is obviously an important item.
(d) The setting: this seems important, but possibly for that reason it might go earlier rather than later in the essay plan.
(e) Author's style: this will involve discussing several smaller issues – vocabulary, literary devices, figures of speech, etc. No set place for it in the plan, but not a good topic to start or end on.
(f) Type of novel (genre): this is a very general topic, and unless you had a lot to say about it, the sort of thing on which to start or finish.
(g) Other works: the same comment applies for this as in (f) – but I think you would only put this towards the *end* of the plan.
(h) Key incidents: since you obviously felt that these illustrated what the novel was 'about' this topic should be closely linked to 'themes'.

So – from these comments I could therefore construct two possible essay plans.

ESSAY PLAN 1
1 Type of novel (genre).
2 The story or plot.
3 The setting.
4 The characters.
5 The themes and key incidents.
6 Author's style.
7 Relation to author's other work.

ESSAY PLAN II
1 The story
2 Themes and key incidents
3 The setting.
4 The characters.
5 Author's style.
6 Relation to author's other work.
7 Type of novel (genre).

Exercise
It is difficult to set exercises on the topic of literary appreciation unless you have already undertaken literary studies, but I will choose a very straightforward poem, make some observations about it, and ask you to put them into some order for your imaginary essay plan.

This is the poem, by Keats – his response to reading Chapman's translation of Homer.

> *On First Looking into Chapman's Homer*
> Much have I travell'd in the realms of gold,
>   And many goodly states and kingdoms seen;
>   Round many western islands have I been
> Which bards in fealty to Apollo hold.
>   That deep-brow'd Homer ruled as his demesne:
>   Yet did I never breathe its pure serene
> Till I heard Chapman speak out loud and bold:
> Then felt I like some watcher of the skies
>   When a new planet swims into his ken;
> Or like stout Cortez when with eagle eyes
>   He stared at the Pacific – and all his men
> Look'd at each other with a wild surmise—
>   Silent, upon a peak in Darien.

Now these are some of the observations I would make about it in an appreciation. You should try to group them together and put them into some order for an essay plan.
(a) Rhymes (gold/hold).
(b) Subject (personal experience of literature).
(c) Rhythm.
(d) Form (the sonnet)
(e) Rhyme scheme (abba/abba/cdcdcd).
(f) Images ('deep brow'd Homer').
(g) Vocabulary (demesne, fealty).
(h) Stress ('Much have I travell'd in the realms of gold').
(i) Syntax ('then felt I').
(j) Tone (Keats's *attitude* to his subject).

(k) Similies (like some watcher of the skies).
(l) Your personal response to the poem.

---

15 minutes   **STOP**

I think you will have noticed that the main problem in creating a   *Discussion*
plan here is the mixture of different types of observation. There
are both small scale technicalities (the rhymes, for instance) and
larger issues like the ideas within the poems and the overall
subject of the poem itself. There are also rather a *lot* of the smaller
observations, and it is difficult to know if one (rhyme) assumes
more significance than another (stress) or not.

The answer to this problem is what I have been trying to stress
throughout this chapter – that you should be prepared to *create* a
sensible plan out of the observations you have assembled, using
common sense and a certain respect for logic of course. In this
example, for instance, it would *not* seem logical to *end* your essay
plan on a minor technical observation. Your essay should surely
be leading towards a general and overall assessment of the
poem's value and meaning, so it would be inappropriate to
conclude with some small-scale considerations. Similarly, an
essay which *began* with an immediate consideration of one of
these small details would seem rather unbalanced by such
abruptness.

As I have said before, there are no rights and wrongs in such
matters, but here I think the most suitable overall 'shape' for your
plan might have been guided by the idea of moving from *general*
consideration of the poem, onto the detail, and then in conclusion to an overall assessment:

(i)   Introduction – some general observation.
(ii) The technical detail.
(iii) Conclusion – overall assessment.

With this basic framework in mind, you could then arrange the
details in whatever seemed the most appropriate manner in
section (ii). I would suggest that if the smaller issues were dealt
with first, the larger ones will then be moving logically towards
your overall assessment in section (iii).

My own plan from the details given in (a) to (l) therefore would
be:
1 Introduction – personal response (l)
2 Form and rhyme scheme (d) and (e)
3 Stress and rhythm (h) and (c)

4 Rhymes (a)
5 Vocabulary (g)
6 Syntax (i)
7 Similies and images (f) and (k)
8 Tone and subject (j) and (b)
9 Conclusion – overall assessment.

7 *Report of an experiment or investigation*

Strictly speaking, this isn't an essay at all, but I'm sure you will appreciate why we are including it in this chapter. To be success-ful, the results of an experiment or investigation require exactly the same sort of consideration as an essay plan. That is: informa-tion, opinion, and observations must be assembled in some sort of order. There will be an intrinsic logic dictated by the activity, and your report will be less effective if it bears little relation to this logic. Even the simplest report will seem confused if its elements are not put in the best order. Imagine receiving a report of someone's visit to a foreign country in which preparations for departure were repeatedly mixed in amongst descriptions of the place visited: the result would be rather confusing, wouldn't it?

I think that by now you should know what we are aiming at in this chapter, so I am going to pass on directly to our practical example.

Imagine that you are writing a report on a survey of traffic density in your locality. I will again give you a list of topic headings and ask you to put them in what seems to you to be the most approp-riate order.
(a)   Where and when survey conducted.
(b)   Definitions of 'traffic'.
(c)   Exclusions or exceptions.
(d)   Analysis of results.
(e)   Conclusions.
(f)   Results.
(g)   Recommendations for action.
(h)   Abstract (summary of report).
(j)   Tables of figures.
(k)   Description of procedures.
(l)   Maps.
(m) Photographs.
(n)   Department of Transport standards.
(o)   Purpose of survey.

15 minutes

STOP

This is another example where the beginning and end are fairly straightforward, but what goes inbetween depends upon your sense of 'form' or your experience in these matters. First I will give my own results, and then say a few words on *why* I chose this particular order.

 1 Abstract or summary (h).
 2 Purpose of survey (o).
 3 Where/when survey conducted (a).
 4 Description of procedures (k).
 5 Definitions and exclusion (b) and (c).
 6 Results (f).
 7 Analysis of results (d).
 8 Conclusions (e).
 9 Recommendations (g).
10 Tables, maps, photographs (j), (l), and (m).
11 Government standards (n).

Discussion

● You may not have known but abstracts (l) are usually given at the beginning of a report, so that the reader can have some overall view of what he is about to read.
● Note that this order puts the topics into groups
    1 –   Introduction
    2 – 5 Definitions and Procedures
    6 – 9 Body of Report
  10 – 11 Appendices

● 2–5   These should come first so that the report reader will know the limits and considerations under which the survey was conducted. It would be pointless offering the results *first*.
● 10 and 11   It is just possible that the tables, maps and photographs *could* appear within the body of the report amongst the results, but it is also *very common* for them to be put at the end so that the results can be read without interruption. And something like a government standard (which might lay down recommendations on road usage) would obviously be added as an appendix to the report.

It should be apparent to you by now that the shape of the report or essay *plan* may often be determined by the subject. You will also appreciate that in this chapter we are trying to cover the most common types of essay question that are set with a view to discussing the important issue of giving shape to your essay plan.

8 *Philosophic analysis*

Don't be alarmed by the term 'philosophic': this is just an academic expression for the process by which we discuss moral questions or investigate the most fundamental principles, causes and nature of things. Questions involving terms like 'should' or 'ought' are usually *moral* problems which are posed for discussion.

'Should parents be responsible for the crimes of their children?'

This is a question which invites philosophic speculation. There can be no 'right' or 'wrong' answer to it. The outcome will be a matter of personal opinion, but more than a 'yes' or 'no' answer is required, and the reasoning process by which we argue the validity of our opinion is essentially philosophic analysis.

Most adult students have little difficulty making a start on such essays because they usually have opinions about questions of 'is' and 'ought'. But they commonly run into two problems fairly quickly:

1 They find it difficult to 'get past' or 'break through' their own opinion to see opposing points of view.
2 They have problems putting their thoughts into a logical plan.

For solutions to the first of these problems I can only refer you to the chapter on clear thinking (Chapter 4) and generating ideas (Chapter 8, Volume I). You must simply get used to the idea of considering points of view other than your own. But *this* chapter is designed to help you with the second of these problems.

Let us suppose you have been confronted with the question I have just made up:
'Should parents be responsible for the crimes of their children?' Applying the guidelines we have been stressing throughout this course you would first of all analyse the terms of the question (Chapter 1). The terms 'parents', 'responsible', 'crimes' and 'children' all stand out as being in need of special consideration or 'definition'. You need to think in advance of any problems which might arise.
(a) 'Parents' – adoptive or biological? Foster-parents? Step-parents?
(b) 'Responsible' – legally? morally? economically?
(c) 'Crimes' – minor misdemeanours, or serious crimes?
(d) 'Children' – up to what age?
There are obviously plenty of complex issues here, and I don't

want to explore the question so fully that I generate an answer to it; what I want to do is use this as an example of how you must generate an essay plan out of the problem itself. You should use your thoughts on the matter as the material out of which you will construct your framework for an answser. Here is what I would do with our example. And I hope my first suggestion doesn't seem like cheating or shirking the issue.

1 'Parents' and 'children': it seems to me perfectly reasonable to impose limits here. That is, to restrict the discussion to the normal, genetic parents and to put an age limit – say sixteen – on the notion of 'child'.

  If you have something to say about exceptions to this, you could always do so separately.

2 'Crimes': be reasonable. The seriousness of a crime is *normally* proportionate to the age of the child.

3 'Responsible': the degree and type of responsibility is likely to arise out of the cases you discuss.

These considerations lead me to think that a chronological approach might be suitable here – always a ready-made structure when no other seems available. It would be quite reasonable to consider cases of very young children (2–5 years) who might commit misdemeanous and then work up towards the more serious instances of 'crime' by teenagers.

I am more or less 'thinking aloud' on paper here to show you the process by which *I* would arrive at some sort of plan. I don't want to follow this through to its conclusion. I will stop at this point to present the first stage of my essay plan:

1 Introduction – discussing terms of question and limits within which it will be discussed.

2 Argument – discussing degrees of responsibility in order rising from small children up to teenagers.

3 Exceptions – discussion of unusual or exceptional cases.

4 Conclusion – this might take into account the current legal position and comment upon it in the light of my argument at 2.

This may not seem particularly impressive, and obviously a great deal more work needs to be done on 2 – the basic argument. No doubt other approaches could have been adopted. But I am trying to demonstrate here is that *some* form of order or logic should be present in your plan, and in questions which don't provide their own plan you must be prepared to generate your own out of the subject under consideration or your own particular approach to it.

That's enough 'instruction' on this type of problem. Now for an exercise in which you should try to create a plan out of my responses to a typical question of this type (already touched on in Chapter 1):

'Is lying always wrong
Here are my brainstormed points.

(a) Lying as a general practice would be counterproductive.
(b) The liar should take responsibility for the results of his lying.
(c) Examples of 'useful' lies: to save life
                                  to ease feelings
                                  to mislead an enemy.
(d) Life is built on an assumption of truthfulness.
(e) Persistent use of 'useful' lies would weaken their effectiveness.
(f) An extreme case: Kant's 'categorical imperative' (tell the truth even to one's enemies).
(g) A difficult case – lying to escape the punishment of an unjust law or one's enemy.
(h) Conclusion.

STOP   **15 minutes**

Now this is my suggestion for a plan.
1 Introduction
    Life is in general built on assumption of truthfulness (d).
2 Argument –
    There are sometimes 'useful' lies (c).
    BUT
3 Persistent use of 'useful' lies would weaken their effectiveness (e).
    AND
4 Liar must take responsibility for the lies (b).
5 Difficult and extreme cases
    Kant's Categorical Imperative (f).
    Escaping unjust punishment (g).
6 Conclusion
    Not always – but usually can be.

9   *The polemical essay*

You will often see in newspapers or magazine articles given over to the prosecution of a particular point of view. If somebody feels very strongly about a controversial topic of current concern (say, nuclear weapons or abortion on demand) they may be given the opportunity to express their opinions on the matter. They will be attempting to persuade readers that such views are correct or praiseworthy, and as such they will be using many of the guidelines I have been discussing in this chapter. But the polemic allows them to be a little more flexible, more overtly subjective – and possibly even a little more entertaining. If it is to be a newspaper article, however, they will probably also need to be more *succinct*.

You may not be asked by the editor of *The Times* or the *Guardian* for your thoughts on such issues – but in fact this type of exercise is often used by teachers to develop students' powers of argument. How does this differ, you might ask, from essays of the type we have covered so far?

In general, I would argue that you might need to give higher priority to *holding the reader's interest*. After all, there is no reason why a reader should wade through two thousand words of polemic unless you have something interesting to say on the subject or present your arguments in a lively and entertaining manner.

It is not possible to lay down any general plan for such an essay. This *must* be determined by the writer and how the subject is approached. But I would offer the following observations on the special characteristics of essays of this type.

1 *Introductions*
   A ponderous introduction would put off the reader immediately. Better a snappy attention-catching start than a long-winded introduction to the subject, even if it is factually accurate.

2 *Keep your readership in mind*
   If you are writing for a reasonably intelligent and well-informed audience, you can assume that the reader will know the basic outline of the subject. This will allow you to concentrate on some of the details or problems you think worthy of extra attention.

3 *Dealing with 'the arguments'*
   You should present your own arguments as cogently as possible and give evidence where necessary to back them up. But you may also need to attack arguments or beliefs held by others in opposition to your own. Handle these as skilfully as you do your own: avoid relying upon sarcasm or *ad hominem* arguments: this could weaken your own case.

4 *Strike the right tone*
   In a polemic this might mean mixing a certain level of seriousness with occasional humour or lighter passages. This will, like

so much else, be determined by your subject. A polemic on abortion or nuclear weapons may not be a suitable subject for jokes; but your critique of slimmers or food-faddists might easily call on a little light raillery to enhance your case. This whole topic of tone is a matter of personal taste, and you will do well to study the work of others to see what is possible or permissible.

5 *Conclusions*

In an essay of this type I don't think you need to *necessarily* summarise the arguments. If the reader has been alert he will still have all these in mind. You might raise the whole subject to a philosophical level, present a new and stunning piece of evidence to defend your particular case, or maybe raise a new question to stump your opponents. It is rather like the introduction: more than usually you can afford to attempt something striking and memorable.

10 *The 'classical' essay*

By 'classical' I mean the sort of essay written, usually by a literary person, which has so many literary values (in addition to its arguments) that it is worth reading even if you don't agree with what is being said. The novelist George Orwell is famous for having produced such work in his essays 'Boys' Weeklies', 'The Decline of English Murder' and 'Politics and the English Language'. The writer, on the other hand, may have used the essay form to offer distilled wisdom on a variety of topics. The essays of the French writer, Montaigne, are very good and very readable examples of this. Serious subjects such as 'Of Liars', 'Of Solitude' and 'That we should not judge our Happiness till after Death' are taken as the occasion for very erudite and humane meditation – but they are marked by the fact of being always lively, thought-provoking, and entertaining.

Alternatively, the writer may have merely set out to be entertaining. The eighteenth-century authors, Addison and Steel, writing for magazines like *The Tatler* and *The Spectator*, used the essay form to take an everyday or contemporary issue and weave whimsical or fanciful ideas around it. They did so in an elegant and witty manner, with great *style* – and therefore their essays are still worth reading even though the subjects on which they wrote were often quite inconsequential.

This type of essay is no longer generally fashionable, either in journalistic or academic circles, but I think it is worth mentioning here for two reasons:

1 To make students *aware* that such a literary form exists, and introduce them to its possibilities.
2 To offer them excellent examples of continuous argument in prose – be it for purposes of amusement or enlightenment.

Further reading

The literary essay
Richard Hoggart, *Speaking to Each Other*, Vol. 2.
Arnold Kettle, *An Introduction to the English Novel.*
F.R. Leavis, *New Bearings in English Poetry.*
　　　　　　The Common Pursuit.
　　　　　　The Great Tradition.

The Polemical Essay
George Orwell, *Inside the Whale.*
　　　　　　The Decline of the English Murder.
Richard Hoggart, *Speaking to Each other*, Vol. 1.

The classical essay
Montaigne, *The Essays of Montaigne.*
Francis Bacon, *Essays.*
Addison and Steel, *Essays from* The Spectator.

Self-assessment exercises

Exercise 1
Without looking back over this chapter, can you list the various types of essay with which we have been dealing?

Exercise 2
Produce essay plans on three or more of the topics below.
1 Describe the process of buying a house.
2 Consider the case for and against vegetarianism.
3 Compare and contrast painting and wallpapering as the best form of decorating.
4 Why do women claim they are 'second-class citizens'?

5 Write a literary appreciation of a poem, novel or short story known to you.
6 Write up a simple investigation (e.g., into household finances) or procedure (e.g., servicing the car) in the form of a report.
7 Argue a case upon which you feel strongly.

Exercise 3
Write up *one* of your plans into an essay of 1,000 words (three to four sides of A4 paper) or more.

Exercise 4
Try to write an essay more or less in the style of Charles Lamb or George Orwell upon either
    'The virtues of a full English breakfast'
or 'Royal weddings and the British public'.

Exercise 5
Describe either (a) a visit to the dentist
            (b) a frightening experience

Clear thinking 4

Profundity of thought belongs to youth, clarity of thought to old
age   *Nietzsche*

When a thought is too weak to be expressed simply, it should be
rejected   *Vauvenargues*

Contents

Introduction

What exactly do we mean by 'clear thinking' – and how is it
related to the other study skills we are dealing with in these
pages? Well, I hope you will have appreciated by now the
importance we attach to essay-writing skills – what we regard as
the cornerstone to academic development at this stage. So far we
have been dealing with the structure or the arrangement of your
arguments in the preceding chapters on essay planning. Now we
have a chapter which is inviting you to consider the clarity, the
rigour, and the validity of your argument themselves. For that is
essentially what clear thinking is about:

● the production of valid arguments and the clear expression of
   ideas
and of course its converse, which is
● the critical inspection and analysis of other people's arguments.

Quite apart from the nature of any subjects you might wish to
study in further or higher education (history, sociology,
languages) this is part of the process in which you will be
engaged – the production of your own arguments and the critical
examination of other people's. This sort of educational 'debate'
will force you to be more careful, precise, and rigorous in what
you say – because *your* arguments will come under the scrutiny
of your tutors and your fellow students. Clear thinking is

therefore a very important skill which you will need to use all the time – but it is not so easy to acquire.

Many people find it more difficult to learn to think clearly than to acquire most other study skills. There are three main reasons for this:
- It can be hard work and mentally tiring, because it involves being constantly vigilant and keeping a close check on our own arguments and those of others.
- It involves learning *a number* of skills and using them simultaneously – skills of analysis, reasoning, understanding, and so on. Like writing essays, clear thinking is the name of a very *complex* skill which naturally takes longer to learn than a simple one.
- It often involves *correcting bad habits* of thinking. Many people have inadvertently become 'sloppy' thinkers: they tend to make false assumptions, jump to conclusions, or to be careless about logic. (In fact most of us are frequently guilty of this to some extent.) These tendencies have to be 'unlearned' – and that takes time.

What this chapter tries to do is simplify matters by considering separately the two key elements of clear thinking. These are:
(a)   Precision and clarity in the use of language.
(b)   The validity or invalidity of arguments.

But before we make a start, let me first offer you a few words of encouragement and advice on tackling this subject.

1   *Clear thinking*

Clear thinking is in fact the plain name for a branch of what might otherwise be called 'philosophy'. It is quite a large and complex topic and many books have been written about it – some of which are listed at the end of this chapter. What follows in Section 2 on 'Languages' and Section 3 on 'Logic' is therefore no more than an extremely brief introduction. I have divided it into these two parts both for the process of clarification, *and* so that you can tackle each topic independently. Indeed, I would advise you *not* to try and work through the whole chapter in one go. You might also try to keep these hints in mind.
(a)   **DON'T DESPAIR** if you are making slow progress. I have already pointed out that you are trying to master a complex range of skills. Don't conclude that you are somehow stupid, or that you have to be very clever to think clearly: in fact many so-called clever people are often confused thinkers.

Anyone can learn to think clearly, but it does take time and effort.

(b) **PRACTISE** conscientiously, and work at it. Don't expect it to 'come right' just by itself or in one go. Try to analyse *why* you are having problems if you find it difficult. Work through the examples in this chapter several times if necessary, and consult other books or study guides.

(c) **BE CRITICAL** of other people's thinking. Whether you are reading a textbook or a magazine, or listening to a discussion on TV or at a party, ask yourself all the time: what exactly is being claimed here? Is it really true? Are there any grounds for it? What does it imply? How could it be challenged? And so on. In this way you will develop the habit of thinking critically and clearly, and it will be less of a conscious effort.

Let's make a start at the sort of thing I mean with a short exercise based upon a very common phenomenon – a letter to a newspaper. This is from an obviously irate reader protesting about the reorganisation of secondary schools. What I want you to do is read it through carefully a number of times, concentrating intently on each stage of the argument it is putting forward. Whilst you are doing this, ask yourself the questions I have just mentioned – What is being claimed? Is it really true? Are there grounds for it? How could it be challenged? Make notes on your observations and your responses, and then later compare them with my own. What you are doing is developing the habit of thinking *critically*.

This is an extract from the letter:

> Recently you said that our schools are failing, something that many parents have felt for years. Let this be the start of a campaign to restore educational standards in our schools.
>
> We once had an educational system which was the envy of the world. Now our schools have been 'kidnapped' by theorists, reformers and the political pirates of the far left.
>
> The first battle of this campaign is already being fought. Parents in Liverpool are engaged in a fight against the Labour council's plans to reorganise secondary schooling, involving the closure of ten of the best schools in Liverpool. These are ones with excellent academic records and traditions which go back beyond the beginning of this century.

---

15 minutes   **STOP**

This is very typical of the sort of everyday argument you might hear in a pub or on a radio or TV discussion. These are *my* observations about it, which I will signal by quoting from the relevant part of the text.

1 'Schools are failing'. Failing to do *what*, exactly? Presumably educate children properly. But *is* there any hard evidence that schools in general are worse than they were twenty or fifty years ago? Many people *think* that this is the case, but they very rarely have any proof to substantiate their claim. And if you think about it for a moment, a hundred years ago most people were hardly educated *at all*, so the general level of the country's education is likely to have risen considerably rather than to have fallen.

2 'Restore educational standards'. The use of the word 'restore' here suggests that either the standards have been *taken away* or that they should be built back up again from a level to which they have allegedly dropped. But it is very unlikely that either of those things has happened. As far as I am aware, it is just as difficult to get a GCE A level in mathematics now as it was twenty years ago – so that is one standard which presumably has not fallen. And the total number of children achieving these qualifications is greater, not less than it was, so that is another.

3 'We once had an educational system which was the envy of the world'. *Did* we? Who says so? (Probably 'we' did.) And if this is the case why have so many countries since organised their education system on lines completely unlike ours? *Some* countries may have envied us, but others had systems just as well developed as ours. Moreover, the 'system' to which the writer is alluding (harking back to the nineteenth and early twentieth century) was one which only dealt with an extremely small percentage of children, all of whom came from the middle and upper classes.

4 'Theorists, reformers and the political pirates of the far Left'. This is called using language *emotively*. The implication here is that people who 'theorise' about something lack practical experience of it and just deal in opinions (though the writer herself is 'theorising' in just this sense); that anyone who wishes to change a given state of affairs (a 'reformer') will spoil it; and that the far Left wish to steal something (isn't that what pirates do?).

5 'Traditions which go back beyond the beginning of this century'. The implication here is that anything which has lasted so long *must* be good and *should* be left unchanged. The traditions may well exist, but that is not *necessarily* a reason for resisting educational reforms. The other weakness here is that which I just dealt with in point three above – traditions for whom?

There are three points of a general nature I would like to add. I hope you didn't think I was taking a sledgehammer to crack a walnut here. After all, these sorts of opinions are often bandied about. We don't expect the person in the street to be a walking philosopher, do we? But this is precisely where we must make an effort to challenge assumptions and arguments (even our own) if we are to make progress on the issue of clear thinking. You should get into the habit of being just as searchingly critical as you can be – although it may seem a somewhat 'negative' attitude to take at first.

Next I should say that despite my observations above, Mrs X of Liverpool *could* still be correct. It is *possible* that educational performance in her locality is falling in some way. The problem is that her own argument is badly flawed and she lacks persuasive evidence or ideas to support it. We will be dealing in Section 3 with this central feature of 'thinking' or logic – that it is important to distinguish between the validity of the argument itself and the conclusion which is reached. It is perfectly possible to go through a logically rigorous argument yet reach the 'wrong' conclusion – if you started from a false assumption, for instance.

My third point is to underline how much of the sloppiness I observed in Mrs X's argument arose from her rather imprecise use of language. Ambiguous, vague, and casual use of language often reflects a lack of clarity in our thoughts. It is for this reason that if we wish to improve our clear thinking skills we must pay close attention to the way we use words. That is why we will now pass immediately to a consideration of language in its relation to clear thinking.

Language   2

According to one common view, words are symbols which express or 'stand for' ideas. This helps to explain why the processes of thinking and reasoning involve language, for although they are primarily a matter of manipulating ideas we can only accomplish them by putting words together to express our thoughts. Unfortunately words sometimes acquire a force and fascination of their own, and because of this they may tend to control or conceal thoughts instead of communicating them. Language can obstruct our thinking in ways like these, for example.

(a) **It may not express any ideas at all.** Recently I bought a bottle   *Discussion*
    of 'family shampoo'. What does that mean? Shampoo for
    people with families? But what about single people – can't
    they use it too? Shampoo for every member of the family?
    But what about tiny babies? Shampoo for most types of hair?
    But surely *any* shampoo which is not designed specifically

for just one type is suitable for that kind of 'general purpose' use.

In this context the word 'family' is actually rather meaningless, for it does not stand for or express any idea. Words are often 'empty' like this, and are used with no real meaning; and then they can mislead us into thinking that something significant is being said when in fact it is not.

(b) **It may seem to express more than it really does.** Some years ago I was invited to a conference of which the advertised purpose was 'to provide the inputs to promote purposive discussion towards the preparation of guidelines for future practice'. After some thought I realised that this meant something like 'to get some ideas which we can talk about in order to suggest what we ought to do next'. That doesn't sound quite so grand, does it?

Language is often used like this to impress us and make us think that something important is being said when (as in this example) the real meaning is actually rather trivial.

(c) **It may stand for a very imprecise idea.** My local paper reported recently that an application to open a chip shop had been refused 'on transport grounds'. Evidently the planning committee felt that the shop would have had an adverse effect on transport in the neighbourhood, but it is totally unclear what that effect might have been. (Obstruction? Congestion? Traffic noise? Danger to pedestrians? Any of these, possibly; or maybe something else again.)

Language used in this way is vague and woolly and is very often a sign that the person using it has not bothered to get clear in their own mind what they want to say. Unfortunately it tends to make other people muddled too, and it leaves room for misunderstandings.

(d) **It may stand for more than one idea.** A good instance of this concerns Richard Hoggart's influential book *The Uses of Literacy*, in which he argued that mass media (such as newspapers and TV) were eroding and destroying the culture of working-class people. Some critics disagreed with him on the grounds that in fact the media were bringing culture to the working classes. You can probably see that the word 'culture' is being used in two senses here: for Hoggart, it meant the songs, stories, etc., created and passed on by working-class people among themselves; for his critics, it meant ballet, drama, etc., which had previously been the preserve of a privileged minority.

(e) **It may express an attitude about an idea.** Imagine that you are arguing with someone who is sticking firmly to their own point of view. They could be described as 'definite' or 'positive'; as being a person of 'principle' or 'integrity'; as 'unyielding', 'inflexible' or 'rigid'; as being 'stubborn', 'obstinate' or 'pig-headed.' All these words (and there are more!) stand for (more or less) the same idea, but obviously they communicate very different attitudes about it, from approval and respect to strong disapproval.

Emotive language (as this is called) can be dangerous when it is used to induce you to adopt an attitude you have not thought about towards something. What that thing is, is one question, and whether it is good or bad is another: emotive language blurs the line between them.

Go through paragraphs (a) to (e) again. Are you confident you understand what is being said in them?

Just to check that you have understood, here are five more examples of the same thing – but put into a different order. Can you say which of points (a) to (e) they illustrate – and how they do so? Concentrate on the way language is being used.
  (i) 'Militants are holding the country to ransom'
 (ii) 'At this moment in time'
(iii) 'Illegitimacy is on the increase due to a decline in moral standards'
(iv) 'Kellogg's Cornflakes – The Sunshine Breakfast!'
 (v) 'More Common Market rules are a threat to our freedom'

---

15 minutes   **STOP**

  (i) This is a very typical example of emotive language (e). When some people stand up for a principle or demand better working conditions, their opponents (and the media) often refer to them in this way ('Militants') which carries very negative connotations and expresses disapproval. Another very common example is that of people trying to liberate their country from foreign domination who are called 'freedom fighters' by their countrymen and 'terrorists' by the oppressors.
 (ii) I'm sure you have heard this expression before: all it means is 'currently' or 'now'. Words have been strung together to puff up the idea and impress an audience, but in fact they add nothing to the basic meaning (b).
(iii) This is rather like our earlier example of 'educational standards', because 'a decline in moral standards' is an extremely imprecise idea (c). Different people have different moral principles, and what exactly is it here that would be

'declining'? Illegitimacy may be on the increase as a statistic simply because less stigma is attached to it and people are therefore prepared to admit it publicly.

(iv) This is very typical advertising copy which uses the positive connotations of a word ('sunshine') even when in this context it means nothing at all. It is exactly the same as 'family shampoo' in example (a).

(v) The word 'freedom' here can certainly stand for more than one idea (d). Having to declare the contents of packaged food may *decrease* the freedom of the manufacturer to add or leave out what he wishes, but it may *increase* my freedom to know what I am buying.

I hope you see now why it is so important to be wary of language. Whenever you encounter an argument or a piece of reasoning in a book, or hear one being presented, ask yourself continually: What exactly is being said? Why is it being said like this? Could it be said more simply/clearly/neutrally? By doing this you will learn to 'see through' language, to see the ideas which are being expressed distinct from the means of expression.

To be able to do that is the first and perhaps the most important step towards thinking clearly. As a great philosopher (Hobbes) remarked long ago: 'words are counters for wise men, who only reckon (i.e. calculate) with them; but they are the money of fools'.

3 *Logic*

Now that we have considered some of the pitfalls involved in expressing ideas clearly, let us turn to those encountered in *connecting* ideas so as to form *arguments* or chains of reasoning which are clear, coherent and cogent.

The study of how to do this properly is called 'logic'. Like most people, you probably have an intuitive logical sense and can usually tell when there is 'something wrong' with an argument; but you may find that knowing a bit of logic enables you to pin down the error precisely. This selection does not attempt to cover the whole subject (for that, you should consult one of the books listed at the end of the chapter); it just aims to make you aware of some of the more common faults in reasoning.

A Two kinds of reasoning
Many errors arise when people fail to distinguish between the

two main kinds of reasoning recognised by logicians, which are called 'induction' and 'deduction'. Here is an example of *induction:*

> In my house there are some cyclamen plants in pots. I notice that those downstairs are flowering well although those upstairs are not. It is cooler downstairs, so I conclude that they do not like to be too warm. I notice also that those in shady rooms do not flower, from which I infer that they like plenty of light as well.

Now contrast the following example of *deduction:*

> I switch on the electric kettle to make tea and find that it is still cold by the time it usually boils. I reason that there must be a fault, and that it must be either in the power supply or in the electrical appliance (or in both). I then plug the mixer into the same socket and find that it works, so I conclude that the fault must be either in the kettle itself or in its plug and lead (or in both).

You can probably see that these two pieces of reasoning differ in several ways. The most crucial difference between them is that the conclusion of the first is much *less certain* than that of the second: I *must* be correct in thinking that the electric socket is not at fault, whereas I may well be wrong in thinking that light and temperature are what affect the plants' flowering – that may be due to some other factor altogether.

The reason for this difference is that the two kinds of reasoning proceed in different ways. *Induction* usually works from a number of observed instances and tries to establish a general rule (e.g., that cyclamen always flower best in cool, bright rooms). Inevitably the rule goes beyond the evidence: it is a statement about what is 'always' or 'generally' the case, based on the (comparatively few) cases actually observed; and therefore it is necessarily tentative, or provisional. In contrast, *deduction* usually works from general rules or principles (e.g., the laws governing the behaviour of electrical apparatus) which it applies to a particular case. Therefore the conclusion reached is as certain as the rules from which it is derived (which, in this example, are very firmly established).

---

5 minutes   STOP

Look at the two examples again and check that you really understand how they illustrate inductive and deductive reasoning. Then read each of the arguments below and decide whether it is an instance of induction or deduction. When you have done that compare your answers with those at the end of the chapter.

(a)   This tin of beans cost 32p. I have given the shopkeeper 50p: *Exercise 1*
      therefore I am owed 18p change.

(b) Not paying what you owe is the same as holding on to what is rightfully someone else's. Keeping what is someone else's is a form of theft. Not declaring income to the taxman involves not paying what you owe. Therefore not declaring income to the taxman involves theft.

(c) There's a rosy sunset. 'Red sky at night; shepherds' delight'; therefore it will be fine tomorrow.

(d) 'If a university be a place of instruction where knowledge is professed, and if in a certain university the subject of religion is excluded, then one of two conclusions is inevitable: either that Religion is not real knowledge, or that in such a university a branch of knowledge is omitted' (Newman).

(e) 'Young of the same litter sometimes differ considerably from each other, though both the young and the parents have apparently been exposed to the same conditions of life: and this shows how unimportant the direct effects of the conditions of life are in comparison with the laws of reproduction and of growth and of inheritance; for had the action of the conditions been direct, if any of the young had varied, all would probably have varied in the same manner' (Darwin).

B Validity

Besides classifying arguments into different types, logicians also study what makes them 'valid', that is, such that the conclusion does indeed follow logically from what has gone before. They have discovered that, especially in deductive reasoning, validity is ensured by the *form* or structure of the argument.

Consider the following examples:

(a) If it's Wednesday today it must be Thursday tomorrow; it is Wednesday today; therefore it's Thursday tomorrow.

(b) If they're divorced they must have been married; they are divorced; therefore they have been married.

You can see that both arguments have the same form:

(c) If P is true then Q is true; P is true; therefore Q is true.

What is more, you can see that *any* argument with that form must be valid: if it really is the case that 'if P is true then Q is true', and if it is also the case that 'P is true', then Q *must* be true too.

That may seem a rather trivial and uninspiring point. But now consider this argument:

(d) If pigs have wings, they can fly; pigs do have wings; therefore pigs can fly.

I hope your natural sense of logic tells you that there's 'something wrong' with this; I hope also that, having read the paragraphs above, you don't conclude that (d) is 'an invalid argument'. It isn't. On the contrary, it's perfectly valid: it has the same form as (a), (b) and (c), all of which are valid; therefore it is valid too.

The important point to grasp is this: *a conclusion can be valid without being true*. All that 'valid' means is 'it follows logically': *If* what goes before is true, the conclusion will be true. If it were indeed the case that pigs had wings, and that if they had wings they could fly, then it would indeed be the case that they could fly.

You can see now that there are always two questions to be asked about any piece of reasoning:
(a)   Are the statements in it true?
(b)   Does the conclusion follow logically from the statements that have gone before?
These questions are quite separate. Logic tries to answer (b) in a general way but has nothing to say about (a). Obviously, you can only tell whether or not the statements are true if you know something about the topic of the argument, and the logician may be completely ignorant about that.

---

20 minutes   **STOP**

Read the preceding paragraphs again. Make sure in particular that you understand how an *argument being valid* differs from its constituent *statements being true*. Then read the following examples of deductive reasoning and decide whether or not each is valid. Finally compare your comments with those at the end of this chapter.
(a)   If Dick and Jane are married to each other, Jane's father will   *Exercise 2*
      be Dick's father-in-law. Jane's father is Dick's father-in-law.
      Therefore Dick and Jane are married to each other.
(b)   If that boy has spots and a temperature, either he's got
      measles or some other disease. If he's got measles, daylight
      hurts his eyes. Daylight doesn't hurt his eyes. Therefore he
      hasn't got measles; therefore he has some other disease.
(c)   All Irishmen are funny. He's an Irishman: therefore he's
      funny.
(d)   If he's honest, I'm a Dutchman. I'm not a Dutchman: there-
      fore he's not honest.
(e)   Deciduous trees shed their leaves in autumn. Sycamores
      shed their leaves in autumn; therefore sycamores are deci-
      duous trees.

So far in this section you have learnt the difference between induction and deduction, and also how the validity of an argument differs from its statements being true. When trying to think clearly yourself it is very important to bear these distinctions in mind. What kind of reasoning are you engaged in? Are the statements true? Does the conclusion follow from them logically? Similarly, when you are confronted with an argument which you think is somehow 'wrong', ask the same questions to pin down exactly where the error lies.

Of course, when something *is* wrong it is not always because of an innocent error or mistake: the reason may be a deliberate attempt to confuse or mislead. Hence we turn to consider finally:

C Some common fallacies

'Fallacy' is the technical name for reasoning which is invalid. Having read the previous section, you will realise that an argument is not fallacious just because its conclusion is untrue: it is a fallacy only when the conclusion does not follow logically from what goes before. Some of the more common kinds of illogical reasoning, which are sometimes used deliberately to mislead or deceive people, are:

(a) *'Begging the question'*. In logic, this means that the argument assumes the truth of what it is supposed to prove.
    Consider this example: 'abortion is murder; murder is wrong; therefore abortion is wrong'. The word 'murder' means 'killing which is wrong' (in contrast to 'manslaughter,' 'execution', and so on, which are supposedly excusable forms of killing). Therefore to say 'abortion is murder' (the first statement of the argument) *presupposes* that 'abortion is wrong': which of course is the conclusion that the argument is supposed to establish. (Incidentally, this is not to say that abortion is not wrong! – just that this is a bad argument to prove it.)

(b) *False dilemma.* Suppose some politician claims that his policies will not lead to the disaster which I think is inevitable if they are implemented. I say: 'If he claims that, he's either a fool or a liar. He's certainly no fool: therefore he must be lying.' As you can see, my conclusion depends on the assumption that there are only two alternatives: either he is a fool, or he is a liar. But in fact, in this kind of situation, there are usually other possibilities as well: he may be sincerely mistaken, for instance. The fallacy consists in ignoring all the possibilities but two in order to give the false impression that a choice has to be made between them.

(c) *False analogy.* Two things are compared which are alike in some (usually superficial) respect; then it is argued (illegitimately) that they will be alike in some other respect.
    For instance, when Mrs. Thatcher became Prime Minister I heard it argued that because she was a housewife who could manage her domestic economy she would therefore be good at managing the economy of the country. Now of course there is a similarity between the two kinds of economic

management; but there are also huge differences, and these make the argument fallacious. (Again, this is not to say that she cannot manage the economy: the conclusion is invalid, but it may still be true.)

(d) *'Post hoc ergo propter hoc'*. A Latin phrase meaning 'after this, therefore because of this' – which is really a summary of this fallacy. It consists in assuming that simply because an event follows another it must have been caused by what happened beforehand.
This fallacy abounds in everyday life. Suppose I get a heavy cold. After a couple of days I am fed up with it so I try the new Wonder Cold Cure. A few days later the cold clears up. Therefore I conclude that the Cold Cure 'did the trick' and I go about recommending it to my friends, etc. What I over-look is the fact (established by much research) that colds usually clear up by themselves within a week or so, so that in fact I would probably have recovered just as quickly even if I had taken no medicine at all.

(e) *'Thin end of the wedge'*. (Also known as 'the slippery slope' argument). It consists in arguing that A will lead to B: that B will be unacceptable: and that therefore we shouldn't do A. There's nothing wrong with that form of argument as it stands, of course, so long as A will in fact lead to B; but it is a fallacy when the connection between them is not inevitable. For example, it might be argued that no new building should be allowed in a given place because it will lead to unrestricted development and eventual overcrowding of the neigh-bourhood. But in fact unrestricted building is not an inevita-ble consequence of one or two new houses: everything depends on what planning controls are exercised locally.

(f) *Selecting evidence*. You have seen earlier how reasoning always starts with statements or facts taken to be true. A common cause of false conclusions is starting with the wrong facts – 'wrong' in the sense that important considerations are ignored.
Suppose for instance that I want to convince you that horo-scopes really predict the future. I tell you about a series of (true) instances when my horoscope said that such-and-such would happen to me, and it did. So far so good: the fallacy occurs when I do not mention (and you ignore) all the many occasions when my horoscope said something would hap-pen and it didn't.

(g) *Demanding impossible proof*. You recall earlier that we distin-guished deduction (which yields absolute certainty) from induction (which at most establishes a very high probability). Sometimes these are confused and an inductive argument is (wrongly) rejected on the grounds that its conclusion is not as certain as the outcome of deduction.

At present, for example, there is a mass of evidence to show that 'acid rain' in Norway and Sweden results from industrial pollution in this country. British authorities are refusing to act because they claim that more studies should be carried out to prove it. Personally I don't know whether they are right or not; but I wonder just how much evidence they want. Are they demanding from inductive evidence the kind of cast-iron proof that only deduction can give? If so, they are committing this fallacy.

STOP **25 minutes** Check through the list of fallacies again. Can you think of any more? Try and find examples of your own to illustrate them. Then see which ones you can spot in this passage (compare your comments with those at the end of the chapter):

Exercise 3 Colleges and universities should do much more to make students attend classes and lectures. At present they do very little to reduce the large number of absences reported every week during term, even though many students end up by failing their examinations and having to drop out. This amounts to a dreadful waste of resources, and yet it could easily be reduced. It is well known that persistent absenteeism usually begins as occasional non-attendance: therefore academic staff should acknowledge their duty to 'check-up' whenever students are absent and, if necessary, to use appropriate means to make them attend. This is an unwelcome task, no doubt, but it is preferable to being lax and indifferent. As many parents and psychologists know, 'spare the rod and spoil the child' is a saying which contains a good deal of truth.

In this brief introduction to the skills of clear thinking you have learnt these fundamental points:
(a) Language can easily affect our thinking. Emotive or vague expressions (for instance) can mislead or confuse our reasoning. It is hard to think clearly unless we express our thoughts in clear, precise and neutral language.
(b) There is more than one kind of reasoning. Induction and deduction proceed differently and establish different degrees of certainty. They should not be confused.

(c)   When a conclusion follows logically from preceding statements the argument is said to be 'valid'. In deduction, validity results from the structure of an argument. A valid conclusion is not necessarily true: the validity of the argument
and the truth of its statement are separate issues.
(d)   Invalid arguments are called 'fallacies'. Sometimes they are
used deliberately to mislead us. Some of the more common
ones have been described.

These are the fundamentals of clear thinking. If you master these
points you will get better at spotting the muddled or misleading
thinking of others, and your own thinking and expression will
become clearer. But, as I said at the beginning, it may take time:
you should practice on the exercises in this unit, and perhaps also
consult one of the books listed below.

Further reading
A. Flew, *Thinking About Thinking* (Fontana). Clear and well-writ-
ten; discusses common causes of confusion.

J. Inglis and R. Lewis, *Clear Thinking* (National Extension
College). Plenty of exercises, but more on language than logic.

P. Shaw, *Logic and its Limits* (Pan). Lively and readable, but more
on logic than language.

R. H. Thouless, *Straight and Crooked Thinking* (Pan). Something of
a classic now, and probably still the best book on the subject: clear
and comprehensive.

Comments on exercises

Exercise 1
(a)   Deduction: given the rules of arithmetic, etc., the conclusion
must be correct.
(b)   Deduction: again, granting the definitions, the conclusion
follows necessarily.
(c)   Induction: the conclusion is no more than probable!
(d)   Deduction: the conclusion follows necessarily from the definitions.
(e)   Induction: 'probably' in the last sentence is a clue.

Exercise 2
(a)   Invalid: assuming that the first and second statements are
both true, the third could still be false: Dick could be married

to Jane's sister, for instance, and still have Jane's father as his father-in-law.
(b)   Valid, but complex! It combines two valid arguments: 'If he's got measles . . . he hasn't got measles', and 'If that boy . . . he hasn't got measles; therefore he has . . .' (write them out in full separately).
(c)   Valid, but the first statement is false.
(d)   Valid, but again the first statement is false (and silly!): what connection could there be between his honesty and my nationality to make it true?
(e)   Invalid. The statements are all true, but the conclusion doesn't follow: replace 'sycamores' by 'chrysanthemums', for instance.

Exercise 3
The main fallacies here are:

'They do very little . . . even though': there is a subtle implication here that students fail because they have been absent. This is a 'post hoc ergo propter hoc': their failure doesn't necessarily result from their absence: both could be the result of something else (disenchantment with their course, for example).

'Many students end up . . .': well, so they do, alas; but equally many don't, despite having been absent quite a lot. Selected evidence!

'It is well known that . . .': is it? I just invented this when I wrote the passage. This is an example of the 'fallacy of assertion' which I haven't mentioned before: It's really just the trick of saying things confidently so that people believe you.

'Absenteeism begins . . .': a 'thin end of the wedge' argument. In fact it's not at all obvious that checking up on every minor absence will do much to stop long-term, persistent absenteeism.

'Acknowledge their duty': well, that assumes that they have a duty which is there to be acknowledged, as it were, which is precisely what the passage is trying to prove: the whole question is begged here.

'It is preferable to': a false dilemma: there are other options besides *either* checking on every absence *or* ignoring all of them – e.g., just checking on those longer than a week.

'Spoil the child': but we're not talking about children: we're talking about young adults of 17+. False analogy.

Self-assessment exercises

Exercise 1
Without looking back over this chapter, can you list all the points
we have covered in it?

Exercise 2
Read through the following passage very carefully and make
notes on the way language is being used in it. If necessary, check
through Section 2 again to remind yourself how language can be
employed to manipulate your response. At the end of the exercise, compare your observations with those in the guidance
notes.

Wooden furniture can be a beautiful feature in any modern
home. Maintenance is easy, since it requires no more than regular
dusting with a soft cloth. If it begins to look dull and lifeless after a
while, a liberal application of polish (preferably containing
beeswax) will be beneficial; but some care should be exercised in
this treatment, since too much polish will be excessive and will
produce a smeary, greasy surface rather than a deep and lustrous
sheen.

Exercise 3
We all know that politicians try to persuade us by using a variety
of techniques: persuasive use of language, dubious analogies,
concentrating on part of an argument only, selective use of evidence, personal attacks, sweeping generalisations and many,
many more. To avoid being taken in we need to be aware of the
tricks of the politican's trade. Clear thinking in this respect is of
crucial importance if we are to use our vote wisely and perform
other roles in our democratic system. Below I have extracted the
first few lines of the three major election manifestos offered at the
1983 General Election. Study them carefully and then write a
critique of the reasoning and persuasive techniques displayed in
each.

A The Conservative Party:
66 **'The Challenge of our Times'**
Foreword by Margaret Thatcher
In the last four years, Britain has recovered her confidence and
self-respect. We have retained the regard and admiration of other
nations. We are seen today as a people with integrity, resolve and
the will to succeed.

This manifesto describes the achievements of four years of Conservative government and sets out our plans for our second term.

The choice before the nation is stark: either to continue our present steadfast progress towards recovery, or to follow policies more extreme and more damaging than those ever put forward by any previous Opposition. **"**

We face three challenges: the defence of our country, the employment of our people, and the prosperity of our economy.

B The Liberal/SDP Alliance:
**" 'Working together for Britain'
PROGRAMME FOR GOVERNMENT**
An introduction by Roy Jenkins and David Steel
The General Election on June 9th 1983 will be seen as a watershed in British politics. It may be recalled as the fateful day when depression became hopelessness and the slide of the post-war years accelerated into the depths of decline. Alternatively it may be remembered as the turning point when the people of this country, at the eleventh hour, decided to turn their backs on dogma and bitterness and chose a new road of partnership and progress. **"**

C The Labour Party:
" 'The New Hope for Britain'
Foreword by Michael Foot
Here you can read Labour's plan to do the things crying out to be done in our country today.

To get Britain back to work. To rebuild our shattered industries. To get rid of the ever-growing dole queues. To correct and enlarge our National Health Service and our other great social services. To help stop the nuclear arms race. Here you can see what Labour is determined to do, and how we shall set about it. **"**

Exercise 3
Facts and values
To analyse and critically assess arguments or pieces of writing we must be aware of the different kinds of statement which can be made. For the purposes of this exercise we are going to distinguish between two kinds of statement: those which are factual and those which embody values.

Factual Statements can either be disproved or verified; some easily, e.g., 'Shrewsbury is in Shropshire'; some with greater difficulty, e.g., 'most' people are in favour of Capital Punishment for murder'; and some are virtually impossible to verify, e.g., 'more Russians eat boiled eggs than Chinese'.

Value judgements can neither be proved nor disproved because they express an opinion or belief. They are frequently prefaced by 'ought' or 'should', e.g., 'life is good', 'dogs should be kept off the street', 'citizens ought to obey the law'.

Bearing these distinctions in mind, state which category the following statements fall into and why. Warning: this exercise may be more difficult than you think!

 1 Fred is a bricklayer.
 2 God is love.
 3 Smoking causes heart disease.
 4 A nuclear war would destroy the world.
 5 Men make better managers than women.
 6 Secretaries should get more money.
 7 Teachers get the pay they deserve.
 8 Of course the opportunities for men and women should be equal.
 9 The motor-car is murdering our big cities.
10 Bricklaying is good for your health.
11 Black people do not want to eat the same food as white people.
12 Philosophy is the prince of academic subjects.

5 *Grammar and punctuation*

It is well to remember that grammar is common speech
formulated.   *W. Somerset Maugham*

Contents

Introduction
1   Punctuation – the basic elements
2   Miscellaneous punctuation
3   Clear writing
4   A note on quotations
5   Spelling
6   Further reading
    Self-assessment exercises

Introduction

As we have said elsewhere in these chapters, many adult
students feel that they have lost or never had the ability to write
clearly and correctly. This often simply a matter of practice. After
leaving secondary school, many people have very little need to
write, apart perhaps from the occasional letter to a relative or
friend. The result is that they lose touch with both the basic rules
and the finer points of grammar and punctuation which they
have been taught. In one sense good writing can be considered
like a sport or physical skill: unless you keep in training or
practice you will not be able to perform so well. We would like to
reassure those people who feel a little 'unfit' in this respect that
with regular practice, the rudiments of good punctuation and
grammar can be quickly acquired or reacquired.

In this chapter we will be taking you through some of the most
elementary 'rules' relating to punctuation and grammar. We will
as usual explain each topic, illustrate it with examples, and
present you with exercises to work on. But before we do so a
preliminary word of warning is necessary.

Apart from these most elementary rules (like beginning each

sentence with a capital letter) both punctuation and grammar are ultimately a matter of *style* and *taste*. That is, they are determined by a sensitivity to language rather than by any iron laws. And good taste is *not* something you can look up in a book: you must acquire it by becoming thoroughly conversant with the medium of language and how it is used.

Many students also feel frustrated when they read work by well-known writers which appears to break the rules or ignore the codes of good practice which convention lays down. If this happens to you, try to remember two things. First, these writers have mastered the basic rules and have thus earned the right to 'bend' them if they wish. When *you* can write perfectly fluent prose you may be able to indulge in a little experimentation. Second, this writing will almost certainly *not* be formal essay-writing of the type you will be producing on this course. We deal elsewhere (Chapter 8) with different types and styles of writing, but you should try to remember that the academic essay is *not* the place for experimentation or idiosyncratic usage. Journalism, fiction, diaries, or poetry may permit unconventional punctuation and grammar, but basic essay-writing of the type we will be dealing with on this course does *not*. You should be aiming, unless you are told otherwise, to produce good, clear, comprehensible prose.

Punctuation – the basic elements   1

There are many ways in which sentences can be punctuated, but right from the start we would like to suggest that – for the time being anyway – you limit yourself to using on the most basic marks of punctuation. These are

the comma	,
the semi-colon	;
the colon	:
the full stop	.

We will deal with things like dashes and brackets later on in this chapter, but since these are often the cause of mistakes if not used properly we strongly recommend that they are left alone until you are quite confident in the use of the basic marks. An excellent little book by Michael Temple, *Get it Right*, has been drawn upon for sections of this unit and is recommended as a more comprehensive treatment.

What *are* these basic elements of punctuation? What function do they perform? If we arrange them in order it might give you a clue.

, ; : .

STOP   5 minutes

They are in fact *pauses* of varying length, ranging from a slight pause indicated by the comma to the complete pause of a full stop. And to illustrate this notion further we might extend the observation to paragraphs and chapters. These are the equivalent of even longer stops, aren't they?

Now let's consider each of the marks in turn. First the comma.

A   **The comma**

The comma creates a *slight pause* in the sentence. It is therefore used when we wish to add a clause, when the individual items in a list of terms are being kept separate, or when there is some change in subject or sense. These are best illustrated by practical examples. We will cover the most straightforward cases first.

(i)   The list of terms.

A long list of terms should be kept separate by the use of the comma:

The store was stocked with fruit, vegetables, meat, bread, and cereals.

This could also apply to a series of adjectives qualifying a noun:

She was a bright, extroverted, confident woman.

But when one of these adjectives qualifies the other, no comma is necessary:

a bright red dress

the small local supermarket

(ii)   A succession of adverbs, verbs, or clauses.

adverbs   She walked out of the room, slowly, heavily, and sadly.

verbs   He was slipping, sliding and falling forwards on the ice.

clauses   We all travelled to town, ate in a good restaurant, went for a walk in the park, then visited a museum.

(iii)   To separate clauses when there is a change of subject or clause.

The boys worked quickly, but not as quickly as the girls.

My friend, who owns a big house, often takes in lodgers.

(iv)   Where a clause is included as a qualification, an insertion, or an afterthought.

A large ornament, well polished and heavily encrusted with jewels, stood in the centre of the table.

To travel alone, as we are often warned, can be a risky business.

82

These sentences make sense, don't they?

There are, of course many other applications for the comma, but I don't think an exhaustive list would be useful at this stage. It is more important that you grasp the basic instances where they *should* be used, and then gradually become acquainted with more sophisticated usages – either through the guides listed under 'Further reading' at the end of this chapter, or through the practice of your own reading and writing. This will apply to all the items of punctuation and grammar discussed in this chapter, but before we move on to one or two exercises here is an illustration of the importance of the simple comma.

What is the difference between these two statements?

(a) The cats, who were hungry, were fed.

(b) The cats who were hungry were fed.

---

5 minutes   **STOP**

In statement (a) *all* the cats were fed. In statement (b) *only* those cats who were hungry were fed, and by implication the rest were not.

Punctuate the following correctly, using commas

(a) I opened the window and breathed in the clear fresh bracing air.

(b) He had a mohican haircut a safety pin in his nose tears in his jeans and "The Clash' tattooed on his forehead.

(c) Mr Ramsbottom livid with rage visibly shaking and emitting strange gurgling sounds marched up the path to my door.

(d) There were six industrious Swedes ten stolid Norwegians six enigmatic Finns and six anarchic Danes on the Nordic Summer School.

(e) A man whom I know well entered the room quickly rubbing his hands and smiling.

---

10 minutes   **STOP**

Comment

(a) I opened the window and breathed in the clear, fresh, bracing air.

(b) He had a mohican haircut, a safety pin in his nose, tears in his jeans, and 'The Clash' tattooed on his forehead.

(c) Mr Ramsbottom, livid with rage, visibly shaking, and emitting strange gurgling sounds, marched up the path to my door.

(d) There were six industrious Swedes, ten stolid Norwegians, six enigmatic Finns and six anarchic Danes on the Nordic

Summer School.
(e) A man, whom I know well, entered the room quickly, rubbing his hands and smiling.

The punctuation in sentence (e) is interesting. You could almost dispense with the first two commas, depending on taste but the location of a comma either *before* or *after* the word 'quickly' alters the sense of the sentence.

B   The semi-colon

This is the punctuation mark which seems to cause the most confusion and give most problems to students. If you are in any doubt about it I would advise you to avoid using it and simply stick to the comma and full stop as your basic marks of punctuation. A series of short, simple but *clear* sentences will always create a much better effect than long ones which are not carefully constructed or punctuated.

The semi-colon represents a slightly longer pause than the comma.

It has two general uses:
(i)   To punctuate clauses which could be separate but are closely related; for example when the second clause represents a development of or a contrast to the first.
  – There are those who have a prejudice against the semi-colon; personally I find it very useful.
  – When we arrived we were tired; we just sat in the car and rested for thirty minutes.
  – I like marmalade; my wife just won't touch the stuff.
Notice that the clauses could stand alone as sentences but too many short sentences produce a jerky, staccato effect. The same would be true if the clauses or phrases referred to different aspects of the same subjects; in the example below semi-colons are again used to add greater fluency and balance.
  – The first man was friendly; the second was amorous; the third was downright unpleasant.
(ii) To punctuate a series of phrases or clauses which themselves contain punctuation.
  – The outbreak of war was caused by a number of factors: Hitler's determination to occupy Austria, Czechoslovakia and Poland; the longstanding desire of Chamberlain and Daladier, as opposed to Winston Churchill, to avoid war at all costs; and Stalin's cynical, last minute deal with Hitler.

Punctuate the following correctly
(a)   I have known more sincere men but I have met few more charming.

(b)   He rushed to the door his hair was awry and his sweater on back to front.
(c)   To understand her properly you have to appreciate that her third husband not to mention her second were alcoholics her parents and her various parents-in-law disowned her after her convictions for drug pushing and she had been unhappy ever since leaving her home town.

---

10 minutes   **STOP**

Comment
(a)   I have known more sincere men; but I have met few more charming.
(b)   He rushed to the door; his hair was awry and his sweater on back to front.
(c)   To understand her properly you have to appreciate that: her third husband, not to mention her second, were alcoholics; her parents, and her various parents-in-law, disowned her after her convictions for drug pushing; and she had been unhappy ever since leaving her home town.

C   The colon
This is the longest pause before coming to the full stop. It is usually used to make a very pointed connection or contrast between the clauses on either sides of it.
(i)   Before a list.
       Three objects lay on the table: a book, a vase, and a shotgun.
(ii)   To make a long pause.
       One good thing came of the inheritance: he founded a hospital.
(iii) To mark a contrast.
       John likes dogs: Mary hates them.

One other popular use is to mark the introduction of a quotation, thus
    The speaker then addressed the crowd: 'Now hear this!'

One way of understanding the colon is to think of it meaning: 'That is to say.'
Now try the exercise below.

Punctuate the following correctly.
(a)   After deep thought I came to a definite conclusion I would have two fried egs and not one.
(b)   Geoffrey was still delighted with the game I was fed up.
(c)   In order to do justice to the garden I needed four things a spade a fork a hole and a rake.

STOP   10 minutes

Comment
(a) After deep thought I came to a definite conclusion: I would have two fried eggs and not one.
(b) Geoffrey was still delighted with the game: I was fed up.
(c) In order to do justice to the garden I needed four things: a spade, a fork, a hoe and a rake.

D   The full stop

Just a brief note on this. A full stop, of course, marks the end of a sentence, e.g., 'The cat sat on the mat.' You should also notice that *after* a full stop your next sentence must always begin with a capital letter. But when does a sentence end? Providing it has a subject, an active verb and (usually) an object, it can be finished when you think it appropriate.

I am aware that this guidance seems rather simplistic but the answer ultimately depends upon judgement and taste. But I will add here a word of advice for anyone in doubt. *In general keep sentences short rather than allowing them to run on at great length.* More students make mistakes through sloppy verbosity than err on the side of terseness.

To repeat my earlier suggestion, I would strongly recommend that if you are in any doubt concerning the use of punctuation marks, you should limit your use to just these basic few. In fact it is possible to write perfectly clear and fluent prose using only the comma and the full stop. Certainly, more mistakes are made by those people who scatter around punctuation marks like confetti than by those who are sparing and restrained in their use of them. This is especially true of the other miscellaneous punctuation marks which we will come to next. I would even go so far as to suggest that to begin with you try to do without them altogether. This will help 'clarify' your writing. Afterwards you can introduce the use of them gradually, and with restraint. You may feel that this advice is unduly puritanical, but it is based on many years of observing students battling with the same difficulties. In one of his earlier units Bill likens this corrective process to that of being coached at tennis. At first the 'correct' instruction we are given feels less comfortable than our old 'incorrect' habits: but these must be eliminated if we wish to improve our skill. I think the anaology is a good one, and for most students the route to good clear writing lies in discipline and practice.

Miscellaneous punctuation   2

We now come to a collection of the other most popular marks of punctuation. You will undoubtedly need these at some time or other, but at the risk of being very boring I am going to repeat my suggestion that to begin with you *use them as little as possible.*

(a)   **The exclamation mark!**

This is used to indicate a tone of anger, alarm, surprise, or a sharp comment or instruction:

> Stop it! Oh dear!
> Certainly not! Catch this!

It can also be used to indicate a tone of heavy irony or sarcasm:

> Oh yes, I'll *bet* you did!

This should only be used if absolutely necessary. Like many of the other punctuation marks which follow, too frequent use seems to encourage a sloppy conversational tone into the writing which is rarely called for. More of this in a moment.

(b)   **The question mark?**

This, obviously, is used to indicate a direct question:

> What do the workers earn?
> Why did they choose him?

But it is not necessary when a question is *reported:*

> I wonder if she will ask me.

Many students often forget to include the question mark at the end of a long question.

> What, given the unprecedented circumstances surrounding the trial, and the unreliability of many of the witnesses, will the outcome be?

(c)   **The dash –**

This is a good example of a mark which seems to cause trouble in direct proportion to the frequency with which it is used. If employed often, it encourages sloppiness. There are two legitimate uses.

(i)   Two should be used to indicate a clause which has been inserted into a sentence:

> When I drew the curtains – I had a terrible hangover – the light seemed blinding.
> All heavy vehicles – cars, lorries, buses – will be banned from this zone.

(ii)   One should be used to indicate a change of thought or an emphasis at the end of a sentence:

> The weather was fine – but I still felt sick.
> The government has again raised taxes – taxes which people cannot afford to pay.

(d)   **Brackets ( )**

These are *always* used in pairs (Don't forget to 'close' brackets), to indicate 'asides' or to enclose illustrative examples:

I completed my stay in Paris (as every visitor should) with a visit to the Louvre.

All the fruit (apples, lemons, and grapes) was piled high in a glass bowl.

You will see that these are used in exactly the same way as two dashes (but they tend to be less abrupt). And note, as in my last statement, that if the final bracket ends your sentence, the full stop comes *outside* it.

(e) **Abbreviations: etc., i.e. viz. &**

Strictly speaking these are not marks of punctuation, but they tend to be used in the same way. I am not going to give you a long list of the most common because – as you by now can probably guess – I believe that they should be used as little as possible. It is perfectly reasonable that you should use them in taking notes for your own use. After all, that is what they are for – to save you having to write out a whole phrase. But in essay-writing they have the impression of laziness. Be prepared to write out terms like 'that is' in full rather than use i.e., and avoid 'etcetera'.

(f) **Italics**

These too are not strictly punctuation, but they perform the same function in helping to give emphasis and convey a *tone* to your writing.

She was *not* the best choice of candidate.

Good writers *seldom* over-use emphasis in their work.

You should note that underlining, is also used to indicate book and play titles.

Lady Macbeth and Duncan are characters in <u>Macbeth</u>.

Fanny Price is the heroine of Jane Austen's novel, <u>Mansfield Park</u>.

They are also used if you wish to introduce a foreign word or phrase into an English sentence.

Without being particularly intelligent, he had plenty of *savoir faire*.

(g) **The apostrophe**

This is becoming a vexed issue as some usage is currently in the process of changing. But you should be aware of the rules governing the two basic uses for it – to indicate either possession or contraction.

(i) *The possessive case*

This is indicated in the case of single nouns by an apostrophe followed by an 's'.

The cat's whiskers.

A man's coat.

A common dilemma is where do you put the apostrophe when the final letter is 's'? In the case of singular nouns it comes after the 's' followed by another 's'.

Mr Davies's jacket.

The watercress's flavour.

But in the case of plurals the apostrophe comes *after* the 's' and stands on its own.

The horses' stable.

The tables' legs.

It is *not* used with the possessive pronouns his, hers, its ours, yours, and theirs but it *is* used with 'One'. For example, 'one's opinion'.

You should be aware that many business concerns are getting around the possible confusion here by eliminating use of the apostrophe altogether from their titles:

Barclays Bank

Harpers and Queen

(ii) *Contraction*

The apostrophe is also used to indicate where a letter has been   omitted:

you're = you are

it's = It is – (not to be confused with 'it's' – belonging to it)

they're = they are

In general you should try to minimise the use of contractions in essays and formal writing.

(h) **Inverted commas** *(or speech marks)*

These are usually (but not exclusively) used to indicate that someone's speech is being reported. They may be double marks (The bride said, "I will") or single ('I will'). There are two important points to remember in connection with their use:

(i)   You should quote exactly what was said and make the quotation fit grammatically with your own words.

(ii) Whichever system of notation you use, once you have started, *stick to it.*

Below are some examples. Read them through and note the punctuation used carefully.

(a) 'I don't really like cheese omelette,' he muttered.

(b) 'Would you like an ice cream?' she asked.

(c) 'Before I can agree to do this,' he insisted, 'a full apology is required.'

(d) 'I asked him who he was,' said Philip, 'and he replied, "I am Sir Cyril Blenkinsop." '

(e) 'First we'll go and see "The Mouse Trap",' suggested Tony, 'and then we'll call into 'The Thirsty Heart' for as much beer as we can drink before closing time.'

---

15 minutes   **STOP**

Comment

(a) Inverted commas indicate the speech reported and a *comma* marks the end of the speech even though it is grammatically a proper sentence.

(b) No comma is necessary when the speech reported ends with a question or exclamation mark.

(c) Commas are used to separate the units of speech. The first word of the second part does not have a capital letter as it is a continuation of the same sentence. Note the inverted commas come *outside* and not inside the full stop.

(d) Double inverted commas are used to indicate a speech *within* a reported speech.

(e) Play titles, tunes and names of pubs, buildings, theatres and so forth are often placed inside quote signs.

(i) **The hyphen**

This is *not* the same as a dash. It is used to make a connection between words. Two basic usages are easily dealt with:
(I)is used to attach prefixes to words:
 Ex-President, Vice-Chancellor
 multi-storey, anti-clockwise

  (ii) and when forming a composite word from two, three or more words:
   lazy good-for-nothing
   get-up-and-go
   an unable-to-get-up feeling.

(j) **Capital letters**

There are a number of basic rules. Capitals are *always* used:
1 To mark the beginning of a sentence.
2 For the first person pronoun 'I'.
3 For names of people, places, months of the year and days of the week:
 John, Manchester, July, Tuesday.
4 For adjectives derived from places and people:
 Indian, Spanish, Thatcherite.
5 For the first word of a title:
 The Judgement of Paris, The Times,
 The Pig and Whistle.

There remain a number of cases where the use of capitals is a question of taste or convention. Terms like 'government', 'parliament', 'bank holiday', and 'army' may or may not take a capital depending upon the context in which they are used or the code of practice of the person using them. You will simply have to become sensitive to such matters through regular attention to detail. In the meantime, whatever convention you decide to follow, *be consistent.*

Finally, in this section, a word of warning against combining elements of punctuation. My advice, as you now know, is to use as little punctuation as possible. Some people, however, will still be tempted into such combinations as:—
These are not only unsightly, but more importantly, *they are not necessary.*

Clear writing   3

You may not necessarily be aware of it, but the structure of a basic sentence in English is as follows:

SUBJECT + VERB + OBJECT (or PREDICATE)
  John   shuts   the door

It may not always be easy to identify these elements (if the sentence is complex or long, for instance) but I am drawing your attention to this basic structure for two reasons:

First – many of the problems in writing clearly arise when one of these important elements is *missing.*

Second – many of the other problems arise because the 'logic' of the connection between these elements is not maintained.

There are many reasons why some students find it difficult to write clearly. These could for convenience be split into two categories: the student is unsure of
(a) points of grammar
(b) organising a sentence
These two categories overlap a great deal, but I have separated them in order to say that the finer points of grammar are best dealt with by studying the texts recommended at the end of this unit.
If you are uncertain about grammar in general there are specialised textbooks which will help you by explaining the finer points of detail. But don't imagine that you need to know all the technical terms of grammar in order to write clearly. It is far more to do with being sensitively attuned to language and the way it is used.

What I am going to offer here are some suggestions of a more general nature under a heading which might be termed 'Organising your sentence'. These suggestions will be based on what are the most common problems. In one sense it is unfortunate that we have to deal with the difficulty in what might seem this rather negative manner, but simply pointing to good practice does not seem to be enough. Many students whose writing is not so clear have a vague notion that something is wrong – but they are not sure what it is.

In my experience people who write badly do so because they are confused, and these following suggestions are offered to help them clear up that confusion. And what the suggestions have in common is an underlying recommendation that writing be kept clear, simple, and straightforward. Most students with writing difficulties can see enormous and immediate improvements in the quality of their work as soon as they begin to simplify it. Let's start with the most common problems.

A   The sentence that goes on too long
Many students, once they have started a sentence, seem reluctant or unable to bring it to an end. This may be because
(a)   they are unsure about punctuation
(b)   they have tried to cram too many ideas into it
(c)   they are simply 'rambling' – adding one thing onto another.
Here is an example which illustrates all these points:
> With all the new household equipment TV's, radios refrigerators, vacuum cleaners dishwashers its a wonder we are not all robots, however they do give a lot of employment, boring as it may be for some poor devil standing on a production line maybe putting one screw in a hole all day, no wonder Ford's go out on strike.

Using my points (a), (b), and (c) above make notes on what you think is 'wrong' about the sentence, and then try to re-write it so that it makes sense.

STOP   **5 minutes**

Comment
(a)   *Punctuation*
   The list of equipment needs a comma after each item, and I think it would be easier to read if it were separated off by dashes after 'equipment' and before 'its a wonder'. The comma following 'robots' should be a full stop – because what follows is a different topic altogether. The same is true for that following 'all day'.
   Two small points of detail: 'its' should be 'it's (because a contraction of 'it is'), and 'Ford's' should read 'workers at Fords'.

(b) *Too many ideas*
     The list of equipment itself is rather long. Just three items
     would have made the point. After 'however' there is a shift
     to a different topic – employment – and then another to the
     boredom of production work. And as if that was not enough
     there is thrown in another – strikes as a result of boredom.
(c) *'Rambling'*
     This 'sentence' has been written without giving careful
     thought to the topic under consideration. The ideas are just
     loosely associated, and there is a suggestion that they have
     simply been put down as they come to mind. The reader can
     guess at a general notion the writer might have, but the
     expression is diffuse and confusing.

     Given these observations, here is how it might be clarified:
         With all the new household equipment – TVs, refriger-
         ators, dishwashers – it's a wonder we are not all robots.
         However, making them does provide a lot of employment,
         boring as it may be for those poor devils standing on a
         production line all day long.

You will notice that I have added one or two words and omitted
some others. Don't imagine that this is 'cheating'! Anything
which helps clarify matters is welcome. And students should get
used to the idea that your first effort is not necessarily the best
that can be done with the idea or the material. Be prepared to
write, re-write, and if necessary re-write again.

B   Too much punctuation
Some students who are unsure about the conventions of punctuation try to compensate by putting in as much as possible – 'just to
be on the safe side'. But too much punctuation can be just as
confusing as too little. This is because marks of punctuation
always introduce a *pause* into the sentence, after which we are
accustomed to expect some grammatical 'shift'. If this is not
forthcoming we feel we have lost our bearings. Here is a simple
example:
    We'd reached the house, by late afternoon; and had thus
    entered directly not even looking up, it was a relief, to be away
    from the city and all its drawbacks.
In fact there is both too much here, and at one crucial point too
little.

Make a note of what is wrong here – just in terms of punctuation –
then re-write the sentence so that its meaning becomes clear.

---

5 minutes   **STOP**

Comment

The first comma is not necessary. The semi-colon could be either a comma or could be omitted. There should be a comma after 'directly'. The comma after 'up' should be a full stop – because what follows is a separate idea altogether. No comma is necessary after 'relief'.

The statement could therefore be clarified thus:

We had reached the house by late afternoon and had thus entered directly, not even looking up. It was a relief to be away from the city and all its drawbacks.

C   The missing item

Apart from a lapse in attention or something like a mental 'blind spot' it is not easy to say why this phenomenon occurs, but some students are given to simply missing important items out of their sentences. It can be the subject, the verb, or the object: the result always seems to be equally confusing to the reader.

Let's look at a typical example to illustrate the point.

The problems, and these are manifold, such as confidence, limited experience, and even lack of opportunity'

This is an easy example. You can imagine what has happened. 'The problems' is the subject of the statement. The student has decided to give examples of them, and has written them down as soon as possible. But then the sentence – statement does not come to an end. It has no principal verb or object. The student perhaps imagines that 'are' is a verb, but this only a subsidiary verb in the list of problems. Perhaps the original intention was to say that 'the problems are not easily solved'. In this case the sentence might read:

The manifold problems – lack of confidence, limited experience, even lack of opportunity – are not easily solved.

D   The conversational tone

An 'incomplete' sentence is often produced because the student slips into a conversational tone, falsely imagining that this will give extra colour to the writing. The result is grammatically shoddy.

Humpty-Dumpty then falls off the wall. All the
king's horses, etc. Just a big mistake.

Avoid this attitude. It is lazy, because you are offering fragments, mere phrases, instead of properly constructed sentences. And it is usually dangerous, because it encourages you to stop thinking carefully about the subject under consideration.

E   Participle phrases

These are a frequent source of problems. Instead of writing *directly* many students seem to think it adds polish to their statements by starting them half way through or writing them back to front. This is a typical example:

Coming in to town, the castle was a splendid sight.

The logic of this statement as it stands is that the castle is coming into the town! Obviously that is *not* what was meant. The statement could be written.

As we came into the town, the castle was a splendid sight.

or

The castle was a splendid sight as we came into the town.

Notice that in both cases the statement is more direct, and in the second (most direct) statement the basis subject – verb – object order is restored.

Here is another example, just to reinforce the point.

Yesterday from my window, gazing down on to the traffic, a horse and cart plodded along the busy street.

This has a horse simultaneously looking from a window and plodding along the street! What the writer obviously *meant* to say (or *should* have said) was

Gazing down from my window yesterday onto the traffic, I *saw* a horse and cart as it plodded along the busy street.

F   Subject–verb separation

This is a problem which seems to arise from over-eagerness. The sentence begins with its subject, but then – perhaps because some new or last-minute idea occurs to the writer – it is immediately qualified in some way. Very often the qualification is itself qualified, and only then, at the end of what might be a very long sentence, is the principle verb added. Here is an example to illustrate the point:

The postman, walking briskly down the tree-lined avenue, along which were two continuous lines of parked cars, suddenly stopped.

You can see how ridiculous the effect of this is. The problem is very similar to that of the missing item. What has happened is that the writer has not thought through and put into a logical order what he or she wanted to say. Items of secondary importance (the avenue, the parked cars) have been mixed up with the most important ('the postman stopped'), and the result is confusing.

G   Case agreement
When the subject of a sentence is singular then the verb must also be in its singular form.

The woman in the picture *is* beautiful.

But problems often arise here when the subject is an indefinite or a collective noun.

No one can know *his* own future.
The team *is* going to win.

Here is an example of incorrect usage caused by uncertainty over the singular/plural question:

Many of us feel inadequate, and that we could not hope to compete with, say, a young student who had just finished their A levels.

You can see why the confusion has arisen. A plural 'many' has been compared with a single 'student' but the notion of plurality has remained in the writer's mind. The sentence should end

either 'who *has* just finished his/her A levels'
or   'young students who *have* just finished their A levels'
       (better)

H   Bad starts
Try to avoid starting sentences with conjunctions like 'and', 'but', 'also', 'through', and 'owing to'. This is not a rule of grammar, but it can be a major source of confusion. Until you are very confident about your control of grammar and syntax, you should stick to simple and straightforward usage. Remember the subject – Verb – Object sequence as a good corrective.

4   *A note on quotations*

How to quote correctly
There are in general two reasons for using quotations:
(a) When you wish to cite evidence from textbooks or secondary sources to support your argument.
(b) When a piece of literature is itself the subject of your essay (say, criticism of a poem or novel) and you need to refer to it in your discussion.

The conventions surrounding accurate quotation and reference are relatively simple, and they are based on the need for *accuracy, consistency* and *clarity*. Keep in mind the idea that a tutor marking your work should be able, if he wishes, to check the accuracy of the quotation you use.

1 Accurate reference

If in an essay you wish to support your argument with the opinion of an expert then you should do so clearly, putting the words quoted between quotation marks (inverted commas) then giving your source of reference. This is done either as a footnote or a reference note at the end of your essay, thus:

References
1. D. McLellan, *The Thought of Karl Marx*, Macmillan, 1971, p. 113.

Try to adopt the conventional order of presenting this information.

Author – Title – Publisher – Date – Page Reference

(This is the order adopted by most library reference systems).

2 How to quote – and how much

Remember that quotations should generally be used only to support or reinforce the argument you are making, or perhaps to illustrate a point of your discussion with 'expert' opinion.

Don't therefore quote so much that either your own argument is drowned, or your essay appears like a patchwork of other people's ideas sewn together with your own occasional connecting links.

Don't be tempted to quote huge chunks from someone else's work, leaving your tutor to spot those few words which are supposed to be significant.

When you wish to quote briefly from another source do it thus:

> As Smith argues in his commentary on community policing: 'the confidence of society is greater the closer it is to its local police force' (p. 212).

Sometimes in more advanced essays it is necessary to quote longer passages in order to discuss an argument at greater length. In this case the convention is to *indent* the quotation thus:

As Smith argues in his commentary on community policing:

> the confidence of society is greater the closer it is to its local police force. We should therefore welcome a return to the policy of the neighbourhood-based force and the scaling down of large scale metropolitan units (p. 212).

What this argument fails to take into account, however, is . . .

3 Quotation in a 'literary' essay

The conventions of quotation are exactly the same in a literary essay, but obviously in the case of any disciplines which involve the detailed examination of a particular text (book/play/essay/poem) where repeated reference must be made to it, slightly more licence is permitted. In the discussion of a short poem the words quoted would merely be indicated in quotation marks:

> When Blake speaks of the 'charted streets' he . . .

If the poem were long, a line number might be given:

> Later Eliot (in *The Waste-land*) echoes Shakespeare:
> 'The chair she sat in, like a burnished throne' (line 77)

One of the many purposes of the literary essay is to demonstrate that you can make linguistically fine discriminations and that you are alert to subleties within the text. Draw attention to just the few significant words by quoting them alone.

> Shakespeare's linguistic compression – 'plated Mars', 'triple pillar of the world', 'such a mutual pair' – (*Antony and Cleopatra*, Act I Scene I) illustrates a degree of poetic density which . . .

4 Incorporating the quotation

It is very important when using quotation to make sure that the grammatical flow and logic of your own argument is not interrupted. Take care that there are no abrupt changes of tense, no gaps, no grammatical inconsistencies or breakdowns in syntax.
You can often make quotations 'fit' grammatically into your argument, as well as shortening them when required, by missing out any unnecessary link words or unnecessary clauses. But when you do this you must indicate the fact that you have done so with the use of the three dots convention.

> Smith goes on to claim that 'the State does not have a *direct* connection with social mores . . . but it does have a decisive influence on public morality'.

5 Using emphasis

If you wish to emphasise some word or phrase within a quotation in order to draw attention to it or stress its meaning, then you must acknowledge the fact that you have done so, indicating that any such stress was not in the original.

> As Henry James claims in his notebook jottings for *The Awkward Age*, he was inspired by a theme suggesting 'the *decadence and vulgarities* and confusions' (my emphasis) which is similar to . . .

5   *Spelling*

Correct the mistakes in the following passage.

Speling is not given much atention on many return to study courses. It is asumed most adults are competant in basic gramar, would be embarassed if there shortcomings were exposed and could not even concieve that any practise might be necesary. In principal this might be justified but in reality we beleive that on most courses a concensus exists in favour of some specefic focussing on the subject. This short section is our attempt to accomodate this rechoirment.

---

5 minutes   STOP

The errors were as follows (in order of appearance)

	Correct spelling
speling	spelling
atention	attention
asumed	assumed
competant	competent
gramar	grammar
embarassed	embarrassed (two r's and two s's)
there	their
concieve	conceive (i before e except after c)
practise	practice (practise is the verb – practice the noun)
necesary	necessary
principal	principle
beleive	believe
concensus	consensus (note *three* s's)
specefic	specific
accomodate	accommodate (two c's *and* two m's)
rechoirment	requirement

Note: You may have thought 'focussing' was wrong but not so: either this spelling or 'focusing' is correct.

If you spotted around a dozen of the sixteen mistakes you did not do so badly, but if you made more than three or four mistakes you could well have a spelling problem on which you need to work.

English spelling is notoriously difficult and it is not just foreigners who complain at its illogicalities and idiosyncracies. Most British people also encounter difficulties in mastering a language which has evolved over the years from an admixture of Latin, Greek, German, Scandinavian and French – not to mention the hundreds of new words which have entered through Britain's worldwide imperial experience. Few people have perfect spelling and there is no shame in making the occasional mistake. So does it matter? As long as one's written words are understood does it matter if spelling is not strictly correct? The answer is that unfortunately it does. Spelling mistakes stand out as highly visible imperfections. Not only do readers make adverse judgements upon the writer but such mistakes distract them from the meaning of what has been written. As long as spelling is judged in this way – and there seems no sign of change in the offing – it is important that you aim for perfect spelling. But this is easier said than done.

The obvious answer is to check and practise, check and practise – but, as we all realise this, is there not a more imaginative and systematic approach one can adopt? The answer here is fortunately, yes. There are several books available on spelling (see bibliography) but two of the most useful are amongst the most recent: Michael Temple's concise *Pocket Guide to Spelling* (John Murray, 1985) and Rhiannedd Pratley's excellent *Spelling It Out* (BBC Publications, 1988). If spelling is a major problem for you then I would recommend either or both of these books. Below are some useful hints selected mainly from the latter text.

1 *Systematic practice.* Try to identify the words you misspell most regularly, write them down and concentrate upon absorbing the correct spellings into your long-term memory.
2 *Does it look and sound right?* Ask yourself this question when in doubt. Probably most of the mistakes you spotted in the opening exercise were diagnosed – almost intuitively – in this way.
3 *Mnemonics can help.* For example, accommodation is one of the most widely misspelt words – judged by signs outside guest houses the length of the land. It seems that millions of people constantly forget that there are two c's and two m's. The following phrase 'To see (two 'c') a tomb (two 'm')' might help you remember. You will recall from Volume I, Chapter 3 that we remember best through the association of ideas and the visualisation of a tomb embodying (excuse the pun) a slightly macabre sense of accommodation helps fix the correct spelling in your mind.
   Rhiannedd Pratley suggests you also look for the *hidden word* as the key to accurate recall, e.g. pro pagan da
4 *Listen for the syllables* which make up the words. Breaking down words into their syllables helps simplify the spelling process, e.g., pos-sess-ive.
5 *Rules.* Despite the near anarchy of English spelling there are a few basic rules – though all are qualified by numerous exceptions.

(a) 'i' before 'e' except after 'c' when making the sound E, e.g., receive, achieve, grief. *But* it's 'e' before 'i' if the words sound A or I are being made, e.g., eight, neither.
(b) Plurals of nouns ending in 'f' or 'fe'. Usually nouns ending in 'f' add only 's' to make the plural, e.g., handkerchiefs. Some, however, end 'ves' e.g. wife, wives. In other cases *either* plural form is correct, e.g., hoofs/hooves.
(c) Plurals of words ending in 'o' usually add 's' but some have an extra 'e', e.g., potatoes. Strictly speaking manifesto has an extra 'e' in its plural form but in recent years this has been dropped by many journalists.
(d) 'All' at the beginning of words has only one '1', e.g., already. Note however that 'all right' and 'alright' are both correct.
(e) 'Full' at the end of words loses one '1', e.g., helpful, useful.

7 *Use the dictionary*

This piece of advice is so obvious you might wonder why we have included it. The answer is that we feel that some extra emphasis and encouragement are required. You need to develop a feel, even a fascination for words: don't feel satisfield until you have clarified the meaning and/or spelling of a new one. Make sure you have a dictionary of your own. Avoid the small pocket versions as well as the very big ones which can confuse rather than enlighten. The *Concise Oxford* or the *Collins Concise English Dictionary* are good, clear compromises. Below is a sample entry from the *Collins*:

> **pos-sess** (pezes') *vt.* [< MFr. < L. pp. of *possidere*] **1.** to have as something that belongs to one; own **2.** to have as an attribute, quality, etc [to *possess* wisdom] **3.** to gain or keep influence or control over; dominate [*possessed* by an idea] **4.** to cause (someone) to have property, facts, etc. (usually with *of*) **5.** [Archaic] to seize; gain —**pos-ses'-sor n.**

As you see the syllables are separated by hyphens in this dictionary. Following the word is a bracketed phonetic version indicating the pronunciation (according to the prefatory guide) found in the 'normal, relaxed conversation of educated speakers'. The full phonetic guide is found at the beginning of the volume. 'vt' indicates this word is a transitive verb ('n' means noun; adj., adjective, adv., adverb, etc.).

Then follows a little history of the word. The symbol < means 'derived from'. MFr means Middle French. '< L. pp. of *possidere*' means 'possess' also derives from the past participle of the Latin verb *possidere*.

Then follow the definitions with bracketed examples. The fifth definition is an older (archaic) sense of the word and the final entry gives the noun – 'possessor' – derived from the verb. There are many more possible abbreviations in this particular dictionary: to learn the full list and the full variety of what you can learn about words, read the guide which precedes the word list. The Collins dictionary contains 85,000 words; the Oxford English Dictionary half a million but only 10,000 words are used in normal written communication and a mere 3,000 in everyday speech.

Further reading

We don't want to burden you with an enormous bibliography of punctuation and grammar. Many books have been written on these subjects, and since grammar is something which changes, albeit slowly, many more will be written in the future. What we offer instead are some firm recommendations, each one pitched at a different level.

1 Michael Temple, *Get it right!* John Murray.
   This is a cheap, simple, straightforward, and very useful guide to spelling, punctuation, and grammar. *Strongly* recommended.
2 G.V. Carey, *Mind the Stop*, Penguin.
   This is more advanced, and deals with problems of 'correctness' and 'good taste'. Although it only sets out to deal with punctuation, the discussion *does* cover many of the items of grammar and syntax we have discussed in this unit.
3 Eric Partridge, *Usage and Abusage*, Hamish Hamilton.
4 H. W. Fowler, *Modern English Usage,* OUP.

These are works of reference which in general assume that the reader knows the basic rules. They deal very comprehensively with all aspects of spelling, grammar, syntax, and good usage.

Summary
In this unit you have learnt: the basic elements of punctuation: the comma, semi-colon, colon and full stop, various other punctuation marks – the exclamation mark, question mark, the dash, brackets, capital letters, the apostrophe, italics, the hyphen, inverted commas – as well as some of the rudiments of clear sentence-writing.

Try to keep these lessons in mind when you are writing essays – and be prepared to use this Unit as a source of reference. If in doubt, *check up.*

Self-assessment exercises

Exercise 1
Without looking back over this chapter, can you list all the points
on grammar and punctuation we have covered in it?

Exercise 2
Punctuate the following *without* using full stops.
1 I ran down the beach to the waters edge the waves lapped over
   my toes.
2 I ordered drinks for us all a pint for Roy a dry Martini for
   Heather a whiskey for Philip and an orange juice for myself.
3 He stared in amazement he had never seen anything like it
   before.
4 He turned to go there was no more to be said.
5 She leapt in the air for joy she felt on top of the world.
6 The reasons for his behaviour were complex he had never liked
   Stephenson an excitable difficult person at the best of times he
   had woken up with a nagging hangover which had deterio-
   rated as the day progressed Davies had hinted that Bolton
   might well be favoured for the planned promotion despite his
   youth and inexperience and perhaps the most important
   reason Rosemary had told him that very morning that she
   planned to move in with Frank.

Exercise 3
False premises. Very often people make statements based upon an
assumption which is not necessarily true. For example 'the boy
who opened the door was obviously ill; his face was very pale'.
The assumption behind this statement is that 'anyone who is very
pale must be ill'. Experience tells us that this is not necessarily the
case as many people naturally have pale complexions but are
extremely healthy. Now try to identify the fallacious or dubious
assumptions behind the following statements:
(a) The sun was not visible so it must have been cloudy.
(b) The boy was an orphan so naturally was very badly behaved.
(c) Socialism is unworkable; you only have to study the USSR to
     see that.
(d) Because they were Chinese they were impossible to tell
     apart.
(e) I couldn't see who was driving the car but it must have been a
     woman because the driving was so bad.

Exercise 4
Clear writing exercises. Correct or improve the following:
1 Once the student has embarked upon the course, having confidence in their own abilities can be a problem.

2 Many of us feel inadaquate, and that we could not hope to compete with say, a young student who had just finished their A levels.

3 For many people studying after work all day does not achieve best results.

4 There will almost certainly be some gain for these others for to study is to become a more alert and interesting companion, becoming more human because to learn is to develop and ultimately perhaps bringing additional income or prestidge.

5 She was born in the East End of London at a period of time during the first and second world wars. Although a loving family, their were no luxurys at all and the auther describes the cold bleak rooms that they live in, and pub across the way.

6 The book describes there relationships and societies rather difficult demands which they find it impossible to fullfil.

7 One problem is knowing ones needs. Another is deciding if a persons abilitys are great enough.

Sentences and paragraphs   6

Words have weight, sound and appearance; it is only by considering these things you can write a sentence that is good to look at and good to listen to   *W. Somerset Maugham*

Contents

Introduction
1   Sentences
2   Paragraphs
3   The topic sentence and its development
4   Linking paragraphs
    Self-assessment exercises

Introduction

As you've already learnt, a well-planned essay must be carefully 'built up' and constructed to form a unified and coherent whole. In this chapter, we will look at some of those elements or 'building blocks', large and small, out of which an essay is put together. The most basic elements of communication (verbal or written) are of course single sounds, which we then combine into meaningful words. But to become more complex and efficient at expressing ourselves, especially in continuous written prose, we have to go further, to combine words into grammatical *sentences*, and sentences into organised *paragraphs*. These larger blocks of developed and coherent meaning are finally combined to produce convincing and flowing prose, as in an academic essay a newspaper article or a book. As the largest, and therefore the most complex and challenging 'bricks' of your essay structure, good paragraphs are crucial; if you can write a sound, coherent and interesting paragraph, you can write an equally efficient complete essay.

Let's start with the slightly smaller elements of expression, and look first at the importance of good sentences. Here we will be going back to the topic of sentence construction covered in the last chapter and expanding upon it a little more.

1 *Sentences*

If you can recognise a correct and proper sentence when you see one, you are well on the way to good writing. But how would you define a sentence, in simple language?

STOP	**5 minutes**

Discussion   Perhaps you said something like 'a group of words' or 'it makes sense' or 'it conveys a total thought', or even something slightly more technical and concrete like 'it has to have a verb in it'. All these are true, and can be combined to form a more comprehensive definition: a sentence is a group of words that makes complete sense and that contains, as a minimum, two basic parts – a *subject*, and a *predicate*, some part of which must include a main verb (see below for explanation of these terms). A sentence is a complete unit of expression that can stand alone *grammatically*, though in fact it may often need other surrounding sentences to make its overall meaning and its context clear. For example, sentences like 'Emma glared at him' or 'It failed to explode' are grammatically sound and complete; they both have a subject ('Emma', 'It') and a predicate 'glared at him', 'failed to explode'), but we would really need to see them in context in order to understand their full meaning properly (who was the 'him' on the receiving end of Emma's glare? What *was* 'it' and why did it not explode?). Incidentally, on a formal written level, it is worth mentioning that all sentences must begin with a capital letter, and end with either a full stop, exclamation mark or question mark.

As you can see, the *subject* of a sentence can be a noun (like 'Emma'), or a pronoun (like 'it'); the *predicate* part must contain a main verb ('glared', 'failed'), through it can also contain a lot of other parts of speech as well. (The only exception to the fundamental rule of *sentence = subject + predicate* is in commands, where the subject is often implied and therefore omitted: in sentences like 'Run' or 'Fasten your safety belt'. The subject 'you' is not actually stated, but completes the sentence by implication.

It is useful to be able to see the structure of a sentence, whether basic or complicated, and to be able to identify the subject part and the predicate part. Remember that the subject is the something or someone you want to talk about, the thing or person you want to name in a sentence; the predicate is what you want to say about it, what it is or does or what happens to it. To find the subject of a sentence, ask yourself, in connection with the verb, '*who* or *what* . . .?' (is doing or being this); to find the predicate, ask what *happens or goes on* or what the subject *does*. For practice, try dividing the following five sentences into their subject and predicate parts:

1 Jesus wept. (The famous shortest sentence in the Bible.)
2 The dog ate the bone.
3 The little red-haired girl climbed the tallest tree.
4 The recent hurricane which swept up from the West Indies devastated several towns on the east coast of America.
5 We will go shopping tomorrow.

---

15 minutes   STOP

---

1 As all sentences (except commands) must have *two* parts anyway, perhaps this first one was not too difficult! The named subject is 'Jesus' and the predicate (what he did) is in the single verb 'wept'.   *Discussion*
2 This sentence falls into one of the commonest patterns for simple sentences in the English language – subject + verb + object. If you take out the subject (what is named, i.e., the dog), you are left with the predicate (what the dog did, which in this case consists of a verb and an object as well – 'ate the bone').
3 This sentence contains a slightly longer and more detailed subject ('the little red-haired girl'), but is of the same common 'subject + verb + object' pattern; the predicate consists of what she did ('climbed the tallest tree').
4 Perhaps you found this one more difficult, as it was a more grammatically complicated sentence, containing an extra clause. The subject consists of the thing named and all the surrounding description applied to it (i.e., 'The recent hurricane which swept up from the West Indies'), the predicate is then all the information left which describes what occurred or happened to the subject ('devastated several towns on the east coast of America').
5 An easier one, I hope, made up of a simple subject which is a pronoun ('we'), and a predicate which consists of a verbal phrase and some information about time ('will go shopping tomorrow'), but which still tells you what the subject's actions are (or, in this future case, will be).

Perhaps you noticed that in this discussion I used two other terms which need definition and clarification. Sentences are also made up of *phrases* and *clauses*. A phrase is a small group of related words, without including both a subject or a predicate of its own ('the red-haired girl', 'on the east coast', 'will go shopping', 'under the table') which functions in the sentence as a single part of speech (a verb, a noun, an adjective, an adverb).

A *clause* is a more complicated unit, built up from related words and phrases, which must include a subject and a predicate of its own. There are two basic types of clauses: the *main clause*, which can stand alone as a complete sentence, making grammatical sense (in which case it would be called a sentence rather than a clause); and the *dependent or subordinate clause*, which, although it too has a subject and predicate of its own, needs to be linked to a main clause in order to complete its meaning and make a proper sentence. I hope an example will make this clear. A clause like 'because I felt ill' has indeed a subject ('I') and a predicate, showing what the subject was or did ('felt ill'), but you can see that the meaning (and the grammar) of the sentence is uncompleted – it is only a dependent or subordinate clause which needs another part of the sentence (main clause) in order to make sense. If we add another (main) clause to it, we complete the sentence proper: 'Because I felt ill, I went home from work early.' The second clause we have added (though notice that in this case it would sound perfectly correct if we put it either before *or* after the first clause is a *main* clause, which functions here as only a part of a sentence, but would make total sense as a complete sentence if it stood on its own – 'I (subject) went home from work early (predicate)'

It is worth thinking carefully about clauses and their various combinations in a sentence, as it can stop you writing a sentence fragment containing only a subordinate clause, however long and complicated – which is not completed by a main clause. Look at the following example; is it a correct sentence, and where is its main (i.e., capable-of-standing-alone) clause?

'Although the weather was appalling, with arctic temperatures, a howling blizzard whipping against the frozen branches of the trees, and a solid sheet of sleet-covered ice over all the roads, which made it difficult to keep upright.'

STOP   5 minutes

Discussion   Even though this example conveyed quite a lot of information, and appeared complicated (*too* long and complicated for a single sentence perhaps) and even though it began with a capital letter and ended (wrongly, in this case) with a full stop, it was in fact *not* a proper sentence, as it never completed its sense by including a main clause. As it stands, it consists of a number of phrases and of subordinate clauses, each of which has its own subject and predicate, but each of which still needs to *depend* on some main clause, which has been omitted. We still are left dangling, as it were, waiting to know what was the consequence of all this information: 'Although . . .' all this, but *then* what? The sentence needs a main clause before it reaches its final full stop: 'Although the weather was appalling . . . difficult to keep upright, *we trudged to the isolated farmhouse.'* This last clause is a *main* one, which could quite well stand independently, and which here completes the meaning and grammar of the sentence.

If your own writing is perfectly sound and clear this may all seem unnecessary or over-theoretical to you, but we have included it because sentences like the last one which run out of control are a very common problem for those people who still need to do some work on their writing skills. Fortunately, there is a very simple solution to it. Write *shorter* sentences. In fact my advice to anyone who has problems with writing – be it with grammar or the construction of sentences – is to keep everything short, clear, and simple. It is far better to err on the side of curtness than to stray into long-winded and over-complex sentences that are likely to lead you into the sort of grammatical traps we have just illustrated. Here is another tip to help you stay out of trouble with grammar and syntax (the arrangement of the words in a sentence). Try to avoid **starting** sentences with conjunctions ('And', 'Though', 'Because'). What you are doing in such a case is starting in the middle of the sentence, and what frequently happens is that you get to the end successfully enough – but forget to include the beginning. If you keep things simple and direct you are more likely to start with what most naturally comes first – the subject ('The man was . . .', 'The problem is . . .').

Paragraphs   2

Now that you have thought about the structure and coherence of your sentences, we can look at how they can be combined in the larger element of the paragraph. I would like to consider four main points about paragraphs here: their function and definition, their basic construction, some possible methods of development and variation, and, finally, ways of linking them together within the total body of the essay. We will look both at how *you* can write your own paragraphs, and also at how you can follow and analyse the handling of paragraphs by other writers.

The function of a paragraph within a longer piece of prose is to link together several related sentences on a main topic – all of which should explain, amplify, defend, support or at least focus on the main idea in some clear way. Like a sentence, a paragraph is a distinct unit of thought, though a larger and a fuller one.

There is no set length for a paragraph: it can vary from one to a thousand words. Paragraphs in current books and magazines are usually from about 50 to 250 words in length, with the average probably only about 100 words. This reflects a change in literary fashion (and in concentration!) from the eighteenth or nineteenth centuries, when paragraphs were typically much longer and more developed than they are today. You should aim (as with sentences) to give your paragraphs a variety in length: a paragraph on a complicated and detailed subject might fill a whole page or more, the next one (for effect) might consist of only a single sentence.

3 *The topic sentence – and its development*

Some students find formal discussion of how to build up and develop a paragraph rather mechanical and restricting; others find it gives them at least a structure, and something to fall back on if they are stuck for ideas. Do remember that these are only suggestions for the bare bones of your paragraphs – the actual writing is enlivened and made unique by the flavour of your own individual style.

A paragraph, in one way, can very much be seen as an essay in miniature, with its own flow and unity, and with a beginning, a middle and an end. But it is also, in another way, similar to the logic and structure of a single sentence – and equally it needs a subject, a point, an overall theme. What would you say was the *most important part* of a paragraph?

STOP   **5 minutes**

There is no 'right answer' to this, and you may have come up with all sorts of suggestions, from 'what it's about' or 'the main idea' or 'the first sentence' to 'the conclusion' or 'the crucial phrases'. But there *are* some fundamental elements which almost all good paragraphs need to contain. The first one is what is usually called *the controlling idea*. Since a paragraph is defined as a major idea around a single theme, it can only have real unity when each sentence in it contributes in some clear way to this central, dominant thought. A sentence which fails to contribute to the controlling idea should be omitted (however much you like the sound of it) because it may destroy the unity of your paragraph. Don't include rambling statements which are only vaguely related to your main central idea. Ask yourself if you can really justify including them in your paragraph, or whether, conversely, perhaps your main controlling idea is inadequate or not thought through carefully enough.

The central thought or main controlling idea of a paragraph is usually conveyed in what is called a *topic sentence*. This crucial sentence, which states, summarises or clearly expresses the main theme, is the keystone of a well-built paragraph. The topic sentence may come anywhere in the paragraph, though most logically and in most cases it is the first sentence. This immediately tells the reader what is coming, and leaves him in no doubt about the overall controlling idea. In a very long paragraph, the initial topic sentence may even be *re*-stated, or given a more significant emphasis, in the conclusion.

It is important to check your own paragraphs for this underlying unity of thought, and safer to make sure that there *is* a clear topic sentence. When offering this sentence as a guide to your reader, make sure it does not only merely describe the content of the following paragraph, but gives specific clues as to your angle, approach, point of view or argument. Look at the following pairs of possible topic sentences; which one of each pair gives the clearest guide to the reader?

(a) Abortion is a very controversial subject.
(b) There are many reasons why some people feel they cannot wholeheartedly support abortion.
(a) The American Civil War began in 1861.
(b) The American Civil War, which began in 1861, had two main causes.
(a) My aunt and uncle live in a remote part of the country.
(b) My aunt and uncle enjoy a hermit-like existence in a ramshackle farmhouse on the west coast of Scotland.
(a) Much of Tennyson's poetry dwells on the world of classical or medieval myth.
(b) A great many of Tennyson's mature poems turn away from nineteenth-century realities and focus on the magic and splendour of classical and medieval myth.

5–10 minutes   **STOP**

In all these cases, sentence b gives a much clearer and more exact guide as to the direction and point of the paragraph to follow. Sentence a is often too open and vague, and doesn't act as a sufficient signpost to the reader, so that he can anticipate or judge intelligently what is to come. It is frustrating and confusing to read most of a paragraph before realising exactly *where* your

Discussion

111

author is going, or what position you are being asked to take in relation to the information you are reading. As an exercise to check whether a paragraph has unity and a firm controlling idea, look at one or two passages from a serious journal or newspaper. Ask yourself the following questions about each one:

1 Has the paragraph got a controlling idea clearly stated? If not, can you supply a topic sentence which neatly encapsulates the theme?

2 Does the main topic shift one or more times? Does this suggest that the paragraph could be shorter, divided differently, or have a broader controlling idea?

3 Does every sentence contribute in some way or another to the main controlling idea?

If a well-constructed paragraph needs a main controlling idea and a clear topic sentence, it also needs a number of *supporting sentences* which develop and expand the central thought and provide the 'meat' or filling for the bulk of the passage. These sentences can develop the paragraph in many different ways. Books on essay-writing, however, suggest for academic paragraph writing a basic pattern of:

1 topic sentence (+ any necessary explanations or definitions of it, which may take several more sentences).

2 support sentences: one main example, developed in detail, + one or two minor examples, mentioned in a sentence or so each, but not expanded.

3 concluding sentence (which re-states, modifies or summarises the controlling idea).

Let me give you an example, taken from a typical student essay, to illustrate this basic pattern. The original question was 'Discuss the case for and against political censorship of the media.'

66 The arguments *against* political censorship however, can be made on grounds which are just as firm. The *moral* arguments usually centre on notions of 'freedom of information' and the individual's 'right to know' as well as the liberty of the individual to discriminate and judge for him or herself. The *legal* arguments point to inconsistencies in the current regulations applied to the various forms of media (books, TV, newspapers) and to differences in law between the UK and other western countries. And there are also a number of social and political arguments ranging from objections to class bias in the composition of the 'establishment' to similar objections to the ownership and control of the various forms of media. Exploring each one of these arguments in turn, it is possible to see that the case *against* political censorship can be just as strong. 99

Irrespective of the content here, how far does this correspond in form (that is, in pattern) to what has just been recommended?

---

10 minutes   **STOP**

I hope you were able to guess that this was the opening paragraph in the second part of our old friend, the 'for and against' essay. The linking word 'however' (about which more shortly) should have suggested to you that the case 'for' had just been made. The first sentence therefore signals that the arguments 'against' are now going to be offered. This is essentially the topic sentence. And the next three sentences indicate what these arguments *are* plus the categories to which they belong (moral, legal, and social). The final sentence then both links back to the first ('just as strong' – as the case 'for') and suggests that what will follow is a detailed examination of the individual arguments ('Exploring each one').

You may feel that there are better arguments in answer to the question of censorship, but the more important point for our purposes here is that the ones under consideration are obviously being well controlled. This is a reasonably good paragraph setting out what will be the second half of the essay. And it follows the basic pattern, which you should try to always keep in mind:
1 Topic sentence
2 Supporting sentences – with examples
3 Concluding sentence

Ideally, you need to aim for an interesting group of related sentences which give enough material to satisfy and inform the reader, without wandering from your controlling idea. A topic sentence plus a couple of brief single-sentence examples would not normally be adequate development of the central thought, and would be choppy and unsatisfying for your reader. This does mean that you have to think and prepare carefully, and know something about your topic, before you launch into a paragraph. The rather 'mechanical' suggestions for development and construction in this section and the next are only formal structures to get you going – they cannot on their own provide ideas and material if you really have nothing at all to say!

As a final point of construction, think about the *order* and arrangement of your sentences within the paragraph. As I said before, a coherent paragraph (like an essay) needs a conscious sense of composition, with a clear beginning (usually a topic sentence), a middle (supporting sentences) and an end (usually some sort of concluding sentence). But variations within this pattern will depend upon your purpose and your material. Whatever you do, there needs to be a clear *logic* and a sequence between sentences, which stems from the main idea, and leads your reader smoothly and confidently to the end.

The same should also be true of the connections between the paragraphs themselves. The logic of this will depend upon the care you have taken with your essay *plan*, but what I want to go on to next is the manner in which one paragraph can be linked to the next.

4   *Linking paragraphs*

Just as a collection of sentences with no clear theme or connection gives a fragmentary or confused impression, so does a group of paragraphs which have not been properly linked to each other. After all, we defined a paragraph as a division of thought, a group of related sentences on a single main theme. A move to a new paragraph thus implies a shift or extension of ideas, and your reader needs to know how it *relates and connects* to the previous ones. This can usually be done quite briefly, in a short sentence or phrase, or even in a single appropriate word which indicates the thematic or logical relationship or change of direction you are taking.

There are two main ways of linking and unifying paragraphs within the larger construction of the whole essay. The first involves a sort of *conscious repetition*. To repeat your main ideas and their relationships within your overall topic or essay helps to guide your reader, and prevents him getting lost in what he might find an abrupt change of subject or direction. It makes sense to use repetition to tie in a new paragraph to the preceding one (linking by *looking back* to what you have already said), or to round off the end of the paragraph by *looking forward* and preparing the reader for the shift in theme and approach that is to follow. Reiterating certain keys words or crucial phases can do this job quite effectively, without having to write a flat and over-obvious re-statement which might be dull or unnecessary.

Look at these examples of the opening and closing phrases of paragraphs from two different essays and try to say in what way they seem to be linked to what comes before or goes after them.
(a) 'The second reason why gas is preferable to electricity is . . .

But if gas is cheaper than electricity, is it as safe and clean?'
(b) 'Yet whilst moral objections on the grounds of cruelty to animals seems to have little effect . . .
. . . Opponents of vegetarianism however have a powerful answer to this argument.'

---

5 minutes   **STOP**

(a) In this example the term 'second reason' tells you quite clearly that the first reason has just been discussed. This is an example of the type of 'repetition' I have just described. It proves that the question is being kept in mind – and it suggests that the essay has been well planned. And the last sentence underlines the topic which has been considered (relative cheapness) but then raises a question – 'is it as safe and clean?' The clear implications here is that this topic will be considered in the next paragraph.
(b) The linking word here is 'Yet' – and it is immediately followed by what seems to be a repetition of what has just been considered ('moral objections'). Moreover the term 'whilst' at the same time signals an alternative argument is about to be considered. The last sentence – especially the linking word 'however' – suggests that the counter-argument will be considered in the paragraph which is to follow. And whilst the subject of the essay may not have been evident from the opening sentence, the phrase 'opponents of vegetarianism' in the last strongly suggests that a case for and against it has been called for.

In both these examples conscious repetition and signals looking forward and backwards help to form links with the preceding and following paragraphs. The second main device which an author can use to link his paragraphs: is to employ simple *transition words and phrases*. These act as clues or signposts to the alert reader as to what is to follow. They are often small and 'neutral' grammatical words, which don't indicate thematic links but *logical* shifts in direction and the way the overall argument is constructed. We use them, of course, to link the smaller elements of sentences together too, in order to give smooth transitions and an easier guide to the reader there as well.

Transitional expressions are of several kinds, depending on the direction of the following paragraph(s). What *sort* of transition words would you expect to use, for example, if your next paragraph in an essay was adding another major idea (of the same kind and with a similar approach and point of view)? Jot down as many as you can think of which merely indicate that your next paragraph is progressing on the same line of thought, but adding new information.

STOP   10 minutes

Discussion   As you may have put down, the commonest conjunction (linking, adding or joining word) in English is the simple word 'and' – but it is usually not thought to be good stylistic practice to start a whole paragraph (or even a sentence) with it. It tends to indicate a very small addition, rather than a major new point. Other transition words, which you could use in your first sentence of the paragraph, and which would show a similar idea was to follow, might include:

in addition, equally important, likewise, furthermore, besides, moreover, again, similarly, a related point is, next, another idea to consider . . .

As part of a whole series of added points, you might well begin consecutive paragraphs with the transition words

first, secondly, thirdly . . . finally/lastly.

Simple and obvious links these may be, but they keep the reader well informed as to the logical progression of your essay.

In contrast, what sort of transition words would you use to indicate that your next paragraph was going to move into an opposing or very different point or argument?

STOP   10 minutes

Discussion   The simplest one to come to mind is the linking conjunction 'but', which always shows (in a minor way) an opposite idea or thought, or a turn in a pro-and-con argument. Others you might have mentioned include:

yet, however, still, nevertheless, on the other hand, on the contrary, notwithstanding, in contrast to this, after all, for all that, otherwise, although this may be true . . .

All these immediately give some sort of clue to your reader that your argument is shifting into a different direction.

Certain transition words or expressions prepare the reader for a result or conclusion, often as part of an overall cause and effect development: hence, accordingly, thus, therefore, consequently, evidently, as a result, since, then, to this end we can see . . . (and many other variations of these). All such transitions indicate the culmination of an argument, a pulling together and a final weighing of the evidence. Transition phrases which introduce examples or illustrations (for example, for instance, to illustrate, as we can see in the following examples . . .) are almost too obvious to mention, as most people seem to use them automatically as a sign-post of actual evidence and illustrations to come.

A transition, towards the end of an essay, into your final points or last paragraph, should also generate a corresponding set of linking or guiding words. Some of these can indicate your following conclusion and final summary, some introduce more a last repetition and intensification of your argument – or both. Can you think which ones these might be?

---

10 minutes   **STOP**

Again, I hope, rather easily, you have come up with a list which   *Discussion* might include phrases like:

to sum up, in sum, in short, to conclude, in brief, finally, on the whole, in any event . . .

all of which would lead your reader to a final conclusion. While phrases like:

in other words, as I have said, as I mentioned, in fact, indeed, as has been noted . . . (and so on)

can tend to introduce a final repetition and perhaps the culmination of your essay.

Many people use a lot of these transition phrases (and many others not mentioned) quite automatically in their continuous writing, and thus make their reader's job easier. Other writers, though, forget that their reader does not know the overall plan and direction as clearly as they themselves do, and they leave out these small linking words which would both clarify and structure their essay. If you fear that you are in this latter category, or even as a way of increasing your self-awareness of these critical transition words, try using them in any longer pieces of writing you produce until you feel comfortable with the construction of your paragraphs and the piece as a whole. It may seem rather mechanical or artificial at first, but the practice will help you develop a sense of structure in your writing, which should lead naturally to a greater degree of control.

Summary (re-cap)
A good paragraph needs:
● unity
● order
● coherence
● variety
and clear links and transitions to related paragraphs.

Its structure should normally include:
- a controlling idea
- a topic sentence
- supporting sentences
- and (possibly) a conclusion.

Related reading
Many study skills books include a chapter on sentence construction, some include material on good paragraphing (or cover it as part of general essay-writing). Ones that are particularly useful are:

Christopher Moor, *Answer the Question* (NEC). Cambridge
Tony Sullivan, *Grammar* (NEC), Cambridge
Waldhorn and Zeiger, *English Made Simple* (W. H. Allen), London
D. J. Collinson, *Writing English*, (Pan) London

Self-assessment exercises

Exercise 1
Without looking back over this chapter, can you list all the major points we have been making about sentences and paragraphs?

Exercise 2
Read through the extracts below and comment upon the use being made of the various constituents of the paragraph.

(a) The Suffragettes' argument was strengthened by the first world war. Women were involved in a large number of essential tasks usually performed by men. They worked in munitions factories, they drove the buses, they even helped run the Government machine. When the War ended they were determined not to lose a moral advantage so dearly won.

They were not disappointed. At first the vote was given to women over thirty but by 1928 the right was extended to all women. The first woman to be elected to The House of Commons was Margaret Astor . . .

(b) The best time for foreign sunshine holidays is late summer. Many people extol the advantages of June, July or August but for me the first two weeks of September are best. Why? Because this is the way to maximise the sunshine.

This might seem contradictory but let me explain. Every summer in Britain, despite all the weather-deprecating jokes we bore each other with, we do have several days or even weeks of sunshine. By the end of August however summer is over; even the occasional Indian summer is autumn by a different name.

Not so in the Mediterranean. Their summer extends through September and if less hot than July and August, is the better for it. In September you have the chance to bask on near secluded beaches unworried by bizarrely-dressed Britons or stern-faced Germans efficiently soaking up their tans. And when you return home, relaxed and gloriously brown, you can enjoy the last laugh on friends whose skins have already taken on an autumnal pallor. A September holiday is one last defiant way of thumbing your nose at the approaching winter.

(c) Last weekend's Test match was my most successful game since Raymond Illingworth led England. In those days the English cricket captain was older than me. And as long as Illingworth remained in charge, the faded dream flickered on. Time had not quite run out. Justice might still be done. The selectors might, even yet, come to their senses. My irrational hope was reintensified by my special status as a Yorkshireman. It seems absurd, I know, but in those days I really did believe that the decadent southerners who make up the majority of Test match selectors would abandon their effete prejudices and come to understand that the salvation of English cricket lay on proper recognition of the Yorkshire qualities of guts, grit and uninhibited self-congratulation.

The Lords Test got off to a cracking start with a genuine Yorkshireman opening the batting and a Yorkshire exile joining him as soon as Graham Gooch had thrown away his wicket with one of those balletic extravagances which pass as strokes in Essex. And then it happened. Bob Taylor was brought out of the lunch tent to replace the injured Bruce French. I could hardly believe it. One of the great fantasies of my boyhood was being acted out before my eyes.

For years I turned up at county grounds early in the morning of match days and waited for the loudspeaker to appeal for me. 'Will Roy Hattersley please come to the dressing room at once and bring his flannels and boots with him?'

Roy Hattersley, the *Guardian*, 2 August 1986

Exercise 3

Choose two of the following 'topic sentences' and develop each one in a paragraph of about 10–15 lines.

1 In many ways our world discourages individual initiative.
2 Traditional moral values have become confused.
3 Daybreak was imminent.
4 The authority of parents has become weakened.
5 This is an age of mass culture.
6 Labour-saving devices are not a recipe for happiness.
7 Democracy works by persuasion.
8 The M1 was littered with wreckage.
9 Our civilisation is a very materialistic one.
10 There is only one way to make Yorkshire pudding.

Exercise 4

Here are some typical examples of sloppy writing. Re-write each sentence to clarify its meaning.

1 This was a rather unique occasion.
2 Two cycles belonging to girls that had been left leaning against lamp-posts were badly damaged.
3 Whether the shell of an egg is white or brown depends solely on the breed of the bird. Generally speaking a brown hen will lay a brown egg and vice versa.
4 You can order our rings by post. State size or enclose string tied round finger.
5 She is the cleverest of the two.
6 This new pot-pourri bowl should be kept in a dark cupboard of the living room to be taken out when the room is occupied and the lid removed.

The A to Z of writing good essays   **7**

A man may write at any time, if he will set himself doggedly to it   *Samuel Johnson*

Contents

Introduction

How to write good essays has provided the central focus of this book. As we explained in the introduction to Volume I we believe written work is not only important as the principal means of assessment in higher education but also as the activity which requires expertise in most of the study skills so far examined.

It is appropriate therefore at this stage in the book to look back, try to refresh our memories on what has been covered and discern some overall shape in the complex task of producing good written work. You will of course be aware that the process involves a number of different stages. From your experience and study so far, try to identify these stages starting with the moment when you receive the title upon which you must write and concluding with the handing in of the finished product.

STOP **15 minutes**

Discussion Fifteen minutes is not long to sum up and organise much of the work that you have already done in this course but I hope you did not find the exercise beyond you. I will give you my own brief list of the ten stages through which I think an essay should evolve and then say something more about each separate stage.

1 Understanding the title.
2 Generation of ideas (if necessary).
3 Preliminary essay plan.
4 Assembling sources
5 Reading.
6 Note-taking
7 Detailed essay plan.
8 First draft of essay.
9 Second draft of essay.
10 Final reading

No doubt your list was similar but not identical to mine: for example, you may not have my stage 3, 'Write preliminary essay plan'. You will also have quickly realised that my stages do not follow the order of topics which you have already studied in the course, e.g. the chapter on 'Understanding the question' was dealt with *after* the chapters on reading and note-taking. Before going on to discuss each stage in turn, I would like to emphasise an important point. Our ideas in this book on how to plan and write an essay have been built up over a number of years experience in teaching study skills; if followed faithfully, they really do work – and often very well. However the path we recommend is not something we ask you to follow slavishly or mechanically. It is not the only way. You may have your own approach to writing essays which produces very satisfactory results and ultimately you may choose to do things your way.

But we are asking you to try our recipe for successful essay planning and see if it works for you. Below we refresh your memory what each stage entails.

1 *Understanding the title or question*

Obviously the starting point of the whole process is the essay title. It is necessary to understand not just the general subject area in which the essay falls but the precise nature of the question asked.

To help you do this we suggested in Chapter 1 of this volume that you use some simple techniques:

(a) Identify the key terms.
(b) Identify the instruction words.
(c) Paraphrase or convert the title into your own words just to make sure you understand it perfectly.
(d) Think through the implications of the title:
    (i) *Knowledge* What will you need to find out?
    (ii) *Questions* What kind of secondary question is the title posing?
    (iii) *Structures* What kind of essay structures will be most suitable?

The title is *very* important. Keep it in the forefront of your mind throughout every stage of the essay-writing process. It may help to write the title out on a piece of paper and have it facing you on your working surface throughout the period in which you are preparing and writing your essay.

Generation of ideas   2

This topic was dealt with in Chapter 8 of Volume I. You will recall that two techniques were explained and practised which were designed to help you articulate ideas and information on all kinds of subjects, but especially essay titles. This stage is only necessary, you will also recall, if you have difficulty in creating ideas on the topic concerned: if you know a great deal about it your problem will lie in organising your ideas, not generating them.

Brainstorming entails writing the topic concerned in the centre of a clean sheet of paper and then filling it with ideas freely associated with the topic and with each other. Organising these ideas involved finding themes or categories into which they could be placed.

The concept tree technique entailed the creation of a diagram in which the topic became the tree trunk, the branches the major points relating to it and the twigs and leaves the supporting or subsidiary points. Remember both techniques can be used throughout all stages of writing your essay: whenever you are stuck for ideas or need to think of new approaches.

3 *Preliminary essay plan*

The desirability of this was touched on in Chapter 2 of this volume when you were advised to 'Think through the question as much as you can and produce a preliminary plan before you start any serious reading'. This you should be able to do either after thoroughly thinking through the meaning and implications of the question or after the brainstorming stage (assuming that you have needed to go through it). A preliminary plan helps you to do three things.

(a) Organise what information and thoughts you do have at this early stage.

(b) Identify the gaps in your existing knowledge.

(c) Focus your search for sources upon those which you really need rather than those you may vaguely think you may need.

Many students spend ages hopefully gathering information of questionable relevance when in fact they should be thinking hard about the question itself. From our own experience we would say that five minutes hard thinking is worth an hour's undirected reading. Certainly, you may find from your reading that your preliminary plan was wholly inadequate, you may even scrap the plan altogether, but the point is that it has served its purpose: it has enabled you to reach a higher level of understanding and planning. How detailed should the plan be? All that is required is a simple plan with an introduction, a main body of the essay reflecting the strategy which you think appropriate (e.g., is it a 'for and against' essay? Is it an essay which 'explains' or 'analyses', 'criticises', etc?) and a conclusion.

4 *Assembling sources*

Most essays require considerable background reading and it is important to assemble those most suitable for the task. The most obvious places are:

(a) Libraries: local, major city libraries, colleges, polytechnics, university libraries (if you have access to them).

(b) Bookshops: the best are usually found in large conurbations, e.g., Foyles or Dillons in London but those connected to polytechnics or universities, e.g. Haigh and Hochland in Manchester, are also very good.

(c) Friends and/or fellow students will usually lend you books (if asked persuasively).

But don't think sources for written work are exclusively in book form.

You should also include: academic journals, weeklies, newspapers, TV and radio programmes, lecture and seminar notes, conversations with tutors and fellow students.

Selecting books
Remember we suggested you develop the skill of *'previewing'* books to find the ones you need. This you can do in a few seconds by moving quickly from title and author to dust jacket notes, contents page, introduction, conclusion, index, etc.

Remember not to overwhelm yourself with too many books, articles or other sources. Our rule of thumb guide is that four or five relevant books are usually a sufficiently good basis for an A level or undergraduate essay in most social science or humanities subjects. Remember also to return library books swiftly to ensure that other students can benefit from them.

Reading   5

All types of the following kinds of reading will probably be used in your essay preparations.

skimming – rather like previewing except that the text is lightly read: chapter subheadings, first and last sentences of paragraphs, selected short passages, especially from the introduction and conclusion.

Search reading – the isolation and identification of particular pieces of information in a text.

Detailed reading – going through the text trying to absorb as much as you can as efficiently as you can – you might very well be taking notes at the same time.

Note-making   6

(a) *The Linear-Logical method* – the traditional form of note-taking based upon; summarised notes, well laid-out on the page, in accordance with a notation system using numbers and abbreviations.

(b) *The Concept-Tree system* – this technique has already been encountered in stage 2: here the subject is written in the centre of the page and major headings added as 'branches' of the tree with subsidiary points as 'twigs', etc.

You will usually need to call upon past notes taken from lectures and books when writing an essay, so clearly written accurate notes, efficiently classified and stored away, will help you immensely. I find that notes taken from books to be used directly in written work can be briefer than lecture notes as what has been read is fresh in the mind and can be supplemented by direct reference to the text: indeed page references might often be all you need in some instances.

7 *Detailed essay plan*

We don't want to give the impression that these stages are something which you can move smoothly through with never a second glance behind at the stages completed. In one sense none of the stages are fully complete until the essay is properly written and submitted; you will regularly be darting back to your books, discovering another key source, taking a few more notes. So it is with your detailed essay plan.

As you proceed through the stages you will probably find your preliminary plan to be unsatisfactory and you will alter it and supplement it with additional ideas and information. This process cannot go on indefinitely, however: you have to recognise the constraints of time and your own energies. You must decide when enough reading has been done and the final detailed plan can be drawn up. As your thoughts have evolved during the reading and note-taking stages you may have altered your strategy or changed your interim conclusions so that your initial plan has already been heavily modified. You may also have noted down some key quotes or thought of a few sentences or phrases for use in the essay. Your final plan, therefore, might easily have been substantially anticipated.

On the other hand, you might choose to delay your final plan until all your reading is complete and you feel in a position to move towards the appropriate structure and judgements on the questions raised by the essay title. Whatever your approach you need to construct your final plan with great care. My view is that it should be as detailed as possible on the grounds that the more you think through your plan the easier the first draft becomes.

First draft   **8**

When you start writing you need to call to the forefront of your mind those qualities which a good essay should ideally possess.

Remember in Chapter 9 of Volume I we examined this and produced eight qualities.

1 Answering the question.
2 Clear structure.
3 Good written style.
4 Evidence of wide reading.
5 Clarity of thought.
6 Well-supported arguments.
7 Good presentation.
8 Original ideas.

If your plan has been properly constructed and if you can avoid digressions from it, you should have little trouble with items 1 and 2.

You should now concentrate upon the other elements, e.g., clear lively style, supporting your arguments with convincing evidence. Casting your thoughts into clear written style (see next chapter) is a tough discipline which often causes you to delve more deeply into your ideas, to rethink them or sharpen them up. You may often find you are forced to go back to your plan and introduce changes there: in other words the evolution of the essay continues even during the first draft. Most people find the first draft to be the hardest stage of all and agonise over it endlessly. They often complain that they take far too long writing, spending hours over just one paragraph. However, don't be distressed by this tendency. Learning new skills takes time and with determined practice you will find your concentration, clarity and thought and fluency of pen improve rapidly.

9 *Second draft*

Some students try to write their essays out direct and hand in their first drafts as their final one. Occasionally these essays are written to a high standard but more often these attempts to take short-cuts come to grief. There are a number of things which your second draft can improve and correct and thereby greatly raise the standard of your final piece of work: grammar, punctuation, spelling, and very important, presentation. You can also ensure at this stage that quotations are properly meshed into the text, that you have remembered to add a bibliography and that the necessary tidying up jobs have been taken care of.

10 *Final reading*

Errors can never be wholly eliminated. Published texts regularly contain spelling and grammatical errors despite exhaustive and expert proof-reading. It follows however that failure to read through even once for minor errors will result in many remaining uncorrected. Some of them may be crucial and affect or distort the sense of what you wish to say. Others may just be careless mistakes which convey a bad impression of haste and sloppiness. Either way failure to check through your essay will lose you marks, the respect of your teacher, or both.

Students often complain that when they have laboured for hours or days over an essay the last thing they want to do is read it through once again. They just want to hand it in and forget about it. But if you have worked so hard, why spoil it all by failing to ensure it is as good as you can make it? Try to become a perfectionist, a pedantic bore if you like, about spelling, punctuation and grammar. Remember too that presentation is crucial. Make sure your handwriting is legible; typewritten essays are always welcomed by tutors and often receive slightly higher marks. Use A4 sized paper and leave a good left hand margin.

Self-assessment exercises

Exercise 1
Without looking back over the chapter, can you list the ten stages in producing an essay we have covered?

Exercise 2
Choose, research, plan and write a 1,500–2,500 word essay on *one* of the following topics.

1 Television does more harm than good. Discuss.
2 Are there any good reasons for thinking it is wrong to wear animal furs?
3 'I think, therefore I am.' Discuss Descartes' famous statement.
4 Explain the rise of a great city.
5 Assess and discuss the contribution made to our national thinking by Mrs Mary Whitehouse.
6 Consider the proposition that the English housing system has contributed to the segregation of social groups in towns and cities.
7 Critically analyse the view that it was Adolf Hitler who must bear responsibility for the outbreak of the Second World War.
8 Assess the qualities of Jane Austen as a writer.
9 Comment on the life either of a great composer or a great painter.
10 'What really matters in artistic judgement is whether or not I like it.' Do you agree that such judgements are ultimately personal?
11 Assess and discuss the impact of the new technology upon society.
12 'I owe nothing to women's lib' (Margaret Thatcher). Are women best advised to ignore the women's movement and concentrate upon self development?

Exercise 3
Write three well-constructed and *well-linked* paragraphs drawing on the topic sentences below.

1 Teachers are not paid enough.
2 The morning air was crisp and sharp.
3 When I opened the door I gasped with surprise.
4 It is everyone's ambition to become old.
5 It is never easy to see yourself as others see you.
6 Painting and decorating is a most satisfying activity.
7 Universities should be expanded rather than run down.
8 Bringing up children properly is an art not easily acquired.
9 We must support our business community.

Exercise 4
Punctuate and correct the following:

1 My dog only wags its tail when its raining
2 The girls bicycles were painted in there favourite colours

3 Many days before Princess Marinas visit, we practiced marching for hours trying to get each step right
4 The groom has been married before, it was one of those marriages that never got off the ground
5 What a marvellous selection their was, Mixers, Sheet sets, towell sets, Pans, crockery & cutlery etc
6 The appartment overlooked a quiet sandy bay, an ideal setting, so peaceful
7 Its Only a Paper Moon was my mothers favourite medly.

Appreciation of written style **8**

Writing has laws of perspective, of light and shade, just as painting does, or music. If you are born knowing them, fine. If not, learn them. Then rearrange the rules to suit yourself   *Truman Capote*

Contents

Introduction

We come now to a subject which at first may not seem directly relevant to study skills in the same way as argument construction and essay-writing techniques. Indeed, it is one of the last major topics we will deal with because it *does* involve many subtle distinctions and a control of language in ways which may not have been possible for you at the beginning of this course. But we can assure you that it *is* directly relevant, and it *is* an important part of being able to write well. To understand and appreciate good style will not only help you both understand and be more critically aware of what other people write; it will also help you produce writing of your own which is more attractive, concise and effective. This in turn can help you to think more clearly and be more discriminating in matters of taste and subtleties of thought.

What the chapter does is take you through an inspection of different *kinds* of writing – newspaper reports, letters, critical essays, and others – analysing the way language is used to produce a *style* appropriate for the message they contain. You will be looking at items of grammar and vocabulary in a more detailed manner than before: this will make you aware how a particular style is generated. Then we will pass on to a similar analysis of 'good style' to show how language can be used to produce some of its finest effects. At this point we will almost be spilling over into the study of literature and linguistics but this is as it should be, since there is an obvious overlap and having reached this stage you will be ready to move on to *apply* the skills you have acquired on this course in the study of other subjects.

1   *What is style?*

Good style is very difficult to define. It is something of which people say 'I can't define it, but I can *recognise* it when I read it.' This is perfectly reasonable, because good style is made up of a number of characteristics, all related to each other in very subtle ways. Think of the analogous 'good style' in dress. When someone is stylishly dressed we often recognise the fact but can't quite say *why*. It may not be a question of that person wearing expensive clothes – just that they have been chosen with *care* and put together in terms of texture, colour, and shape in a way which is elegant and pleasing. Very often the simplest choice of clothes can seem like good style – because they are *appropriate* to the situation in which they are being worn. And think how often the converse is true. People who are overdressed for a particular occasion (flamboyant clothes at a funeral, for instance) are guilty of 'poor taste' because they have not been sensitive to the *context* in which their clothes were being worn. The same outfit for example, might have been perfectly suitable for a party in the evening.

The same is true for good style in writing. First of all it must be *appropriate for the context in which it is being used*. Let's illustrate this idea with a couple of examples: Imagine you opened a cookery book and read the following recipe for baking a cake:

> Allow the beautifully soft flour, of a delicate off-white colour, to trickle lovingly through the sieve onto the eagerly expectant pats of bright yellow butter nestling together in the bottom of the bowl.

You know immediately that something is wrong here. What *is* it?

STOP   5 minutes

This sort of writing is simply not appropriate for a cake recipe, the whole purpose of which should be to give you brief, clear *instructions* on what to do. The writer here has clogged up the instruction with quite unnecessary descriptions ('beautifully soft', 'delicate off-white', 'bright yellow') as well as fanciful attitudes of his own to what is going on ('lovingly', 'eagerly expectant') and superfluous locations ('bottom of the bowl'). What we expect in such a piece of writing is *brevity* and *clarity*, uncluttered by anything which smacks of 'fine writing', e.g.: *Discussion*

'sieve flour on to butter'

Next, let's go to the other extreme with an example from an imaginary student essay on 'The Origins of the Industrial Revolution':

Easy access to raw materials – coal, iron, etc. And cheap labour too, all exploited of course! What do you expect from a Tory administration and total bourgeois hegemony'.

This is obviously sloppy writing, but can you say *why*, in terms of style?

---

5 minutes STOP

The extract begins with an incomplete sentence – more like a note you would make in a lecture than the sort of continuous prose which is appropriate to essay writing. The second sentence, as if taking its cue from the first, begins to slip into a conversational style. It offers a very loose opinion ('all exploited') – and slips out of correct grammar in doing so. And the third sentence not only poses a question (though without using a question mark) but suddenly slips into the jargon of political theory ('bourgeois hegemony'). We cannot say that this expression is *wrong* but we can say that it seems inappropriate here. It is certainly not the same sort of language in which the rest of the essay seems to be written. *Discussion*

So the imaginary extract is an example of bad style because the writer is not being sensitive to what is appropriate for an essay of this type. It is sloppy because it mixes two other modes of writing (note-taking and conversation or letter-writing) which are out of place in an academic essay.

Let's just reinforce this point by illustrating how these two other modes are not *bad* in themselves and might be quite acceptable in a letter to a close friend.

Cause for alarm? Oh, my goodness! There was confusion everywhere. Pots, pans, food-stuck-to-the-floor, A real *mess!*

133

You can see here that the breathless, telegraphic brevity of these grammatically incomplete statements is *meant* simply to transmit a sense of shock or excitement. Accuracy is not being aimed at, and the writer knows that the reader will understand both the context and the subject.

This is perhaps the most important point about good style. We have a vast range of literary effects to choose from, a range of vocabularies, and a number of different *tones* or voices we can adopt. The important thing is that they should be appropriate for the piece of work in hand (which for the purposes of this course is generally the essay). Think of the analogy with dress again for a moment. Asked to a formal dinner dance we would not go dressed in a bathing suit, just as we would not wear evening dress on the beach – yet both forms of dress are suitable in their appropriate setting.

As I have just said, you can often recognise good style or a particular style without being able to say why. One of the purposes of this chapter will be to help you identify the devices which are being used – particularly in 'fine' or effective writing. From this we hope you will be more able to exclude bad style from your own work and produce writing which is more elegant and effective.

2 *Different kinds of writing*

Now let's get under way with an exercise which is designed to lead us one step further towards the identification of points of good style, whilst at the same time illustrating the importance of *appropriateness*. What follow are examples of different *kinds* of writing, that is, extracts taken from different sources. The aim here is to show how each separate objective calls for a different style of writing. You will probably be able to identify the origin of each extract without too much trouble – because you are used to reading. But what I want you to do is say what are the characteristics of the style and why it is appropriate, which you might find more difficult because you are probably *not* used to analysing language and the way it is used.

Where do you think this extract is from – and what can you say about its style?

(a) Prescription charges will go up by 20p an item to £2.20 from April 1, Mr. Barney Hayhoe, the Health Minister, announced yesterday. The latest rise means they have gone up by over 1,000 per cent since 1979 when a prescription cost 20p.

---

5 minutes   **STOP**

You probably guessed from the content alone that this was taken   *Discussion*
from a newspaper news report. In terms of style this is evident
from the predominance of facts and figures in the statement, the
absence of any colouring adjectives or adverbs and the placing of
the important information at the start of the first sentence – so as
to arrest the reader's attention. We could also add that it is
probably a 'quality' newspaper since the first sentence is composed of four separate clauses. The popular tabloid newspaper
would probably have split this information into at least two
separate sentences. The use of numbers for money, percentages,
and the year are quite justified here since they make for clear,
rapid understanding.

So the style is plain, 'factual', and unadorned – which is appropriate for the rapid communication of news.

Now here is another straightford example:
(b)   There were many kinds of dinosaur. They lived long before
      the first men. Some were very small and moved quickly.
      Others were big and moved slowly. The dinosaurs in this
      picture were very heavy and slow.

---

5 minutes   **STOP**

Even if you had not already guessed, the phrase 'in this picture'   *Discussion*
should have told you that this was the explanatory text in a book
for children on prehistoric animals. But the style itself should be
enough. Each sentence is quote short and contains just one idea.
(That is, just enough information for a young person to absorb.)
The sentences are not complicated by dependent clauses. The
two beginning 'some' and 'others' have the same syntax (the
arrangement of the words) but carry contrasting information; and
the similarity of their composition highlights the contrast, which
is obviously what the writer wants the reader to note.

So, although this is simple, almost naive writing, it is again
appropriate, in style, for its purpose.
(c)   Now a different genre altogether:
      You would have been amused at McGee's performance –
      over the top as per. And Doris's reaction. Shock! Horror! I
      am a woman most sinned against. Offending pooch
      clutched against her Oxfam jumper.

135

<table>
<tr><td>**STOP**</td><td>**5 minutes**</td></tr>
</table>

Discussion   This is rather like my 'Cause for alarm?' example, isn't it? You can tell it is from a jokey and facetious letter exchanged between two people who know each other well. In terms of style this is evident from the direct address to another person ('You'); the use of idiom ('over the top') and slang ('pooch', 'jumper'); and the lack of formal syntax in using abbreviation ('as per') and exclamations ('Shock! Horror!') obviously thrown in to entertain the reader. In fact many rules of conventional grammar are broken here – but in a letter this is often permissible. First, because the writer is obviously in control of the language and his principal objective is to amuse the reader. Second, since they obviously both know each other well, information can be hinted at or telegraphed without lengthy explanation.

I wouldn't hold this up as an example of a particularly elegant style, but it is acceptable *in this context*

This example may be harder to identify, but you should concentrate not so much on trying to guess its origin, as on observing its stylistic characteristics.

(d)   Poe's philosophy of the short story deeply influenced his practice as a writer, and an examination of one story 'The Case of Amontillado' (1846) will reveal how he embodies his principles of unity in his own art. The revenge theme is common-place enough, but it is how Poe treats the theme that makes this story interesting. The first paragraph established the situation, and the reader calls to mind Poe's dictum that no one word in a story should be wasted.

<table>
<tr><td>**STOP**</td><td>**5 minutes**</td></tr>
</table>

Discussion   It is principally the vocabulary which is noteworthy here. Terms like 'principles of unity', 'theme', and 'dictum' tell us that the writer is addressing an intelligent well-educated reader. This is reinforced by the length of the sentences, each one of which contains at least three items of information: they are well controlled however, and they follow a normal, logical pattern of syntax. The fact that the passage contains units of information (the title of the story and the date it was published) and also uses a vocabulary of *evaluation* ('deeply influenced', 'examination', 'reveal') suggests that some sort of exposition and judgement is being offered. And the fact that there are no decorative frills, no linguistic flourishes present, reinforces the impression that the writer is principally concerned the reader takes a serious interest in the argument. The extract is in fact from an academic essay, an article which offers a critical assessment of Edgar Allan Poe's work. And the style is appropriate because it is well adapted to the writer's purpose.

Here is a slightly tricky example which may not be so easy to identify as you might think – but again you should concentrate on the elements of style, which might give you a clue.

(e) one of the most important things you can learn from a lecture, I mean if the lecturer is any good, and to my mind a good lecturer is someone who makes himself seen and heard properly, he knows how to project himself and the like, is how to get your message across and, well, just communicate with people.

---

5 minutes   **STOP**

Whatever your specific observations, I hope you will agree with   *Discussion*
me that this is very poor written style indeed. At a technical level
this is one overlong sentence, punctuated in a way which makes
it difficult to read, let alone understand. The weakness here arises
from a stylistic device which often spoils student essays – using a
long string of clauses, each one with less and less grammatical
connexion to the subject. And the dependent clauses sometimes
go on for so long that they actually shift the sense on to a new
subject. But what you may also have noted was the use of 'filler-
words' ('I mean', 'well', 'like') which add nothing to the sense
and are used in *speech* rather than writing.

You can pat yourself on the back if you spotted that this example
is in fact speech written down. If you didn't, then read through
the example again with this revelation in mind and I'm sure you
will almost be able to 'hear' the speaker.

I include this example precisely to illustrate the danger of including speech habits in writing. The two modes are quite different
and you should keep this in mind if ever you are tempted to inject
'life' into your writing by the inclusion of slang (which usually
disrupts the tone) or expressions and constructions which are not
appropriate to written language. The use of 'to my mind' and
'and the like' here are examples of this sloppy usage.

Very few people can *speak* with exact grammatical accuracy. We
allow for this by permitting the odd 'er', 'um', and unfinished
sentence but in writing there is no need and hence no justification
for this. And don't forget that when speaking to somebody we

also make our meaning clear by emphasis, tone of voice, facial expression, and even the use of gestures.

None of these – except perhaps emphasis – is available to us when writing, so it is important that we are as exact and grammatically correct as possible so that our meaning is quite clear.

I apologise if this sounds rather pedantic, but this is quite a common fault and you will do yourself a useful favour if you can keep in mind the lessons of this example.

Now let's finish off this section of the chapter with a final example to illustrate the point that the appropriateness of a style will be determined by the context in which it is used.

(f)   LIBRETTO. (Italian dimunitive of *libro*, Latin *liber*, a book. The book or words of an opera, oratorio, or long musical work. Lorenzo de Ponte uses the librettist of Mozart's *Le Nozze di Figaro, Don Giovanni*, and *Cosi fan tutte*.

STOP   5 minutes

Discussion   You probably guessed without much difficulty that this was an extract from a dictonary or an encyclopedia. But *how* did you know that, in terms of style? Well – the fact that the first word is printed in capital letters and stands alone, marked by a full stop, suggests *visually* that this term is about to come in for special treatment. And it is. What follows is one sentence giving the origin of the term, one defining its meaning, and another offering illustrative examples. But look at the first two statements. Neither of them contains a verb. This is because they are both preceded by *implied* statements. In the first sentence 'This word derives from . . .', and in the second 'It means . . .'. But since the dictionary is defining and explaining a long succession of such terms these expressions are omitted on the grounds that (a) constant repetition would become tedious, and (b) as much information should be (tightly packed) into the dictionary as possible.

Thus rules and conventions which we have pointed out to you (each sentence should be complete, with subject, verb, and object) are here being contravened. But that is because the context makes it permissible to do so. The tight, abbreviated style which results is appropriate for definitions in dictionaries.

What to look for   3

If the previous section contained notions which for you were at all new, your response might be 'well – I understand the general idea, but I'm still not quite sure what I ought to be looking for'. And if this *is* the case *don't worry*. At this point, as I mentioned earlier, we are pushing you into realms of linguistics and literary criticism. And we are doing so in the belief that a knowledge of how language works is bound to be of assistance to the sharpening of your study skills – no matter what subject you are eventually going to use them on. There are hardly any subjects, in the academic sense, which will not at some point involve your having to pay close attention to what other people have written, and to produce good writing yourself.

It is also at this point that we are able to point to the usefulness of terms which many people forget after they leave school – the technical terms of grammar. Don't worry, we are not going to plunge you into the business of parsing and clause analysis. What follows is really just a reminder of the *names* given to different parts of language and some suggestions on how to approach what is essentially the skill of *close reading*. In fact it is at the seemingly elementary level of reading that we begin.

(a) Careful reading
If all we need from a piece of writing is information (say, looking up somebody's number in the phone book) then we need not pay much attention to the style in which it is written. But as soon as we begin to consider the *quality* of writing we must be prepared to consider it more carefully. This will probably mean reading it *more than once*, reading some sections of it *slowly, paying more attention to details,* and even considering individual items like single words or points of punctuation.

We will be coming onto what exactly we might look for next, but at this stage I wish to give very strong emphasis to this idea of *reading carefully*. Many students find it a difficult habit to adopt, but in essence what it means is *slowing down* and *paying attention to detail*.

Obviously, if you are going on after this to study mathematics or geography you won't be particularly concerned with matters of style and even if it is to be sociology or history you will naturally be more concerned with the *content* rather than quality of writing. But let me suggest to you that you will still not be wasting your time by paying attention to the exercises in this chapter. It is always useful, in a culture so heavily based on language, to be aware of the way it can be used. And if your chosen subject is one of the more traditional topics in the humanities – the study of literature, languages, philosophy, theatre, history of art – it is essential that you are able to deal with the quality of language-usage and the question of style. So for the rest of this chapter you will have to forgive me if I write as if we are *all* intending students of literature. Only in this way will it be possible to illustrate the *detail* I have been speaking about. Students in other disciplines should if they wish just regard what follows as useful exercises in acquiring a skill they *might* find useful.

So – to repeat – careful reading means that you must be prepared to read it a number of times. Where this is not reasonably possible (say, with a long novel) you may instead dwell at length upon a single page.

Next we come to the nature of that reading – which should be *active*

(b) Active reading

What I mean by this is that you should be alert and participate in your reading. You should be all the time asking questions of what you read, and noting any special effects in the language and the way it is used. This will mean making notes on the things you observe. We have covered this point in other units. You should get used to the notion that – *so long as the books are your own* – it is a good idea to make notes on what you are reading. Just as a quick reminder in case you had forgotten, use a pencil, not a pen, and try to comment as perceptively as possible on what you wish to note (don't just underline).

In terms of the appreciation of style you may at first not be sure what to do with an item you notice. You may not know what it is going to contribute to your analysis or judgement. Don't worry about this: make a note of it anyway. Be prepared simply to note those words, effects, or phrases which strike you as interesting, unusual, or in some way worthy of note. Eventually you will get into the habit of doing this automatically as you read, and you will not then need to stop to make notes: but to begin with, be prepared to go through with what might seem like a rather tedious exercise.

Let me give you an example of the sort of note-making I mean. What do you find linguistically noteworthy in the following piece of poetry? You don't have to make an analysis of it. Just say what seems interesting or requires explanation.

Thou, Nature, art my goddess. To thy law
My services are bound. Wherefore should I
Stand in the plague of custome, and permit
The curiosity of nations to deprive me,
For that I am some twelve or fourteen moonshines
Lag of a brother?

5–10 minutes   **STOP**

Going through line by line, the most obvious details or queries   *Discussion*
you might have noted are as follows (I have added the explanations of the obviously archaic language which you might not
know yourself):
(i)   'Thou' – this use of the second-person pronoun is obviously
        old-fashioned, and it is often used by poets.
(ii)   'Nature' – the fact that this is spelt with a capital indicates
        that it has special importance.
(iii)   'Wherefore' – old-fashioned and poetic usage again. This
        reinforces the effect of 'Thou' and 'thy'.
(iv)   'in the plague of custom' – this is an interestingly
        compressed expression, with 'plague' being used in an
        unusual sense.
(v)   'curiosity of nations' – the same is true of this expression.
(vi)   'For that' – this is being used where we might expect
        'because'.
(vii)   'moonshines' – this is a poetic substitute for 'months'.
(vii)   'lag of' – another unusual expression, which is being used
        instead of the more prosaic 'short of'.
Much, much more could be said about even such a short passage
(which is from *King Lear*, by the way) but at this stage we are not
concerned with analysis, just with making a note of that which
seems interesting, unusual or significant. And let me repeat –
even if at first you are not sure what it adds to the style, if
something strikes you as interesting or even puzzling, *do make a
note of it*. Later on, it may be possible to fit this detail into the
overall 'picture' of your appreciation.

Now let's look at another example just to reinforce what I have
said. Again, read the following passage through a number of
times and say what you think worthy of note, purely in terms of
the language of the passage and the way it is being used. The
extract is taken from the first page of Dickens's novel *Bleak House:*

❝   London. Michaelmas. Term lately over, and the Lord Chan-
    cellor sitting in Lincoln's Inn Hall. Implacable November
    weather. As much wind in the trees as if the waters had but
    newly retired from the face of the earth, and it would not be

wonderful to meet a Megalosaurus, forty feet long or so, waddling like an elephantine lizard up Holborn Hill. **"**

STOP   **5–10 minutes**

Discussion   It is often more difficult to define the elements of style in prose writing for the paradoxical reason that we are so used to reading it. But whatever you spotted here I hope you will agree with me that this is rich and impressive writing. Here is my list of the points you might have noted.

(i)   'London' – an opening 'sentence' to the novel only one word in length!

(ii)   Sentence length – four sentences of varying length, from one word to forty-three words.

(iii)   'Michaelmas Term' – many names here in capitals (Lincoln's Inn, Megalosaurus, Holborn Hill).

(iv)   Sentence construction – none of the first three sentences has a main verb. Technically they are 'incomplete'.

(v)   'Implacable' – unusually strong word to describe 'weather'.

(vi)   'as if the waters' – this is an allusion to the primeval world.

(vii)   'wonderful' – being used in its original sense of 'something we wonder at'.

(viii) 'or so' – the introduction of a slightly conversational tone.

(ix)   'waddling' – appropriate verb, but it also makes the megalosaurus seem almost amusing.

(x)   'elephantine lizard' – 'large' noun converted into an adjective and amusingly coupled with something unusually small ('lizard').

You will have noticed that in merely noting what I thought worthy of attention in these two examples I have had to use some of the technical vocabulary of grammar – noun, verb, adjective, pronoun, and so on. This is where, in order to extract as much as possible from a passage in terms of appreciating its style, you should be prepared to make the effort *to put an equal amount in*. This will involve your taking the trouble to learn the basic terms you will require to discuss the subject. It is no good simply pointing to a piece of writing and saying 'This seems to be good.' You should be able to say *why* it is good, *what* its good qualities *are*, and exactly *how* they are expressed in the piece under consideration that is, *which* particular linguistic devices create the effect you wish to point to.

At this stage therefore, I think it would be useful to remind ourselves of a few basic terms we will need in discussing points of style. These fall into two categories: (i) parts of speech, and (ii) literary terms.

Parts of speech 4

I am going to limit this list to only the most elementary items you will require. (Adapted from M. Temple, *Get it Right*, p. 51.)

(a) A NOUN is the *name* of a person, thing, or quality: house, David, sparrow, beauty, honour
(b) A PRONOUN is used in place of a noun (to avoid having to repeat it)
he, she, me, it, they, you, anyone
(c) A VERB expresses an *action:* it is a *doing* word:
he *runs*, she *sings*, we *shout*
and it expresses states of *being:*
I *am*, he *is*, we *will*, they *might*
(d) An ADJECTIVE describes a noun or pronoun:
a *black* cat, a *big* house, the boy is *tall*
(e) An ADVERB modifies a verb (or an adjective):
he ran *quickly*, she sings *beautifully*,
an *unusually* tall boy
(f) A CONJUNCTION joins words, phrases, or clauses:
bread *and* butter, poor *but* honest,
he played well, *although* he was injured
(g) A PREPOSITION introduces a phrase, and is followed by a noun or pronoun:
Put it *on* the table, *by* airmail, *over* the top

There are many more technical terms concerned with grammar, but I think it would be counterproductive to list them all here. Instead, I will refer you once again to Michael Temple's excellently clear *Get It Right!* if you want further information on the topic.

Let us now move on to a similar list of the most commonly used *literary* terms you will need in considering good style. Again I am going to limit us to a very selective list suitable for the non-specialist – that is, the intelligent and inquiring student who is not necessarily making a special study of literature.

Literary terms 5

I want to emphasise that this is only a *selection* of some of the commonest terms used in the discussion of good style. But to know them and to understand their use should enhance both your own ability to discuss language and the way it is used – and it should help you become more aware of the way you write yourself.

1 ALLITERATION – the repetition of consonants (often at the beginning of words) to echo the sound or sense of the thing(s) described. 'She sells sea shells along the sea shore.'

2 ASSONANCE – the repetition of vowel sounds – a common method of producing a musical effect in poetic rhymes: store/floor, lies/eyes, moon/swoon

3 IMAGERY – a term used to suggest the creation of striking pictures in words: 'O my love is like a red, red rose.'

4 IRONY – a statement, made with humorous or satirical intent, which implies the opposite of what it says:
'So you've lost the key? That's *fine!*'

5 METAPHOR – a comparison of two things in which we say one thing *is* the other:
'He is a tower of strength.'
'They are the salt of the earth.'

6 ONOMATOPOEIA – the use of words which sound like the things they are describing:
pop! crack, buzz, plop

7 PARADOX – a statement which appears to be contradictory yet contains some sort of truth:
'The child is father to the man.'

8 PERSONIFICATION – giving ideas or objects personal attributes:
'The kettle sang merrily.'
'She is a fine boat.'

9 PUN – a humorous play on words to suggest two meanings at the same time:
'The central heating salesman *radiated* charm.'

10 SIMILE – a direct comparison of two things, usually introduced by 'like' or 'as':
'He was as strong as a lion.'
'The twins were like two peas in a pod.'

11 SYMBOL – an object or phenomenon which represents something else:
'The lily is a symbol of innocence (or death).'
'The portcullis is the symbol of Parliament.'

12 SYNTAX – the arrangement and grammatical relation of words in a sentence.

13 TONE – the attitude, manner, or prevailing outlook in a piece of writing determined both by the subject, and the terms in which it is presented.

14 VOCABULARY – the author's particular choice of words, and qualities they may have in common.

Do not imagine that in making an analysis of style you are *merely* searching for such devices in a piece of work. And please remember that the list could be ten or twenty times as long as it is. What I am trying to suggest is that in pointing to what you consider an element of good style, you should make as much effort as you can to name or describe exactly what it is that is producing the effect. For instance, in one of the examples I have just given:

'O my love is like a red, red rose.'

You could no doubt spot that the comparison here is a *simile* (love/rose) as well as being a striking *image*. But be prepared to state the obvious as well. In this case the effect of the line (by Robert Burns) is strengthened by the *repetition* of the word 'red'.

Good prose style   6

What we are going to do now is look at a number of examples of good prose style – that is, writing produced by authors of generally acknowledged skills and refinement. The pieces I have chosen are largely from the world of literature, but I don't want to suggest that writers of fiction have a monopoly of these skills. Many historians, biographers, and essayists have been admired for their style. I have chosen the following examples because the element of good style in them should be strikingly obvious. After all, it is often an important part of the quality of good fiction. And I should also add a word of warning. Good style can ultimately be a question of personal *taste:* qualities we admire in a writer may not appeal to somebody else. Nevertheless, it should be possible to describe and analyse the style of a piece of writing fairly neutrally, and leave the question of whether it appeals to us or not as a separate issue.

Your objective in each of the examples which follow is to see how much you can say about the way language is being handled. Put into effect the suggestions I have been making in this chapter. Read through the passages two or three times at least, and give close consideration to the way language is being used. Make notes of everything you find of interest. You are not being asked to make a comprehensive analysis: to do that you would need to know the whole work from which each one is extracted.

In my comments I will offer, not in any particular order of importance, some of the observations you might have noticed. Don't worry if your list doesn't correspond exactly with mine. This type of exercise takes time to get used to, and there are no absolutely 'right' or 'wrong' answers. Just try to observe as many facets of style as possible.

A This is the opening of Jane Austen's *Mansfield Park*, published in 1814.

“ About thirty years ago, Miss Maria Ward of Huntingdon, with only seven thousand pounds, had the good luck to captivate Sir Thomas Bertram, of Mansfield Park, in the country of Northampton, and to be thereby raised to the rank of a baronet's lady, with all the comforts and consequences of an handsome house and large income. All Huntingdon exclaimed on the greatness of the match, and her uncle, the lawyer, himself allowed her to be at least three thousand pounds short of any equitable claim to it. She had two sisters to be benefitted by her elevation; and such of their acquaintance as thought Miss Ward and Miss Frances quite as handsome as Miss Maria, did not scruple to predict their marrying with almost equal advantage. But there certainly are not so many men of large fortune in the world, as there are pretty women to deserve them. ”

STOP   **25 minutes**

Discussion   (a) *Sentence length and construction.* What might strike you here is how long those sentences are – though they become progressively shorter. The first has several subordinate clauses, but they are arranged in a logical time sequence which makes the sense easy to follow. Since the syntax is similar in the first three, the fourth receives part of its force from following the same pattern but being shorter.

(b) *Vocabulary.* It may not have struck you at first, but many of the terms here are drawn from the worlds of *money* and *class*. 'Seven thousand pounds', 'large income', 'equitable claim', and 'large fortune' all help establish a financial consideration in the passage. And this is reinforced by the language of class and social status: 'raised to the rank', 'baronet's lady', 'elevation'.

(c) *Comic effects.* It should be obvious on re-reading that Austen's placing 'only' before 'seven thousand pounds' is slightly ironic, as is the whole notion that Miss Ward needed the money to 'captivate' Sir Thomas. The terms 'elevation' and 'did not scruple to predict' are slightly comic in being so abstract and inflated for the topics they are describing. The final sentence – a comic epigram in itself – is a good illustration of Austen's wit.

(d) *Alliteration.* In 'comforts and consequences' and 'handsome house', the repetition of initial consonants helps us along at the end of this rather long sentence.

(e) *Names.* Notice how many names there are in this short passage, both of people and places. All these help to create the sense of realism which gives Austen's writing much of its attractiveness. And note how the illusion of reality is strengthened by the quite fictitious Mansfield Park being discussed in the same manner (and the same sentence) as the factual Huntingdon and Northampton.

B From Thomas Hardy's *Tess of the D'Urbervilles* (1891)

The outskirt of the garden in which Tess found herself had been left uncultivated for some years, and was now damp and rank with juicy grass which sent up mists of pollen at a touch; and with tall blooming weeds emitting offensive smells – weeds whose red and yellow and purple hues formed a polychrome as dazzling as that of cultivated flowers. She went stealthily as a cat through this profusion of growth, gathering cuckoo-spittle on her skirts, cracking snails that were underfoot, staining her hands with thistle-milk and slug-slime, and rubbing off upon her naked arms stickly blights which, though snow-white on the apple-tree trunks, made madder stains on her skin; thus she drew quite near to Clare, still unobserved of him.

---

25 minutes   **STOP**

(a) *Sentence length*. As in the last example, we are struck by the   *Discussion*
    length of the sentences. There are only two here, both
    essentially catalogues of the contents of the garden. Modern
    usage would probably split them into smaller sense units.
    But Hardy maintains control through clever use of punctu-
    ation, notably the two semi-colons and the dash. The length
    of the sentence reinforces the sense of lushness in the pas-
    sage. It does this in a way which would be impossible using a
    series of short abrupt sentences.
(b) *Vocabulary*. Notice Hardy's vigorous use of adjectives to
    qualify his nouns: 'juicy grass', 'tall blooming weeds', 'offen-
    sive smells'. The nouns are earthy and physical, the adjec-
    tives describing them are not quite what we might normally
    expect. In the second sentence the effect is even more
    marked: 'cuckoo-spittle', 'thistle-milk', 'slug-slime', and
    'sticky blights' are both scientifically specific *and* sensuously
    evocative. Notice too for instance that 'cuckoo' is *onomato-
    poeic*, 'slug-slime' almost conjures up what it describes by the
    sibilant repetition of the 'sl' sound, and there is a crackling,
    musical effect in 'sticky blights' which echoes the other
    expressions with its 'st' and 'ts' sounds. Much of the life in
    the passage is imparted by this use of *verbs*: 'sent up',
    'emitting' 'dazzling', 'gathering', 'crackling', 'staining', 'rub-
    bing off', 'drew'. And it is significant that these verbs all

147

belong to roughly the same *register*: they are generally of a gentle and subtle nature.

(c) *Imagery*. This is a common category in the analysis of prose. Remember, it means the creation of a striking picture. Each one of the clauses in the second sentence – 'gathering cuckoo spittle on her skirts', and so on – is a sort of image, but the last one is particularly strong: the blights which are snow-white on the trees become 'madder stains' on her naked arms. Again, Hardy chooses a term ('madder') which is both scientifically accurate and poetically expressive; for it means both the plant and the (red) dye that is made from it.

(d) *Tone*. It is obvious that Hardy is here deliberately trying to conjure up the lushness of a neglected garden, and he does so principally with the elements of vocabulary and syntax I have just mentioned. But this effect is strengthened by his use of one or two poetic devices: the repetition of 'weeds' in the first sentence, the expression 'rubbed off *upon*' (rather than the more prosaic 'on'), and the slightly archaic 'unobserved *of* him'. Tone is rather difficult to describe, but I would say this passage has a sensuous and poetic tone.

C from Joseph Conrad's *Heart of Darkness*, 1902

The sea-reach of the Thames stretched before us like the beginning of an interminable waterway. In the offing the sea and the sky were welded together without a joint, and in the luminous space the tanned sails of the barges drifting up with the tide seemed to stand still in red clusters of canvas sharply peaked, with gleams of vanished spirits. A haze rested on the low shores that ran out to sea in vanishing flatness. The air was dark above Gravesend, and further back still seemed condensed into a mournful gloom, brooding motionless over the largest, and the greatest town on earth.

STOP **25 minutes**

Discussion (a) *Vocabulary*. There are two striking features here in Conrad's choice of words. First the terms 'sea-reach', 'offing' and 'tide' suggest an intimate knowledge of sailing and the sea: like Hardy in the previous extract, he is writing for an intelligent and literate audience. Second, his use of large, powerful, and often abstract qualifying adjectives ('interminable', 'vanishing', 'mournful') impart a sense of seriousness to the writing and give it a sort of moral 'charge' or tension. This is reinforced by his choice of unusual nouns: 'waterway' is rather old-fashioned (echoing the Anglo-Saxon term for the sea – 'whales-way') which, curiously, imparts a certain dignity or loftiness in the passage precisely because it seems more elemental. This is also true of 'town' where we might normally expect 'city'.

(b) *Figures of speech*. As in his choice of vocabulary, Conrad imparts solemnity and power here by his selection of rhetorical devices. 'Welded together' is an unusually technical expression to describe the joining of sea and sky, but since they will both be flat at the horizon it seems logically possible. (Others might wish to argue that it is disruptively inappropriate). 'Vanishing flatness' comes close to not having much meaning, but since he is describing a view stretching out towards the horizon this again seems to work. 'Mournful gloom' has both the onomatopoeia of 'gloom' itself and the rhythmic alliteration of the 'l' and 'm' and the echo between the 'ou' and the 'oo' which create such a strongly rhythmic effect, even in the space of two words.

(c) *Rhythm*. It is rather difficult to discuss rhythm in prose writing because there are no regular stresses as there are in poetry. But anyone with a musical sense will be able to detect movement, stress and certain emphases which are occasionally imparted to prose writing. Here, the last sentence possesses what I would call a falling cadence. This begins with the 'oo' sound in 'gloom': there is then a pause signalled by the comma, the repetition of 'oo' in 'brooding', another clause arrested at 'biggest' for the emphasis of 'and the greatest' before falling to end on the words 'on earth' – a suitably large-scale concept (which incidentally is reinforced by the point I made about 'town' above).

Conclusion

At this point you may be wondering why we have strayed so far into the realm of literary criticism and analysis. What has this got to do with study skills, you might ask?

Our answer is that we think students should become sensitive to language and the way it is used. We believe that style is one of the most subtle instruments in the range of skills we have been encouraging you to acquire. And although you may be able to scrape through some course of study with a knowledge of the bare 'facts' it is unlikely that you will ever get very far (especially in the humanities) without becoming sensitive to subtleties of vocabulary, tone, and linguistic usage in general.

I don't want to make this sound daunting. What I am trying to explain is that even if you are going on to study politics, philosophy, or history you will produce better written work if you appreciate how well some other people have written, and even better if you can write well yourself.

We don't expect every student to become an original 'stylist'. In fact your own style will emerge naturally as you gain confidence and give a clear and accurate articulation of your thoughts. What we hope is that you will appreciate that 'good style' is very largely a question of its being appropriate to the subject and the form of expression (letter, essay, article) under consideration. Sensitivity on this point will help you to develop the ability to discriminate and be alert to subtleties which study in further or higher education will involve.

Style checklist
The following are a list of questions which can be used to make a stylistic analysis of any piece of writing.
1 What *kind* of writing is it?
2 *Vocabulary*: what *types* of words are used? Do they belong to any particular genre?
3 Groups of words: how are phrases, clauses, sentences built up?
4 *Grammar*: What kind of punctuation and syntax are used?
5 *Rhythm*: Are the sentences short or long? What kind of internal rhythms do they have?
6 *Figures of speech*: What kind of imagery is used? Are they original or merely cliches? From what sources are the images drawn?
7 *Literary devices*: What use is made of alliteration, assonance, puns . . .?
8 *Tone*: What kind of attitude does the writing reflect? Is it witty, serious, conversational . . .?
9 *Intention*: What do you think the piece of writing sets out to do? To inform, entertain, enlighten, communicate, dramatise . . .?
10 *Quality*: To what extent do you think that the writing achieves its apparent objective?

Self-assessment exercises

Exercise 1
Without looking back over the chapter, can you write down an

explanation of the points we have been covering? Don't just tabulate this time. Write out short digests of each section. I offer my own for purposes of comparison in the guidance notes.

Exercise 2
Read through the following pieces of writing and assess them according to the checklist on style which we offered at the end of the Conclusion to this chapter.

Extract A
Yesterday on the Centre Court, Boris 'boom-boom' Becker blazed his way to a brillaint victory over Ivan 'stone face' Lendl. At times it seemed the all England Club's premier stage had caught the measles – like a red rash. Becker was everywhere! Grinning with delight the fiery-haired German said afterwards 'I played great, I feel great, life is great.'

The question now is who can shoot down Becker's blitzkrieg attack on the world's top titles? And when will Britain's tennis establishment realise that our young players are just not good enough? I'd still back Fred Perry against the lot of 'em.

Extract B
All Personnel in Category 3 ii (technical), employed in the department for not more than three years from the 30th April are hereby given notice that as from 4th May inst. they are eligible for additional tax equal to one-sixth of their statutory allowance according to Section 65 of Standing Regulations 9 of the Corporate Finance Act 1953 providing they have been out of the country for more than thirty days during the calender year since the last mentioned date and providing they have not been members of any other employment category than that aforementioned apart from those in category 2 iv (admin). Claims forms will be issued on application to Heads of Units.

Extract C
I will tell you.
The barge she sat in, like a burnish'd throne
Burn'd on the water. The poop was beaten gold;
Purple the sails, and so perfumed that
The winds were love-sick with them; the oars were silver,
Which to the tune of flutes kept stroke, and made
The water which they beat to follow faster,
As amorous of their strokes. For her own person,
It beggar'd all description. She did lie
In her pavilion, cloth-of-gold, of tissue,
O'erpicturing that Venus where we see
The fancy out-work nature. On each side her,

Stood pretty dimpled boys, like smiling Cupids,
With divers-colour'd fans, whose wind did seem
To glow the delicate cheeks which they did cool,
And what they undid did.

Antony and Cleopatra

Extract D
London. Michaelmas term lately over, and the Lord Chancellor
sitting in Lincoln's Inn Hall. Implacable November weather. As
much mud in the streets as if the waters had but newly retired
from the face of the earth, and it would not be wonderful to meet
at Megalosaurus, forty feet long or so, waddling like an elephantine lizard up Holborn Hill. Smoke lowering down from chimney-
pots, making a soft, black drizzle, with flakes of soot in it as big as
full-grown snow-flakes – gone into mourning, one might
imagine, for the death of the sun. Dogs, undistinguishable in
mire. Horses, scarcely better, splashed to their very blinkers.
Foot passengers, jostling one another's umbrellas in a general
infection of ill-temper and losing their foothold at street-corners,
where tens of thousands of other foot passengers have been
slipping and sliding since day broke (if this day ever broke),
adding new deposits to the crust upon crust of mud, sticking at
those points tenaciously to the pavement, and accumulating at
compound interest.

Exercise 3
Clear writing exercise
Correct or improve the following statements.
1 It seems to be socially acceptable now to get a divorce, perhaps
   couples do not work hard enough at repairing a breakdown in
   their relationship.
2 Ethnic and religious groups also view divorce in different
   lights, and how the home is affected.
3 People should have a responsible attitude towards marriage
   and this should be mirrored in their attempts to seek a solution
   out of it.
4 Situations develop to hurt and upset the children of divorced
   parents that neither they or the parent left to cope can prevent questions from other children at school for
   instance situations where everyone else has two parents
   except them, everyday little things which never let them forget
   they are different.
5 However, usually two people do not become entirely dis-
   enchanted with each other at the same time and an over hasty
   decision can lead to a long period of regret; both for the one
   who was left, and for the partner who cannot build his/her life
   as clearly as he/she thought because of the residue of misery

with which the offending spouse has been left.

6 Marriage although not taken as seriously of to-day is still widely accepted as social norm. The attitude to divorce has become much more relaxed in the modern world.

Exercise 4

The weekly journal *The Economist* recently published extracts from its internal style sheet. It began by quoting George Orwell's six elementary rules from 'Politics and the English Language', an essay written in 1946.

1 Never use a metaphor, simile or other figure of speech which you are used to seeing in print.
2 Never use a long word where a short one will do.
3 If it is possible to cut out a word, always cut it out.
4 Never use the passive where you can use the active.
5 Never use a foreign phrase, a scientific word or a jargon word if you can think of an everyday English equivalent.
6 Break any of these rules sooner than say anything outright barbarous.

The Economist added a number of additional rules, e.g.,

7 Don't be stuffy or pompous: use the language of everyday speech.
8 Don't be hectoring or arrogant.
9 Don't be too pleased with yourself.
10 Don't be too chatty.
11 Don't be too free with the use of slang.
12 Avoid Americanisms.

Prominence is also given to the following piece of advice:

'Clarity of writing usually follows clarity of thought. So think what you want to say, then say it as simply as possible.'

Write two or three paragraphs commenting on the advice offered by George Orwell and *The Economist*. Should such advice only apply to journalism or is it more generally applicable to other forms of writing such as academic essays, scientific reports, novels and so forth? Do you think the checklist above leaves out any important elements? If so, try to formulate them yourself.

9 *Examinations*

Examinations are formidable even to the best prepared, for the greatest fool may ask more than the wisest man can answer   *Charles Cobb Cotten*

Contents

Introduction

Working through the materials up to this point I hope you have become enthusiastic about applying them to the different tasks you have to carry out as a student. We can all see the value in careful reading and essay writing. We can all see the need to maximise our performance by following useful guidelines. And we have all felt the warm glow a satisfactory result can produce. When we come to examinations it can be very different. Students often experience a range of feelings from mild apprehension to utter panic when in the last part of their course their tutor says: 'The examinations are now getting quite near.' For many of us an approaching examination is far worse than a visit to the dentist. Everybody has memories – even years later mild nightmares – of the last-minute revision; the nailbiting; the interminable cups of coffee; the missed bus or train; the missed question; the claustrophobia in the examination room; and a lot more besides.

We have all known people who were excellent students until the pre-examination period arrived, whose activities are disrupted by the approaching ordeal and who failed to acquit themselves as successfully as their previous study record suggested they might.

The purpose of this chapter is not to suggest that the examinations can be made painless.

It *will*

● *argue that many* of the problems we associate with examinations can be overcome if examinations are regarded not as a final obstacle course at the end of the study process but as *an integral part* of your course of study to be confronted and thought about as soon as your course begins.

● *attempt to convince you that* by applying many of the techniques of study you have acquired through this course, the examination can become a valuable part of your learning experience, not something that puts you off learning for life. But before we discuss the practical problems of preparing for examinations let's think a little about what examinations are for.

Why have examinations?   1

Make a brief list of the arguments for having examinations as part of a course and the arguments against.

10 minutes	**STOP**

In their defence: *Discussion*

(a) They are a means of *assessing progress*, especially when used during a course. They thus provide a guideline for both tutor and student.

(b) They are a means of *motivating students* to work hard. When you know that you have a thorough examination of all aspects of your studies to face then you apply yourself and make sure you know your stuff.

(c) They are a means of *grading students* according to their progress and selecting them for suitable further education.

(d) They are a means of *protecting standards*. If at the end of the course you are to receive a qualification, whether an A level, a diploma or degree which will guide others as to your progress, your abilities and your competence, then exams maintain the value of that qualification.

(e) Because they provide an objective test with conditions the same for everybody, exams avoid personal factors and favouritism and are *a fair means* of achieving these ends.

The prosecution replies:
(a) Examinations, by placing so much importance on formal written interrogation at the end of the course or parts of a course, *distract from the course as a learning experience.* There is often a tension between developing oneself educationally in the broad sense, being interested in a subject for its own sake and the requirements of the examination system.
(b) Examinations all too often show *not* the degree to which the student has developed educationally but *the degree to which the student has crammed* his or her mind full of facts and arguments which will evaporate the day after the test.
(c) Examinations are *not objective.* The content of the examination and student performance in it can be influenced by a variety of factors from cultural background to pre-menstrual tension.
(d) *The marking of examinations is unreliable* because it cannot completely exclude personal factors. There will, despite rigorous attempts by examining bodies to control the situation, always be differences of opinion, temperament and judgement and, therefore, always 'hard' markers and 'easy' markers and differences between different examining bodies and institutions granting similar qualifications.
(e) Because of these problems examinations are *not a wholly fair means* of assessing progress, grading students and protecting standards of qualifications.

The debate is a very old one and it will continue. Very broadly the last two decades in Britain have seen some movement away from the idea of the formal examination as the *only* means of assessment and some movement towards a *mix* of examination and continuous assessment. Nonetheless, the formal examination still possesses a central role in further and higher education in this country. As a mature student you need to be aware of some of the questions in the continuing controversy about formal exams. However, if you are taking certain courses and you wish to complete them successfully you will have to *accept* the need to meet course requirements by taking a formal exam, whatever your personal views on its validity as an assessment technique. You either do the course as it stands or you don't. It is no good presenting the world with a biting critique of the examination system the day after you have failed!

It follows that the two key points to be made in relation to success in examinations are: *Think Positively* and *Think Early*.

Examinations as an integral part of the course   2

To help you think about these key points, briefly comment on the attitude of these students:

> Jill is studying on a one-year diploma course. The course begins in October and culminates in June with four written three-hour exams. Like many of us Jill dislikes the idea of exams. 'I'll put them completely out of my mind until after Easter', she says, 'otherwise I'll just get depressed and thinking about them will interfere with my work.'

> Bill, who is on the same course, has a somewhat different attitude. 'That's leaving things too much to the last minute', he claims, 'I start doing a little revision over the Christmas holidays, reading through my notes, nothing too strenuous as it's still early days yet. During the Easter vacation I begin in earnest. That's when I seriously examine what the exam involves. I treat it scientifically. I get hold of past examination papers. I always reckon that what came up two years ago might come up again. Once we return after Easter then I really go into the training camp. Now it's time for real revision. I skip the remaining lectures and classes and just revise, revise, revise.'

---

5 minutes   **STOP**

Well, what did you think about Bill and Jill? Have they got the right idea? Neither had really, but Bill was obviously much closer to it than Jill. Thinking *positively* and thinking *early* means that you should actively consider what the course examination involves as part of your overall consideration of the course *before* you decide to take the course. Bill thought that a scientific approach meant looking at past examination papers almost a couple of months before the exam. But a thoroughly scientific approach would mean that as soon as the course begins you have in your possession, and have read, not only copies of syllabuses and reading lists, but also copies of past examination papers and of model answers.

Discussion

Jill's idea that you put exams out of your mind until they loom large is even more dangerous. *Confront the reality of exams as an integral part of the course as soon as it begins.* As you work through the course relate each part to the kind of examination question that comes up within that particular area. It is much better for somebody in Jill's position to face what she thinks of as an unpleasant reality in October than in April or May. If she puts exams completely out of her mind until near the end of the course she will not only be unprepared but the idea of exams will possibly terrify and paralyse her already inadequate last-minute preparations. If, however, she thinks about the exams right at the start of the course and throughout its duration and relates her routine work to them, then the idea of exams will become more natural, something familiar, less foreign and less frightening.

By refusing to think about her exams through her course Jill is also forfeiting another very good means of controlling and limiting her anxieties. We discussed earlier on how useful it is for students to form informal *study groups*. It is very helpful if such groups discuss the relationship of what they are studying to exams, rehearse exam questions and discuss educational and personal problems in relation to exams *from an early stage*. By sharing her anxieties Jill may find solutions to them. She should also, of course, be allocated a personal tutor or have access to a course counsellor, someone who is there to give personal advice and guidance. If Jill has problems with exams she should discuss this with her tutor, not *leave it until the last minute*.

If the *'mañana* mentality' – putting off until tomorrow what we should do today – is a major factor in the forbidding image of exams it also applies to revision. Both Jill and Bill see revision, like exams, as something *external* to the ordinary process of study. From what you have learnt already you will know that this breeds an inefficient approach. Revision should be a regular recurring built-in part of the study process, not a last-minute link between that process and the examination.

Revision is not, as both Bill and Jill seem to think, even at best a matter for Christmas or Easter but for the whole year round. Revision should take place regularly: for instance, at the end of each week or month, when you should go back over what you have recently studied whilst it is relatively fresh in your mind and relate it to the other components of your course. The time for *real* revision is all the time!

But if revision is *continous* we can distinguish between revision and *special* revision. Bill used the phrase 'going into training camp'. The period immediately before the exams should represent a break from our normal study routine in that we are now gathering the threads together for a final effort; we need to step up the process. But remember, 'going into training camp' will only produce the finely tuned athlete in perfect shape if the contestant was reasonably fit beforehand!

If you think *positively* and think *early*, relating each part of the course as you do it to your final examination in that part of the course, then your examination *can* became a useful integrated part of the learning process.
Two final points:

Bill says: *'Look at the last two years' exam questions.'*

Fatal: Look back over a longer 7 or 8-year period. Examiners like to experiment and ring the changes. The idea that the same questions come up bi-annually is nonsense. In, say, politics or economics, where the subject matter is constantly shifting, examiners are constantly asking new questions (we will look at using past papers a little later).

Bill says: *'Once you start special revision miss any remaining classes and lectures to concentrate your attention and energies.'*

Fatal: In a couple of hours of a lecture or a discussion class you may pick up vital information, a new slant on the subject, an essential component in the overall course structure that you may overlook completely in your private study or which might take you many hours to acquire. *Always complete your course.* Apart from anything else it is not unknown for tutors in final classes and lectures even those not specifically organised for revision purposes to provide valuable suggestions and hints on examination content and technique.

To sum up: You should be preparing for your examinations right from the start of the course. Preparing for exams involves:
● regular attendance at classes and lectures
● regular preparation for classes and lectures
● regular revision of classes and lectures
● regular completion of essay and exercise assignments
In short, it involves following assiduously the rules of studying discussed in these chapters. It is not something that can begin in the immediate period prior to an exam – at least not if you wish to do yourself justice.

Different kinds of examinations 3

Before we go any further in talking about preparing for exams it would be useful it we briefly listed some of the different methods of examining students used in the British educaional system.

1 *Essay examination*
The argument behind this approach is that writing an essay under time-tested conditions where you have no access to books, notes and articles is the best and most flexible means of assessing student understanding of a subject.

2 *Examination by thesis*
Sometimes students can take a higher degree by writing a long thesis on a specified subject instead of taking an essay-based exam. Sometimes a shorter thesis is required in addition to an essay-based exam to complete the course requirement. Sometimes, as with a Ph.D. the qualification consists almost totally of writing a thesis. The justification for this method is that it tests a student's capacity to read, research and write in a *sustained* fashion, to synthesise a mass of complex information and ideas and perhaps to come up with a new and original advance of knowledge.

3 *Short question examination*
These involve *multiple choice questions* where candidates are asked to select from a number of possible answers, *matching questions* where the student has to match each term with its counterpart; and *'true-false' questions* where the need is to again select one answer. Whilst these exams can test knowledge and exactitude they fail to explore the wider range of skills tested by the essay-based approach.

4 *The open book examination*
This is a more recent development in which you are entitled to use your books and notes in the examination room. The test of memory is less rigorous but, it is argued, the student has a better chance to show creative, analytical and presentational skills than with 'unseen' exams.

5 *The practical examination*
These examinations are usually intended to provide a complement to the classroom test. For example, science students may be asked to perform an experiment or identify material under laboratory conditions. Language students may be required to carry on a short conversation with an examiner. The aim is obviously to see if you can apply your knowledge in simulated situations. You have shown that you can write good Spanish, but can you also *speak* good Spanish?

6 *The oral examination*
This is sometimes called a *viva* and is most commonly used with students who have taken an examination by thesis. It is again intended to satisfy the supervisors and outside experts that their grasp of the subject that they have studied in depth is not confined to the written page.

In this chapter we deal largely with the essay-based examination. This is the most common in British higher education and tends to cause more problems to more people. However, where relevant, we will refer to the other types of test.

Revising for examinations   4

Whatever kind of examination you are facing you will need intense and efficient preparation. We have already said that any course will require the use of both constant revision and *special* revision in the pre-examination period. Think about the kind of guidelines you would suggest for those facing an exam.

---

10 minutes   **STOP**

If you have studied hard and efficiently throughout the course you may still feel tensed-up as exams approach. But your anxiety in this context is more likely to be *creative* anxiety which will set the adrenalin flowing and thus work to your advantage. All too often it is those who have not studied and prepared properly who suffer from crippling anxiety as the exams approach. If you have pursued the assiduous or 'professional' approach the following guidelines should further complement your efforts.   *Discussion*

1 *Revision materials*
   Make sure that you have available
   ● Copies of your course outline, syllabus and reading list.
   ● Textbooks and other required reading.
   ● Essays and exercises you have completed as part of the course together with comments, corrections, assessments from tutors.
   ● Past examination papers.
   ● Past examiners' reports. (in the case of A levels available upon request from the examination board).
What haven't you got that you need? How can you get it: from fellow students, or tutors, or the library?

2 *Make sure you know*
   ● The form of the papers set, eg., compulsory sections to be completed.
   ● Who sets the exams and who marks them.
   ● The grading system to be used.

3 *Revision arrangements*
By the time you come to your special revision you should have

mastered an effective study routine covering *when* and *where*, *what* and *how*. You should now examine your routine. If, for example, you have previously found it convenient to study in college, will it now be more efficient, as classes and lectures end, for you to study at home; or in a library near your home; or a mix of both? Is time spent travelling to college outweighed by the advantage of discussion with fellow students? Or is the latter for you simply a means of socialising and wasting valuable study time? But is it necessary for you to break up and vary your place of study so as to stimulate freshness and efficient effort?

Remember to discuss your coming exams with your partner, parents and friends. In the pre-examination period many of us feel that we need more time than our previous study routine required. This must be discussed with those we live with and if a temporary change of responsibilities is required, bargains must be made. Similarly, most of us wish to limit our social life during our special revision and it is important that friends and relatives understand. But *note*: you *need* some time for relaxation. If you work too hard too long you may quickly reach the top of your productivity curve. Get some free time. On the other hand if you overdo your 'relaxation' you'll be in no shape for the challenge of three-hour examination papers. Try to 'reward' your hard work with appropriately small breaks: watching a television pro-gramme, playing your favourite sport, etc.

4 *Revision schedule*
(a) *Drawing up your timetable*
If you have built the examinations into your study schedule you will be aware when the time has come to move into top gear. Each three-hour paper will require at least one week's full-time revision, possibly more. Six papers will require therefore 6–8 weeks' intensive preparation. As you approach this period, examine *what is to be done* and assess *the amount of time you require to do it.*

This involves a brief survey of your syllabus and your course work as a preliminary to drawing up a revision timetable to be pinned up over your desk. Plan your time on a daily and weekly basis. Set yourself daily and weekly targets but continually review progress. Pace yourself. There are, of course, questions involved here which only you can answer although you can discuss them with fellow students. For example, should you study one or two subjects in a day? You need to weigh variety against the possiblity of a sustained onslaught on your subject. If you have made an important breakthrough with one subject on Monday, should you continue on Tuesday, breaking your original pattern?

(b) *Sequence and time allocation*
What sequence of subjects should you follow? What time allocation should you give to each exam and each question? These are judgements only you can make.

My advice is *not* to neglect the subject or questions you find unattractive or difficult in favour of those that you find attractive and stimulating. I was once studying for an examination in the *Sociology of Crime*. The paper was divided into two parts, *Criminology* and *Penology*. I found criminology a more interesting area whilst the way penology was taught decreased my already minimal enthusiasm. As a result I saturated myself in the first subject area and prepared inadequately for the second. The exam required two answers from each part of the paper and awarded equal marks for each question. My answers in the first section were comfortably above distinction level. the mediocrity of my performance in the second part of the paper dragged my overall mark down so that I missed that coveted accolade of a distinction. Remember, life and study do not terminate after your exam; if, as I did, you find a particular area of study exciting you can carry on with it later. Do not allow your specific interests to blur the overall task you are facing and distort your preparation for it.

(c) *Spotting questions*
The same kind of thing goes for spotting questions. There is nothing wrong with placing a little more emphasis on the specific subjects that come up with regularity. But you should only do this in the context of revising a fair part of your syllabus well. You cannot rely on Luck. The student who picks four 'regular' questions when the paper requires four answers and scarcely looks at the rest of the syllabus is fighting for survival when only two of the prepared topics come up. However, if you have covered twenty topics in a course and will be asked for questions in your exam you could probably concentrate, with some safety upon 10–15 topics. Select those subjects on which you feel strong and have put in work: eg., project essays.

Think about these points and draw up a detailed timetable. Once you have done this try to give it a fair trial. Obviously, you will need a modicum of controlled flexibility: if you are feeling 'low' on a particular day studying a subject different to the one scheduled may help raise your morale. Only you can take the final decision but if you do depart from your timetable return to it and the difficult subject at your next session.

Finally, do you need to change your normal study schedule?

Given that you are likely to be studying longer do you need to change your normal habits of working more in the morning than in the evening or vice versa, the times you take your breaks, sleeping patterns, etc.? And given the differences between special revision and normal study can you work longer without a break? Or do you need more breaks?

If these problems are recognised and confronted, you will be in a much stronger position to do well.

5   *Revision methods*
Your revision methods must be *active* ones. The student who simply sits at his or her desk passively reading through notes will quickly become bored and will take little or nothing in. Instead here are a few suggestions:
● While reading your notes underline key points and jot down your comments on a fresh piece of paper.
● Switch to your textbook and use the same method.
● Produce summarised versions of your notes (possibly in an alternative form, for instance, if your notes are Linear-Logical change them into the Concept-Tree approach). Then produce summaries of your summaries so that eventually large topics are represented by a few key points. Your whole course will then be reduced to a few key 'trigger' words, each representing a pyramid of information, arguments and theories.
● Make lists of names, dates, definitions and concepts, cross-reference for different essay topics.
● Try using record cards for your note summaries and lists.
● Talk key points into a tape recorder. Play it back once, listen, play it back twice, and check with notes simultaneously.
● Become question-orientated. Get into the mental habit of posing yourself questions . . . and answering them. Pose yourself examination style questions too, and work through structured responses. You can do this mentally, counting off the points on your fingers if this helps.
● Form revision syndicates. A group of fellow students often agree to work through topics collectively, sharing and exchanging their revision preparations. Some people claim that the most enjoyable and effective learning takes place in this context. The hard spadework of assimilating your subject has to be done by you alone. These are just some methods people have found useful. Remember, variety is the spice of life, so try a mix. A lot of this is basic memory work and the memory works in funny ways. You will find it helpful to turn back to Volume I, Chapter 3 but here are a couple of techniques I have found helpful.

Memory aids

Memory by association
It may be difficult to recall that the important legal case of *Bents Brewery* v *Hogan* was heard in 1945. If you think of it in the context of the end of the Second World War it may stick in your mind. Similarly, the *Bridlington Agreement* governing the relations between British trade unions may not be instantly recallable as the product of the 1939 Trade Union Congress. If you connect it with the year war broke out you'll probably remember it better. Of course it all depends upon your interests and background: some of us would find it easier to remember that 1933 was the year that Hitler came to power by linking it with the fact that it was the year Everton beat Manchester City in the FA Cup, whilst for others the process would be reversed!

Memory by mnemonics
Some people feel that this method of creating words by taking the first letter of each idea, definition or concept is a good means of remembering the structure of an exposition or essay. One might recall Marx's first four laws of motion of capitalism (a) the concentration and centralisation of capital, (b) the progressive proletarianisation of the work force, (c) the growth of the organic composition of capital and (d) the tendency of the rate of profit to decline as . . . CPCP. Alternatively, Mary Tudor's religious policy – the Counter-Reformation, the Acts of Repeal, the Act of Six Articles, the Heresy Laws, the attempts to revive the monasteries – could be remembered as CARSHM, noting the 'chasm' between her policies and those of her predecessors and successor.

So far we have discussed some of the problems of drawing up a special revision schedule and how to make a start on your special revision. Having broken the ice and completed the groundwork of familiarising yourself with your material, what other methods can you use to deepen your understanding, strengthen your preparation, question yourself even more effectively? Make a list of some of the other methods you might use as the revision period develops.

---

15 minutes   **STOP**

---

1 *Talking it out*   *Discussion*
If you hit difficulties first discuss them with fellow students. Explain the problem, the issue, the arguments, to a reliable friend and let him or her comment.

2 *Using the tutor*

Some tutors state at the end of classes: 'That's it, I've done everything I can. Now it's up to *you* . . .' Well, not quite: if you hit problems, if certain issues defy your understanding, then *talk to your teacher*. Most tutors want their students to do well and are prepared to help, often right up to the exam itself.

3 *Practice questions*

This is a very important and much neglected part of revision. You will be tested on your performance within the examination room and, as everyone knows, performance improves with practice. It is therefore essential to rehearse the examination experience in advance. This can be approached in a variety of ways.

(i) *Practise analysing past examination questions.* Look for the key instruction words and try to fathom precisely what is being required. Try paraphrasing questions in your own words. Where meanings appear elusive use 'brainstorming' techniques to help unblock your thinking and clarify understanding (this entails scribbling down freely associated ideas on a particular topic).

(ii) *Note form answers:* Try planning responses to past questions in outline form. If time is short in a particular exam you may in any case be advised to adopt this approach so practice will be doubly useful. Try to develop a feel for the correct strategy, e.g., does the question posed require a descriptive, an analytic or a 'for and against' approach?

(iii) *Write out full answers working to a time limit.* This will help prepare you physically and mentally for the examination and help you to enter the examination room with confidence. Think carefully about the tone and level of the writing required.

(iv) Don't forget to check:
- Overall time allowed?
- Overall number of questions?
- Different sections within the paper?
- Any compulsory questions?
- How many questions must you answer?
- How are marks divided amongst the questions?
- How much time should you allot for each question?
- What are you allowed to take with you into the examination rooms: calculators, tables, books?

To repeat, performing well in examinations is an acquired skill. My own recollection is that my first two or three papers in my degree exams were not an entirely happy experience but my performance then began to improve markedly. I should have taken the advice I am now giving to you! If you have practised examinations in the run up to the big day you will be warmed up and more likely to display your full potential.

4 *Summary revision.* Try to allocate two or three days before the examination period to review all your revision work to gain an overall grasp of your revision activities together with a sense of perspective. Extended last-minute revision into the small hours is not advised as this is likely to confuse and tire you.

How to handle the examination   5

Let us suppose we are now approaching the examination itself. Here again a little thought as to technique and presentation can help you immeasurably and mean the difference between excellence and mediocrity; success or failure. To help you think about examination technique consider the following statements.

- 'The night before the exams go out, relax, have a good time, even have a few drinks.'
- 'I always arrive at the exam room a little late, missing all the butterflies and the nervous chatter.'
- 'Look at your paper. Pick out quickly your best question. Start writing immediately to give yourself confidence.'
- 'Describe, discuss, analyse . . . it's all the same really: a signal to tell you to bang down everything you know about the subject.'
- 'Spend as long as you can on your best questions. That's the road to success.'
- 'It's essential to get in a good six sides of script for each question.'
- 'Keep writing until they force you to stop – that's my advice!'

You win no prizes for spotting that all the statements contain bad advice – the truth is however that many students behave in practice as if they have followed it. The period immediately before the exam can be a difficult time. Resist the temptation, for example, to concentrate myopically on your first exam. It is helpful if you have completed the substance of your revision a few days before the curtain rises and can concentrate on examination rehearsals or skimming through your sum-marised notes. If you are attacked by last-minute nerves try to relax with people you know will boost your confidence. Keep away from the worriers and the merchants of doom.

The night before the exam is largely a matter of individual choice.

Some people prefer to combine relaxation with light revision. Going out for a drink can be unwise as a few drinks can lead to other things. An early night is far preferable. Certainly before you do anything check.
● You know where the exam is being held.
● You know how to get there and how you are getting there.
● You know any checking-in procedure.
● You know the examination instructions.
● Your schedule for the period between your first and second exam is planned and fixed.
● You have everything you will need for the exam from money for fares to any registration slips or cars for the exam, to *two* biros, pencils, a rubber and any materials allowed. Don't forget a reliable watch!
● You know the procedure if you are taken ill or have some other problem that will stop you taking the exam or affect your performance in it in an important fashion. Even at this late stage you can still talk to your tutor or counsellor.

If you follow this checklist you will ensure that your last-minute worries are minimised and that you feel calm and efficient rather than flustered and rushed.

To sum up: the best advice the day before is: relax but don't push the exam out of your mind.

Many of us are more alert when we have been up and about for an hour or two and it may be a good idea to get up a little earlier than normal on the day of the examination. This also provides some insurance against little things going wrong at the last minute. Make sure you have an effective alarm system and don't sleep in.

It is *FATAL* to arrive late. In fact ensure that your travelling arrangements mean that you will arrive *early* in case of any problems. If having arrived, found the building and found the room, you wish to go off by yourself that is a different matter but make sure that you are in the exam room on time. Don't make a fetish of where you sit – if someone sits in 'your' seat first your calm will be disturbed – but find somewhere where you feel you are unlikely to be distracted.

Many examinations require you to fill in a registration slip giving details of your course, institution, date of birth, examination centre, and so forth. Follow the instructions carefully. Many examinations today give you a specific period of time to read the examination directions and study the questions. Use this precious time. Check first of all that you have the right paper, then read the directions . . . slowly . . . twice. Check that they have not changed in small ways since previous years for instance, check whether you start each answer on a new page, whether each section of the examination requires different answer books, whether you should write on one side of the page only.

It is *FATAL* to then pick out the best questions and start writing as soon as you can. Instead:

1 Read the whole paper through . . . slowly . . . twice
  Do read each question carefuly.
  Don't rush from one question to another briefly scanning each but not taking in its detail and meaning.
  It is in these first few minutes that a calm, precise businesslike attitude sets the scene for the successful examination. Move slowly and methodically.
2 When you read each question the second time: underline key instruction words and be on the look out for the double direct- ive – for example, 'Describe and assess' . . . 'Discuss, illustrat- ing from' . . . Check the precise meaning of instruction terms in Chapter 1.

You should, by now, be familiar with all these terms – compare, contrast, evaluate, review, justify, etc. But *go over them again carefully before your exam.* You will know by now that it is *fatal* to see that a question is about a particular event such as the Norman Conquest or a person such as Harold Wilson and take this as an invitation to simply write all you know about each. Look at the two examples below:

(a) Examine in detail the changes in landownership and systems of tenure which occurred in the two decades after the Norman Conquest.

'Norman Conquest' strikes you immediately but the key words are in reality 'Examine', 'landownership', 'tenure' and 'two decades'.

(b) Compare and contrast the economic policies of Harold Wilson's governments between 1946–66 and the two 1974 elections.

Again the temptation is to see 'Harold Wilson' and ignore the key instruction word, 'economic' and the very specific dates given. This question is limited:

 (i) To the first and third Wilson governments.
(ii) To economic policy.

But how widely or narrowly do I define economic policy? Do I know enough about the motivating principles and the detailed practice of economic policies in these two periods to bring out the continuity and discontinuities the similarities and the differences? You are *not* just being asked to regurgitate what happened but to analyse it in a comparative way.

3 Now sort out the sheep from the goats. Eliminate the questions you simply cannot do or will find great difficulty answering and select those you can tackle.

4 Now select the three or four questions (or whatever the examination requirement is) you can do best.

5 Now check the timing of your questions. You will find that it is *FATAL* to spend too much time on your best questions(s).

Allocate your time according to the marks attached to each question.

For example, if, as is common, you are informed 'Answer five questions' in a three-hour examination with all questions carrying equal marks, then allocate approximately 35 minutes for each question. If you are asked to 'Answer four questions' then it's 40–45 minutes per question. The extra five minutes is to plan your answer although you will be able to do some mental preparation if you are in addition given an allocation of reading time. I use the word 'approximately' because a wise student will also want a further five minutes at the end to check the paper. If marks are allocated equally between questions then remember *the marginal rule*: ten minutes on a new question will produce more marks than not touching that question at all and lavishing the time on a question that you have already done well. Always make an attempt at the required number of questions. If you are really in trouble jot down your last answer in semi-note form. At least the examiner will know that you had a grasp of its essential points.

6 It is still *fatal* to start writing your first answer. Instead, quickly sketch out a skeleton plan on a piece of scrap paper, your exam paper or the answer book for each question, before you begin writing your answers.

Example:
Compare and contrast the *internal structure* of the Transport and General Workers Union with that of the Amalgamated Union of Engineering Workers.

Give *an example* of each *in operation*. Account for the *differences* between the two.

Sketched outline
1 (a) TGWU established trade group structure. AUEW problems of amalgamation, different sections – still own structure. Focus: on TGWU and engineering section of AUEW.
  (b) Large lay executive vs small full-time executive.
  (c) Powers of TGWU General Secretary vs AUEW President/General Secretary split function.
  (d) Relation of latter to small AUEW conference meeting annually, method of elections vs TGWU large, biannual, different mode of elections.

(e) Appointment of full-time officers vs election of full-time officers.

(f) Shop steward system in both unions.

2 Use TGW on incomes policy 1974–9 and AUEW on government money for ballots 1980.

3 Analyse development of AUEW from roots as craft union and compare with TGWU origin as amalgamation of general unions. Compare and contrast different traditions but changing environment.

In practice, of course, you would jot this down using a form of shorthand. Such an exercise sketches in the dimensions of the question – it is not asking you to write everything you know about the two unions. It is asking *three* questions. You have given yourself a broad structure and at the same time touched on the mainsprings of your knowledge and reminded yourself what you know. You may wish to plan *all* the required questions before beginning to write or you may wish to write *each* answer directly after the plan.

7 You can now start writing your first answer. Start with what you consider to be your strongest question; this gives you confidence, will get the adrenalin and the memory flowing, and build your confidence. Once again, remember the rules of essay-writing. You do *not* need to write a certain number of pages for each question. What you have to sell is measured in quality not quantity. Most examiners want less writing, more thinking.

● Make sure your answers have a clear but brief introduction. Do not waste time repeating the question.

● Define the key terms (if this is necessary).

● Use paragraphs to emphasise each key point in the main body of your answer. First point . . . second point . . .

● Check for relevance as you develop your answer. Be as crisp and concise as possible and avoid padding.

● Emplify your points with examples. Justify assertions. Take up counter-arguments, introduce relevant statistics. Use brief, pertinent diagrams, tables or graphs.

● End with summary of key points and your conclusion, perhaps referring back to the question and using its actual words.

8 It is not advisable to keep on writing until the last minute. Presentation is important. Poor spelling, sloppy punctuation and slips of the pen may create an unfavourable impression. Checking your answer is also vital. So try swiftly to go back over each question at least making sure you have committed no major abominations – you have answered the right number of questions, you have covered all the points within each question – and your paper looks at least reasonably in order. Keep

working on this until you have to stop.

Physical problems

9 *Nerves.* Volume I, Chapter 3 advised you on how to relax but occasionally panic occurs in a examination. Be aware what is happening if this occurs and reasure yourself that it won't last long. Let your muscles go limp and breathe in deeply, holding your breath for five seconds. Then release your breath, also taking five seconds. Repeat the exercise five times and you should be in a mood to continue. If not repeat the whole exercise once more.

Memory blocks. Don't panic and don't give up. Try to relax. Think back to when you prepared the particular area, the particular lecture it came up in, the particular class it was discussed in. Use your mind's eye. What can the blocked item be related to? Keep jotting down related points and you will find in most cases it will jump back into your mind. But don't get stuck. Keep to the timetable. Some students find the point will emerge as they work on the next question.

Writer's cramp. The best antidote is lots of preparation, under exam conditions before the real thing. Brief pauses will usually help ease the problem.

Illness. Try and overcome feelings of nausea or exhaustion that suddenly arrive during the exam by concentrating on the work. If it is overpowering, stop, breathe in relax. If it is insuperable, inform the examiner quickly.

10 If you have successfully completed your exam do not over relax or go out on a spree. You have won one battle but, after a brief rest, you must return to the fray. Once you have completed your exam programme, file your notes away carefully. Consider what you have learned from the experience but avoid lengthy and unhelpful collective post-mortems. If you are going on as a student try to resume work from the higher plateau a good examination performance will have provided you with.

Finally, here is a brief checklist of tips to help you in the run up to an examination.

Examinations checklist

Preparation

(a)   Be aware of the syllabus studied.

(b)   Check past papers.

(c)   Be aware of the form of the examination.

Revision

(a)   For major examinations begin 6–8 weeks beforehand.

(b)   Plan timetable of topics to be studied.

(c)   Revise at periods throughout the course.

(d)   Get into the habit of 're-learning': straight after learning; at regular intervals after initial learning; and in the final run up to the examination.

(e)   Be aware that the learning requirements differ from subject to subject being studied, e.g., mathematics is very different to history.

(f)   Last-minute cramming can be effective but can also confuse: analyse your own performance and act accordingly.

(g)   Take and store notes efficiently: take notes of notes.

(h)   Avoid passive learning: recite into a tape recorder, form revision syndicates, do mock examinations.

(i)   Check the type of question which recurrs in the examination concerned.

(j)   Plan answers to past papers.

(k)   Leave time for 'top up' revision in the two or three days before the examination.

Avoiding anxiety

(a)   Anxiety originates usually from fear of failure combined with high motivation.

(b)   Take regular exercise and diversions during the revision period.

(c)   Devise relaxation techniques that work for you.

In the examination room

(a)   Make sure you have a good night's sleep before the examination and arrive prepared with all equipment you need.

(b)   Read the whole paper through, noting instructions carefully.

(c)   Divide up the time available for each question and stick to your timetable.

(d)   Mark the questions you *can* do: choose the easy questions rather than the difficult ones and choose the ones that you think you can best do justice to.

(e)   Make sure you have interpreted the question correctly and have identified the key words in the question.

(f)   Produce a brief plan for every question and make sure you stick to it. Make sure that the main points in your arguments are clearly indicated.

(g)   Don't prevaricate in your answers: get stuck into the question straight away. Avoid long introductions.

(h)   Do all the questions and finish them in note form if necessary.

(i)   Try to write as legibly as possible.

(j)   Leave time to check answers: read them all through and correct spelling and grammatical errors. Whatever you do,

don't leave before the end of the examination; use every minute available. Remember the examiner can only mark what you have served to place in front of him.
(Adopted from Maddox, *How to Study*, Pan, pp. 109–23.)

Self-assessment exercises

Exercise 1
Without looking back over this chapter, can you list all the major points we have been making in it?

Exercise 2
Below you will see the first two paragraphs of an examination answer – by an anonymous student – to the following question:
'The New Technology will transform society more radically than any set of political ideas.' Discuss.
Read through the answer and make a note of all the mistakes, both major and minor.

The new technology

66 I'm not sure what the New Technology is. What is it? but people who belong to trade unions have got to realise that you can't stand still whilst the Japanese and West Germans are constantly innovating. The name of the game these days is introducing the best and most modern production techniques before the competitors. Instead of moaning about job losses and low wages. The problem with Trade Unions is that Marxism does not work. Stalin proved this with twenty million killed in slave labour camps in Siberia.

Reducing the problem to basics it's obvious that they want to protect their jobs. How can they be so shortsighted when protecting jobs only produces poor products that no one wants to buy and destroys jobs in the end anyway. Trade unions must recognise reality and adapt to it otherwise they will bring about their own ends. The old technology is dead and should be buried in favour of the latest which semi conductors, robot technology and advanced computer systems can provide. The potential benefits to mankind are immense. Equipped with the new technology, within a few years backward peoples could achieve all the advantages of advanced civilisation with cars, cities, fast food and television. 99

Exercise 3
Now write about 200 words of your own as the beginning of an

answer to the same question – then compare them with the example we offer in the guidance notes.

Exercise 4
Can you list seven important qualities to aim for in an examination essay answer?

Exercise 5
This is an examination exercise. *Don't read the questions yet!* Organise a quiet room and a free period of over 1½ hours (take the phone off the hook!) Then 'set' yourself the exam and try to perform as if you were sitting under examination conditions.

Making the grade: examination paper TIME ALLOWED 1½ *hours*
Write essays on two of the subjects below.
 1 Define the characteristics of an ideal living partner and assess the validity of marriage in present-day society.
 2 On average British people watch twenty-four hours of television every week: why is this too much?
 3 Do you agree that capital punishment is the appropriate sentence for the murder of policemen?
 4 Assess and discuss the contribution made by the trade unions to our national thinking.
 5 'A tightly controlled environment and routine are essential for satisfactory personality development in children.' Discuss.
 6 Is it accurate to see the poor as trapped in a 'culture of poverty'?
 7 To what extent do you consider inequalities in society to be inevitable and also desirable?
 8 Evaluate the respective merits of 'pop' and 'classical' music.
 9 To what extent does someone's style of dress betray their social class?
10 Consider the implications of the theory that plants have feelings.

10 *Opportunities for further study*

Better ask twice than lose your way once   *Danish Proverb*

I keep six honest serving men
(They taught me all I know)
Their names are What and Why and When
And How and Where and Who
                                        Rudyard Kipling

Contents
I

Introduction

If you have stayed with us to this last chapter you will be aware by now that our primary objective has been to introduce you to those study skills which we regard as *essential* if you are going to undertake any form of further/higher education/training in a serious manner. And even if your objective was just to refresh those skills or to prepare yourself for something entirely different, I hope you will agree that the ability to organise yourself and your time, to think more clearly, read more attentively, to express yourself more fluently, and to present coherent arguments in written form are all skills which will be useful to you in many aspects of life.

However, I think we are probably right in assuming that most students undertaking the course have some form of further education or personal development as a possible future objective, so in this chapter we are going to concentrate on helping you to answer questions such as 'Where can I go from here?' 'Am I ready for higher education?' 'What courses are available?' 'Do I need entrance qualifications? 'What level am I at right now?' 'How long would it take?' 'And even if I succeed, what jobs are available?

We will not necessarily be answering these questions *for* you but helping *you* to find the answers, pointing you in the right direction, telling you where to look, and showing you how to dig out the information or the guidance that you need. There may not be simple and easily available answers to your queries or immediate possibilities of gratifying your ambitions, and I would from long personal experience counsel equal amounts of *persistence* and *patience* at this stage.

I would suggest as a general rule that you seek the advice of as many people as possible. The process of making choices will be more successful the better informed you are. You will certainly be annoyed if, two or three years hence, you find that you overlooked a more suitable course or discovered that you were all the time eligible for an extra grant.

So what will be offered in this chapter?

Section I
1 *A revision exercise.* I think it is important to review the course and help you assess the progress you have made to date. You may find that certain sections of the course need to be looked at again more closely. It may be that there were some points you didn't quite grasp and you may need to refresh some of the lessons covered in the earlier units.
2 *Taking stock.* This involves a realistic assessment of your own progress to date and abilities as they now stand.
3 *Further studies.* You may already have some firm idea of what you would like to do or where you would like to go, but I would still advise you to read this section.
4 *Entering higher education*

Section II
5 *Education and future employment.*
6 *Further recommended reading.* We cannot answer all your

questions in one short chapter but we hope to point you in the direction of more detailed guides and sources.

1 *Course review exercise*

What follows is a list of questions relating to all of the chapters in this volume, which brings us to the end of our study programme. As usual, we would like you to be honest and rigorous: don't be tempted to look at the answers until you have come to the end of the exercise. And in common with the other exercises you have been doing throughout the study programme – *write down* your answers.

By now you should have a reasonable idea of how to assess yourself. We certainly don't expect you to come up with the correct answer to every single question, but the percentage of right answers will give you some idea of how well you have absorbed the lessons of the chapters in this volume.

Do not imagine that we are out to trick you or to pose especially difficult questions. Everything will be based on what you have read in these pages. All we want to do is give you the chance to check that you have grasped some of the most important lessons in each chapter. And don't worry if you sometimes use slightly different terms than those we have used: just be honest with yourself when assessing your answers.

If there turn out to be some sections that you have understood less well than others, do not hesitate to go back over them. Re-read whichever chapters are concerned, and do the exercises again until you are sure of the points being made.

Questions
1 What are the three main processes suggested for proper understanding of essay questions?
2 What are the four most common mistakes in understanding essay questions?
3 Can you offer definitions for the following terms commonly used in essay question instructions:

Compare	Discuss
Contrast	Outline

4 What is the basic structure of a 'for and against' type of essay, using what we called the Strategy I approach?
5 What are the essential features of the Strategy II approach?

6 Can you list five out of the nine types of essay we discussed?
7 Name the two basic kinds of reasoning we discussed in the chapter on clear thinking
8 Can you list four out of the seven examples of common fallacies used in argument?
9 What are the four most basic marks of punctuation?
10 For what two purposes do we commonly underline words we write?
11 Can you give four instances where capital letters are always required?
12 What are the basic elements of a simple sentence written in English?
13 What is it that unites all the elements of a single paragraph?
14 What basic elements are commonly found in a well written paragraph?
15 Can you list the ten basic stages in producing an essay – from A to Z?
16 What is the first and most important element of 'good style' in writing?
17 What is the difference between an adjective and an adverb?
18 Define 'metaphor', 'simile', 'syntax', and 'irony'.
19 Can you list four good reasons for having examinations?
20 What materials should you have to hand when revising for an examination?

Taking stock   2

I want to consider the topic of self-assessment at this stage under two separate headings:
(a)   Your own personal self-assessment.
(b)   Your potential for further advancement.

(a) Personal self-assessment
This cannot be undertaken scientifically but, as a first step, it might be worth noting the following. If you have managed to complete all chapters up to this point then you have – at minimum – managed to:
1 *Understand the units* – although you may have found difficulty in some sections.
2 *Keep up with the work.*
3 *Work regularly* and establish some kind of routine.
4 *Derive some enjoyment* from your studies (otherwise you would not have completed them!)
5 *Sustain your motivation* and concentration.

In addition you may have discovered:

1 *Hidden talents* or skills of which you were unaware, for instance, creative writing, planning essays, appreciating written style.

2 *New interests*. The course dips into a wide variety of academic disciplines – history, philosophy, literature, politics, sociology – any of which may have captured your interest and given you ideas for further study.

3 *Transferability of skills*. Study skills don't exist in isolation: they are applicable outside the study in the various realms of everyday life. You may have found that you feel more confident in writing letters, in expressing yourself verbally to others, in grasping ideas, and in assimilating information in newspapers or broadsheets.

4 *Sense of self*. Many people return to study from a position of 'I'm not sure if I can do this – and what will other people think of me if I do?' If completion of the course has helped you find out more about yourself and to refine your ideas regarding future study then your sense of identity has been strengthened: your confidence in overcoming a new range of challenge has been increased.

(b) Potential for future development

This is very difficult to assess, and I would strongly recommend that you only make such an assessment after close consultation with a tutor. Your potential in terms of academic *ability* will largely be a combination of the sort of judgements I have just been discussing in the two foregoing sections. Potential in this sense is largely a matter of *ability* combined with *capacity for work*, and, ultimately, *intellectual ambition*.

But there is another sort of potential which often bothers the adult student. It is this: students are often aware that they may have a reasonable level of ability, but they are not quite sure how best to apply it. That is, they have not fixed their attention on any one subject area in particular. They are not sure what they are best suited to. And worse still, they feel slightly guilty about this, envying the conventionally young students who seem to know exactly what subjects they wish to study.

My advice here is straightforward. *Stop feeling guilty*. After all, why *should* you know what you are best suited for if you have not tried studying a number of subjects? Next, stop envying the young school leaver. Many of them are equally unsure; some will even finish further education wishing they had studied something else; and don't forget that their ability levels and their suitability for certain subjects have been carefully and regularly scrutinised by their teachers during the previous two years!

Remember too, that you are not alone. Many other adult students will feel the same.

What can be done about this state of uncertainty? Let me suggest that the problem has two parts which in the student's mind become understandably mixed together.

(a) The problem of which subject(s) to study.
(b) The future *use* of the knowledge acquired – which usually centres on the notion of a possible career or employment prospects.

You can see why these two questions become so easily intertwined. If you are not quite sure which subject you are best suited to study, how can you plan your future, knowing that employment prospects often depend upon having the 'right' qualifications? Alternatively, if you are not sure what future employment possibilities are open to you, how is it possible to select a subject which might open them up to you? The complexities in this problem are manifold, and they are compounded by the fact that society today is changing so rapidly. It is very difficult to state with any degree of certainty the relationship between academic study and employment prospects.

How then to cut this Gordian knot? My approach (derived largely from my own personal experience: I was in exactly this position myself as an adult student) is to at least begin by looking at them separately. Let's do just that. First, the choice of further study, and after that its possible relation to future employment.

Choosing courses for further study
I am going to begin by assuming that most students at this stage fall into one of three categories:
(a) Students who are still uncertain about their academic ability, choice of course, and their own potential.
(b) Students who are more confident in their own ability but don't know which subject to choose.
(c) Students who know what subject to choose, have a specific course of training in mind, or want to pursue a definite career.
Let's deal with these possibilities one at a time – though I am aware that there may be a great deal of overlap between them.
(a) *Still uncertain*
If you are still quite uncertain it is possible that you need to do some more preparatory study before you embark on anything at a higher level. There are a number of options open to you.
  (i) Another preparatory course.
 (ii) Evening or daytime classes to put your study skills to use and 'taste' a number of different possible subjects.

(iii) Taking a GCE O or A level.

We will be dealing in a moment with the nature of these courses and where they can be found. For now, take your time in consolidating what you have learned so far. It is far better to spend another twelve months or even two years practising skills and exploring possible subjects of study than to dash forward in an ill-prepared manner. After all, more study will help you broaden your horizons and the practice should help strengthen your confidence.

Which type of course you choose and the length of time you take over it might depend on one other thing – your age. If you are, say, in your mid to late twenties another year or two will not make much difference, even if you have some new career in mind. Similarly, if you are nearing retirement age it probably makes little difference to you because you are engaged in this process as a gentle means of self-exploration without any career prospects in mind. It is the middle period which is more difficult – say between thirty and forty-five – when you are more likely to feel that every year counts and the chances of embarking on some new career or path in life are decreasing very rapidly (though I should say that even younger and older people might feel this just as strongly).

This is where you need counselling, guidance, patience and persistence. It will depend on how determined you are. If your plans for future study are just a recreation or hobby, then you can afford to try anything you wish. If they are more focused – say you *do* eventually wish to go to a polytechnic or a university – then you must be more careful and positive.

At this stage we often recommend that students should consider taking one (or two) GCE A levels or some equivalent examination. The admissions tutor in universities will almost always recommend the same thing – for three reasons:
   (i) Achieving a reasonable grade at GCE A level will show that you are serious about further study.
  (ii) It will prove you have the academic ability.
 (iii) It will demonstrate that you know something about the subject.

If you have completed this course reasonably well you should be able to take on A levels with little difficulty.

There are *other* ways of qualifying for university entry, and we'll be dealing with some of them below. But remember that GCE A levels are a recognised way of proving that you are a suitable candidate *from the admissions tutor's point of view*. Some A level courses in FE colleges are well taught but some are rather mechanical and pitched at young rather than mature candidates.

(b) *More confident – but still uncertain*

This category embraces the vast majority of adult students who wish to proceed to further study and higher education. The problem here is that you might be equally interested in, say, history, literature, and art, but unsure which to pursue further. There are two pieces of advice I would offer here.

Firstly – you don't have to choose between a number of possible interests. Increasingly, these days polytechnics and universities offer courses which allow you to combine a number of subjects without necessarily specialising in any one in particular. There are even courses which allow you to choose a specialisation as you go along.

Secondly, if you just want to study one subject – say history – you should not approach it hapazardly, as if you just as easily might have chosen art or chemistry. If you are applying to an institution of higher education, you should be able to communicate some genuine interest in the subject itself, and a desire to study it.

So if you are in this category of student – reasonably confident of your ability and your study skills, but still uncertain what subject to choose, you should
  (i) Consult a tutor and seek counselling and advice.
 (ii) Be prepared to keep your options open.
(iii) If necessary, try to choose the subject for which you are best suited.

This last option – you may well observe – of course begs the question, 'How do I know for which I am best suited?' Well, here you really do need to think hard and carefully about where your skills and your interests lie. Try to decide what is, for instance, that persistently gives you pleasure or interests you. Here are some obvious examples.
  (i) You spend lots of your spare time reading novels by Dickens, Thomas Hardy, the Bronte sisters, and you even read poetry with a sense of enjoyment.
       Choose to study *Literature* or a course with a strong literature component.
 (ii) You keep abreast of current affairs, follow the political development of foreign countries, know what is going on in government and parliament.
       Study *Politics* or some branch of the social sciences.
(iii) You are interested in biographies and the social conditions of previous ages.
       Study *History*.

I'm sure you will have grasped the idea, even if these examples are very straightforward.

(c) *Decided*

This is the easiest category of all because, provided the student has the required ability, all that is necessary is to find the right course. For instance, if you wished to embark on a career in banking you would know that a degree in economics would be a logical choice. Or if you wanted to take up teaching or social work there are quite definite qualifications you would need in order to do so. You would need to seek counselling and guidance, then select the appropriate course and the institution where it is taught – the line of procedure is quite direct. You will need to know the entrance qualifications required, maybe what grant you will be entitled to receive as a student, and maybe what the future employment prospects are in your chosen career. I am not suggesting that there will be no difficulties in negotiating this process – merely that the element of uncertainty is minimised.

At this point I would like to turn to another group of factors which might have a bearing on your choice. In every case there are a number of considerations which might have to be borne in mind – family commitments, finance, the amount of time available, and so on. Each individual will have a different set of circumstances to consider: the choice will involve weighing these alongside the more academic questions of ability and ambition.

Most students find that these other considerations tend to become tangled together; they are very difficult to measure or assess; there seems no easy way to give them 'weighting' and they seem rather amorphous and difficult to grasp. One way we can help you is to consider them separately, one at a time.

Other factors to consider

I am going to put my observations in this section under four separate headings.

(a)   Part-time or full-time study.
(b)   Finance and grants.
(c)   Age.
(d)   Further advice and counselling.

(a) **Part-time or full-time study**

This, of course, will depend on your circumstances. If you need to continue in full-time employment, then part-time study is forced upon you. But many other people opt for part-time study: disabled people, those with heavy family commitments, those with irregular work patterns (shift workers, armed forces personnel) or those who simply do not wish their lives to become over-burdened with academic study. Many older people for instance – those near or beyond retirement age – choose to take up part-time study as a form of intellectual 'relaxation' to occupy their later years. Full-time study is more likely to bring a major change to your life. Let's deal with part-time study first.

There are both advantages and disadvantages to part-time study. The advantages are that you are more likely to be able to continue your present life (your full-time job) without any major disruption, you can probably spread your studies over a longer period (which should be easier) and you may even be able to take them more seriously in that you could do more reading around your subject than you could when undertaking full-time study.

The disadvantages are that you are more likely to have to study on your own and you probably won't have much contact with tutors or fellow-students. (People who are used to working alone and independently have an advantage in this respect.) Another disadvantage is that many part-time students feel that the sheer volume of work in six years' part-time study adds up to more than that in three years' full time and in some cases they may be correct – which points us to another obvious disadvantage. Part-time study takes a long time: completion of a degree course might take anything from five to ten years, depending upon the workoad you undertake each year and the number of 'credits' you start with (there are usually allowances made for any qualifications you might already have when you start). Finally, part-time students are currently not entitled to full maintenance allowances.

The types of courses available to you in this respect fall into two principal categories: correspondence-based courses, and college-based courses. I will say a few words about each, choosing the typical examples.

The Open University operates part-time degree courses on which the student works largely alone under the distance learning supervision of a tutor. There are tutorial meetings once a month and the student is fed with learning materials by post. These are supplemented by radio and television programmes. The student works at a predetermined rate, but you can 'drop out' for a year if you so wish. There is another feature of the OU system which can be seen either as an advantage or a disadvantage. There is a very wide selection of courses to choose from at any given time – something to suit everyone. But since the course is 'modular' (you build up to a required number of credits) you cannot really specialise in one subject. Your degree at the end is more or less bound to be a general one.

College-based courses are operated where polytechnics or

universities offer part-time degrees, certificates, work related diplomas and so forth, which are either put on specially or are built up by part-time students joining the normal courses attended by full-time students. These have the advantage of more contact with tutors and fellow students. There is the 'reassurance' of an institution to hand, with access to its library, personal advice, and other facilities. The disadvantages (which are few, I believe) will be mainly those created by the need to be physically present at tutorial meetings.

There are many other things to be said about the pros and cons of part-time versus full-time study, but at this point I don't think it is possible to go on listing advice in this chapter. You must seek further guidance and counselling appropriate to your own particular case.

(b) **Finance and grants**
This section applies principally to those who are contemplating full-time study. Many people say 'Yes – I'm interested – but how can I possibly afford it?' There are two answers to this question.

The first is that if you are a typical adult student (over 21) you will normally be entitled to a government grant payable to you for three years whilst you study for a degree. I am going to leave *you* to find out exactly how much this grant will be. You can discover this from the reading list at the end of this Chapter (specifically the DES leaflet 'Grants to Students' and the section on 'Money' in *Second Chances* by Parks and Good). But a typical mature student might receive anything from roughly £2,000 to £4,000 per annum (1990 prices) depending on circumstances and number of dependants.

Whatever these are, it is certainly not a *lot* of money, but what I am going to say are a few words on how some people manage to survive three years on such a low 'income'.

If you have a partner who is working there shouldn't be as much of a problem, and don't forget that the student in such a couple will have a more flexible timetable to undertake some of the job-sharing which is likely to be necessary. But even if you have not, you would be surprised how many people manage to get by. Many adult students take in a lodger to help with household costs (maybe another adult student) or take vacation jobs to supplement their income. When I was taking my degree as a mature student I worked as a freelance engineer in the long summer vacations; a friend of mine now works as a 'temp', shorthand typing whenever she needs extra money. And if you know well in advance that you will be taking up full-time study, you could save up for it. To use my own experience again; I prepared for two years by working overtime in my job, putting the extra earnings to one side for what I knew would be lean years to come.

Then, as well as extra money, you can try to make do with *less*. Most students expect to have a fairly meagre life-style: they buy second-hand books, learn to cut costs, study in the library instead of heating a room at home, do without luxuries (cars, expensive clothes), travel by bicycle to save on bus fares. You could do the same and you will also feel that you are doing so in a supportive environment because the people you mix with will all be in the same position. Perhaps the best advice on this is to talk to other mature students who have made the adjustment successfully.

(c) **Age**
I have already mentioned this earlier, but now a few extra observations.
   (i) If you are a *younger* mature student (21–30) you still have more or less the same options as the conventional student of 18–22 years of age. The disadvantage is that you have been outside the education system for a while, but the corresponding advantage is that you are likely to have life and work experiences which can amply compensate for this. You still have the possibility of making a study choice which can relate directly to a career ambition. You are less likely to have accumulated personal and domestic ties (marriage, family, house-ownership) which limit your choice of institution. And you would not find yourself very much different in age and interests to the ordinary students at a polytechnic or a university.

   If you left school young (15–17) and have few formal qualifications *do* be prepared to undertake some formal preparatory study (A levels) if you are advised to do so. Another year will not make a great deal of difference and patience will be well rewarded. If you took A levels but either got poor results or didn't go on to further education immediately, this course has presumably been a refresher course for you, and you should be able to go on now and take up your studies at the level where you left off.

   (ii) The *typical mature student* is aged between 30 and 45: people wishing to make a career change; people wishing to take up educational opportunities they missed; people whose children have now started to grow up, who have developed intellectually since leaving school; those who wish to expand their intellectual horizons – the list is much longer.

If you are in this age range and undertaking further education as a means of exploring your favourite subject on your own intellectual possibilities – then all well and good. But many students understandably want more than this. They might like it to lead to a job; or they might want to study their favourite subject and *thereby* enhance their career prospects. And many of them will be fuelled by the anxious recognition that the years are passing quickly.

My advice here is to seek as much advice as you can, take a clear objective look at yourself, and be *realistic*. In your early thirties it is not *too* late to make that start you always wanted – but you will have to recognise that you will always be ten years behind those who started at the more conventional point of the early twenties. At the other end of the scale, towards your mid-forties, your ambition is likely to be more modest – to swop one career for another more congenial if less lucrative, or (if you have been a housewife, say) to undertake paid work for the first time. This is a very difficult age-band about which to generalise. All sorts of personal development are possible. I will give you three examples, from each part of the spectrum.

My own experience was to leave engineering, study between 29 and 35 with no clear idea of what I wanted to do, and to discover that I enjoyed teaching whilst I was doing so part-time as a research student. Linda, a single parent in her mid-thirties (who had previously been an ice-skating instructress) studied a New Horizons course, entered Manchester University and discovered whilst studying that she had a talent for mathematics and computer studies. After graduating, she has now been taken on to the University staff to teach. John, formerly an accountant, gave it up to take a degree and a Certificate in Social Work. He now earns less money but has job satisfaction working in the social services.

I am not suggesting that further education will automatically lead to a more pleasant occupation. But in general, the enhanced sense of confidence and personal worth which it seems to induce in people helps them discover what they want. And I should also add that quite a few go back to what they were doing before, quite content with the intellectual and personal enhancement they have gained through study.

(iii) The older age-band (45 and upwards) are likely to be

housewives whose children have grown up, people who have taken early retirement, people who have been made redundant, and those who because their lives and careers have become settled, wish to explore their intellectual potential. Not many people in this band will expect further education to catapult them into a brand new career in some glamorous occupation. Their worries tend to be of the 'Is it too late?' or 'Am I past it?' variety. And the answer is, generally, no. It is certainly never too late. There are under-graduates in their sixties and seventies and with such life experience it is easy to imagine how much more such people can both put into as well as get out of a course in further education. You may well work and think more slowly at this age – but this will probably be compensated by increased powers of concentration and maturity of judgement.

(d) Further advice and counselling
I have already stressed the importance of seeking advice at every stage of your approach to further education; from a tutor regarding your capabilities and from the institution where you might be thinking of applying regarding opportunities. Let me extend this a little now to include *all* possible sources.

You should write to or phone as many colleges, polytechnics, or universities as you can to obtain their prospectuses. Check the content of their course carefully to see which ones would suit you best. When you have narrowed down your options concerning your choice of courses, you should make an appointment and go to speak to the admissions tutor for that course. Ask for any reading lists, the course options, the written work requirements, and any special requirements.

You should, if you can, talk to students who are currently engaged on any courses you intend to take. They will tell you what the reading load is like, what the quality of teaching is, and if there are any hidden pitfalls on the course. If you have a definite career ambition in mind, it would be especially useful if you could speak to any ex-students who are now employed in your chosen field. The labour market fluctuates considerably and it doesn't always follow that employment will automatically follow in the wake of qualifications.

3   *Further studies*

Courses available

The most comprehensive lists of available courses are included in the further reading at the end of this Chapter. What I am going to do here is say a few words about those which are most likely to be of interest. The actual range of courses available is enormous: the problem remains one of finding a course which exactly fits your requirements.

For the sake of clarification and simplicity I am going to deal with the options under four headings.
(a) Liberal adult education.
(b) Higher education.
(c) Correspondence courses and flexistudy.
(d) Other courses and institutions.

(a) *Liberal adult education*

This expression is used to describe the pursuit of 'knowledge' or education for its own sake, without any particular goal in mind except the intellectual and personal development of the individual student. It might be called 'leisure' education and include anything from yoga and flower-arranging at the 'recreational' end of the spectrum to classes on politics or philosophical theories at the more cerebral end. The range of subjects on offer is very wide, they are usually open to anyone, no entrance qualification is necessary and they are part-time; usually a couple of hours in the daytime or evening on one day a week. They do not generally lead to any qualification, there are no examinations and the level at which they are pitched can vary from 'introductory' to 'advanced'. These terms are rather vague, I know, but beginners' classes will assume that you have absolutely no previous knowledge of the subject (say, if you wanted to learn a foreign language) whilst an advanced class may assume that you have already been studying the subject for two or three years at least.

A number of institutions offer such classes, but the principal providers are the LEAs (Local Education Authorities), University EMDs (Extra-Mural departments) and the WEA (Workers' Educational Association). There is a good deal of overlap in the type of courses these three institutions put on, but LEAs (offering courses in schools, evening centres and colleges of further education) tend to concentrate upon skills – car maintenance, yoga, cookery, woodwork, sport – whilst the WEA and EMDs (offering courses on campus, as well as schools and evening centres) concentrate more upon courses requiring wider reading and intellectual activity – philosophy, politics, history, biological sciences. WEAs tend to target some of their courses at specific groups – trade-union studies, women's studies – whilst EMDs offer some specialised courses – The Philosophy of Immanuel Kant, Advanced Computer Studies. All institutions offer many variations on these themes – study days, excursions, study groups trips abroad.

If you wish to discover what is on offer, all three institutions usually issue a prospectus in August or September, outlining the courses they will be offering for the forthcoming autumn and spring. Classes are usually run in one term before Christmas, a second *after* and then a shorter third term after Easter. However, this tradition, based on academic practice, is beginning to change in many places now. Costs for these courses are usually low. (In 1990 around £1.40 per two-hour class meeting) and there are often concessions or even free places for the elderly or the unemployed.

(b) *Higher education*
This expression is used to describe education of a type beyond GCE A level, it describes the sorts of courses which are offered at universities, polytechnics, college of higher education and the Open University. Most of these courses are full time and have some sort of entry requirement. For instance, if you wished to study French Literature at a University you would be expected to be able to speak and write French, and to already have some knowledge of its literature. This is why universities usually rely heavily on GCE A level passes as an indicator of a student's ability.

For many adult students this poses a problem. If they have no A level passes, they may not be too keen on going back to what they often see as 'night school' to obtain them. As already suggested many A level classes have atmospheres and approaches which are not altogether appropriate for fully mature students. But you will not normally be expected to achieve the higher grades, and many admissions tutors will look sympathetically at your application if you are prepared to submit yourself to this sort of 'test'. Here are two real-life examples. Debby (25) applied to study American Literature and Society at a university. The admissions tutors were so impressed with her at interview they offered her a place if she gained 'C' or even 'D' grades in English Literature and Sociology. (She got an 'A' and a 'B'). Karen applied to study Ancient History. The department wanted a reasonable grade at A level History, but when she only got a D they admitted her on the strength of this and a long essay she submitted to them for assessment.

(c) *Correspondence courses and flexistudy*

So far we have dealt with the two extreme ends of the spectrum as far as further education is concerned – leisure study, and full-time university study. But many students at the preparatory, the intermediate, and the advanced stages want more than leisure study, but are unable to undertake full-time or even college-based part-time study. For these people there are an increasing number of courses available as correspondence courses and what is coming to be known as flexistudy.

(i) *Sub-degree courses*

You can take GCE A level courses by correspondence if you wish, but in addition there are now a number of courses which are geared to people in full-time jobs or those with circumstances which force them to undertake study at a distance. I have already covered the advantages and disadvantages of this type of course. I once undertook an A level correspondence course with the National Extension College and was lucky enough to be given a very diligent tutor whose marking and comments encouraged me a great deal, but when my circumstances changed I switched to a college-based part-time course and was glad of the contact with other students which this provided.

'Flexi-study' is an 'open-learning' system geared to meet the special requirements of a student. In other words, the student may submit a couple of essays then, by telephone, arrange to meet the tutor for what amounts to a private tutorial. Alternatively, if the tutor is college-based, the student may 'drop in' by arrangement at irregular intervals. The idea, as the name implies, is to be as flexible as possible to meet the requirements of the student. The South Manchester Community College, for example, currently has 1,500 flexistudy students on its books, three-quarters of them studying courses leading to qualifications.

(ii) *Advanced level courses*

This usually means the Open University. The OU does not have any formal entry requirements. Provided you can read and write to a reasonable standard, you can be admitted. There is often a waiting period of up to a year or so – but this can be put to good use in undertaking some sort of preparatory courses (something which the OU often advises). You should know that the OU academic year runs from February to November. Don't imagine that you can decide in the autumn and start immediately the following year. Make your mind up and apply in plenty of time.

As an OU student you will be deluged by printed materials – outlines, course units, wall charts, illustrative material, reading lists, a radio and TV broadcast calendar – and this in addition to the set books is as much as most students can cope with. You can take up to two full credits (i.e. courses) per year; currently courses cost £150–£200 per year. Some courses are only half-credit rated, but beware – many students complain that taking two half-credit courses is much harder work than just one single credit course.

Students submit essays to a tutor who marks the essay and sends them back with extensive comments. You meet the tutor at occasional tutorial sessions and can phone the tutor privately to iron out any individual queries. In addition to a tutor you will also be allocated a counsellor who will help you with any personal problems, queries relating to your programme, and questions on the fairly complex administrative system the OU needs to keep itself going.

The OU is ideal for those mature students who cannot afford to give up their jobs so as to undertake full-time study. It may take you a number of years to obtain your degree, but provided you are not in any hurry you will certainly gain a broad educational experience.

(d) *Other courses and institutions*
(i) *Colleges and institutions of further and higher education*
These put on a whole variety of courses ranging from GCE A level and 'craft' courses, through specialist courses for builders, plumbers, electricians, dressmakers and cooks, to degree courses similar to those offered at polytechnics and universities.

The mature student who wants to pursue a very definite and probably narrowly defined field of study (like one of the occupations I have just mentioned) should explore this possibility. If, for instance, you wish to gain a Certificate in Cabinet-Making (a sort of advanced 'woodwork') or in cookery (these days called 'Food and Beverage Preparation') then these colleges are likely to be for you. See Brian Heap's guide for further information.

(ii) *Adult residential colleges*
These are, as the name suggests, colleges where adult students go to *live* and study. They offer one and two-year courses of study which are of a preparatory nature, noremally leading on to higher education. None of them demand formal entry qualifications. Selection is by a combination of interview, perhaps a piece of written work, and evidence that you have already been helping yourself by attending other courses. Most of them offer a qualification which is accepted as satisfying higher education entrance requirements. You can obtain grants to cover the cost of fees, residence, and maintenance allowance. And this will not affect your right to further grant(s) if and when you go on to full-time university study. (See final section for address list.)

(iii) *Access courses*

Alternatively, the adult student can undertake an 'access' course specifically designed as preparation for further education. This will not normally result in formal entrance qualifications, but the practice in study skills, the advice and counselling which make up such courses will be very useful in preparing and guiding students towards the possible alternatives. These courses come under a number of different names and titles so read the course information carefully to make sure they are suitable for you.

This leads me on to the complex and thorny process of entry procedures which the following diagram attempts to simplify. It takes as its starting point someone who has completed preparatory studies and wishes to enter higher education.

Entering higher education   4

Flow diagram illustrating typical stages between completion of course and entry into higher education

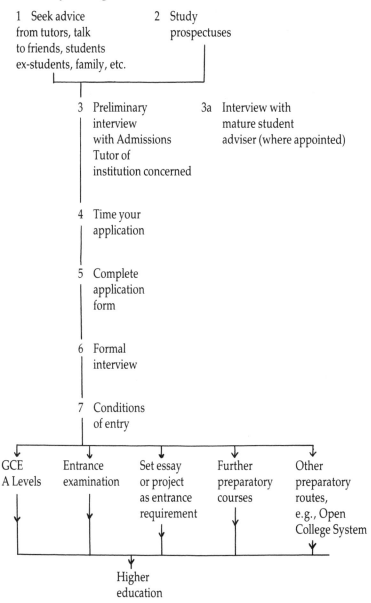

1 Seek advice   2 Study
from tutors, talk   prospectuses
to friends, students
ex-students, family, etc.

3 Preliminary   3a Interview with
   interview   mature student
   with Admissions   adviser (where appointed)
   Tutor of
   institution concerned

4 Time your
   application

5 Complete
   application
   form

6 Formal
   interview

7 Conditions
   of entry

GCE   Entrance   Set essay   Further   Other
A Levels   examination   or project   preparatory   preparatory
                             as entrance   courses   routes,
                             requirement   e.g., Open
                                                             College System

Higher
education

Stages in application procedure
1 Seek the advice of a tutor or someone experienced in the field to
   check that you are ready to apply. You may be advised to wait a
   little longer but if you receive positive advice you have nothing
   to lose by making preliminary enquiries.

If you are studying on your own and have no access to an objective opinion, then at least be prepared to write a standard academic essay (1,500 words) in your chosen subject area or something you know about. This will give those people you are going to speak to some idea of your capability. Talk also to friends, family and other mature students to acquaint yourself with all the challenges and problems with which you will be faced.

2 Get hold of and study carefully as many prospectuses as you can. Many adult students apply to their 'home' college but if you are able to move away to study make sure that you choose the institution best suited to your interests. Many universities, polytechnics and colleges give special emphasis to some sub-jects, or have a character or atmosphere of their own.

3 Next, try to make an appointment to see the *Admissions Tutor* in the department which you wish to apply to. Remember that at this stage you are going for a preliminary and exploratory conversation in which you hope to establish two or three things:

(a) What *courses* the department has to offer which will suit *you*.

(b) What the department will require of you in the way of entrance qualifications.

(c) If you are at a suitable stage of readiness to make a formal application.

Remember, that an admissions tutor will usually be a normal member of the Department who is paid to teach there, but for one or two years has got the extra job of vetting applicants. If the department to which you are applying is very popular or prestigious they may have as many as a thousand applications a year for as few as fifty places. *You*, therefore, have got to persuade them that you have something special to offer, or that you have a special degree of enthusiasm or ability in the sub-ject. But I should also add, to encourage those students with what might be called 'minority interests', that the opposite is often the case. That is, if you were interested in a subject which is not especially popular – say classics (Greek and Latin) – then those departments are likely to have fewer applicants, and your chances of being offered a place will be that much greater. Admissions tutors are not obliged to grant such preliminary interviews but in our experience they are most helpful.

3a At this stage you might also arrange an interview with the Adviser to Mature Applicants (or equivalent) if one exists at the institution you are applying to. The purpose of doing this is to give you another opinion about your readiness to apply, further advice on what is available and guidance on different entry routes.

4 A word about the *timing* of this application procedure. You will

196

have to get used to the idea of *thinking a long way ahead*. You should go for your preliminary interview at least a *year* in advance of wishing to take up full-time study. So, by the autumn of the year before you wish to start, begin the process I am outlining here. Once you have done that you will have to make a formal application (on the UCCA form) which must reach the university by mid-December. However, most universities allocate places before this time so try to apply *as soon as possible*, preferably in September.

Polytechnics and colleges have later closing dates – usually March or April. In some cases it has been known for exceptional students to be admitted at the last minute – only a couple of weeks before the course is due to start – but they have been very much the exception to the rule.

5 *The application form*
This is called the UCCA form for universities and the PCAS form for polytechnics. Most institutions, like Colleges of Higher Education or adult residential colleges have similar forms. Full details of how these are to be filled in will be found in the accompanying leaflets and the guides listed in further reading.

I want to stress just a couple of points here. *Do* fill this in as carefully and neatly as possible – because it will be photocoped and used by a number of different people. It might be a good idea to assemble all the information required on a separate sheet of paper first, then transfer it to the form. If you cannot type, then write as carefully as possible.

Many adult students feel embarrassed by how *little* information they are able to put on the form. There are two answers to this. Certainly do *not* omit any professional qualifications you have. You may be applying to study the history of art, but include qualifications you may have gained as a nurse, a social worker, an engineer, or local government worker. Secondly, make sure that all the positive aspects of your life experience are recorded for those who will be looking at your application. Remember that you are being assessed along with (largely) young people who have just finished their sixth-form studies. If you have travelled widely, held a number of different jobs, excelled in some sport, run a small business, or done anything unusual – then make sure that these appear on the form. Of course you should also highlight any intellectual or cultural interests which are compatible with the subject(s) you are applying to study. In short – make the most of your own life history and your interests.

6 *The interview*
The next stage in the normal procedure is that an applicant is

called for a formal interview. Remember, its purpose is to give admissions tutors a chance to see your qualities. They have to decide if you will make a good full-time student. Are you really interested in learning? Does the subject really seem to be of interest to you? Are you able to study at the requisite level? Will you make a positive contribution to the department?

Obviously, many people are nervous about being so carefully scrutinised. And of course a great deal (for the student) rests on the outcome. But try to be as relaxed and natural as possible. Don't feel that you have got to try and impress the people interviewing you. Just respond positively, openly and creatively to their questions.

By this stage in the process you should have some idea of the set books for the course(s) you wish to study – and it would obviously help if you could show familiarity with some of them.

If you are turned down then as a mature student you will quite possibly be told at the interview why they cannot offer you a place. Perhaps they need more proof of your ability, or you need to prepare yourself more fully. It is very likely that they will tell you what to do to improve your chances.

But even if you *are* offered a place, it will often be conditional on fulfilling certain conditions – and this, especially for mature students, is where we come to the thorniest point of all.

7 *Conditions for entry*
If you are a typical mature student without formal entrance qualifications, the department to which you are applying has to have some other way of satisfying itself that you are a suitable candidate. Regulations on the grounds of acceptability vary from one university to another, but in general the department has a number of possibilities for satisfying itself. It can ask you to
(a)   take GCE A levels
(b)   sit an entrance examination
(c)   submit a substantial piece of work
(d)   take some other preparatory course.

This is not an exhaustive list: there may be other possibilities.

(a)   *GCE A levels*
This is often the most disappointing news! They will accept you – but you still have to go through the very hoops you were probably hoping to avoid. This means that they are not very sure of you and are playing safe – but it shows they are interested in you. They may require good

grades – like three Bs – but in the case of mature students a more moderate performance is often asked for: for example, two Cs or maybe one good pass in the subject concerned.

For guidance on standard 'A' level requirements by all polytechnic and university departments see the excellently detailed *Degree Course Offers* by Brian Heap. This annual compendium reveals, for example, that if you wish to study English, Oxford and Cambridge universities usually ask for three As, Manchester two Bs and a C, Bristol two Bs, the North London Polytechnic a B and a D, while Bath College of Higher Education requires two Ds. If you wish to study engineering grade requirements range from three As at Cambridge to two Es at Sunderland Polytechnic.

(b) *Entrance examination*
Some universities have what is often called a 'mature matriculation' examination, that is, an examination set especially for mature applicants. If you pass the examination you satisfy the university that you have the necessary academic ability to study at the higher education level.

What is in this examination paper? This varies – but you could normally expect a section on general knowledge, certainly some essay questions and probably a special section dealing with the subject you wish to study. At Manchester University the Mature Matriculation examination can comprise three 3-hour papers but discretion is often exercised as to the papers a candidate must sit. Before taking such an examination work through Chapter 9 once again and try to find fellow mature students who have successfully passed the test. Even though these examinations are not very difficult mature students often work themselves up to a pitch of anxiety – possibly because their earlier experience of examinations has been unhappy. Some advice and reassurance from a tutor or ex-tutor should be sought and some systematic preparation along the lines advised in Chapter 9.

(c) *Submitting a piece of work*
Some of the more welcoming departments might well give you the option of submitting a piece of work to prove your ability. This might be anything from a standard academic essay (1,500 words) on a subject either they or you choose, to a longer (2,000–3,000 words) project or extended essay.

Again, you would be well advised to consult with your tutor on such a piece of work – but I have no hesitation in saying that this is a *very attractive option*. If you have the writing skills you will need for further and higher education, all this option requires is that you display them! You may need to read reasonably widely around your topic but you can work at your own pace, check and rewrite what you have written, all without feeling under pressure. Make sure, however, that the presentation of your finished work is as neat and attractive as possible.

(d) *Preparatory courses*
As already mentioned, many universities are now beginning to recognise a whole variety of preparatory courses as being legitimate qualifications for entry. These can vary from Return to Study-type courses which the University has decided to formally (or informally) recognise, to courses run by other institutions.

These possibilities are currently changing so rapidly and vary so much from one institution to the other, that it is not possible to give hard and fast guidelines. You should be prepared to make thorough enquiries and don't expect all admissions tutors necessarily to be aware of them!

(e) *Other methods of entry*
The traditional qualifications for entry into higher education are being supplemented by other systems – many of which vary from region to region. The Manchester Open College Federation, for example, enables adult students to receive 'credits' for a whole range of courses studied and to use them as qualifications for further study.

5 *Section II*
Education and future employment

The motives of adults who 'return to study' are complex. Some wish to study for study's sake; others maybe, to jolt their brains into activity after years of relative neglect; others to try the challenge of higher education; and still others to move into occupations with more intrinsic and financial rewards. Indeed, the vocational (or 'job-related' motive) is often closely intertwined with all the others; we have all to eat and unless retired, we want the jobs to which our interests and talents best suit us. If you have just completed this course you might be looking at further educational activity with employment very much in mind. If so, this section may be of help in directing your thoughts and actions.

Self-assessment for employment
Earlier in this Chapter we encouraged you to assess your performance. If employment or a change of employment is now your objective a different kind of self-assessment is necessary. You need to take stock of what you have to offer potential employers. Some courses funded by the Manpower Services Commission (MSC) enable you to do this as part of a job-seeking package but the useful book by Godfrey Golzen and Philip Plumley, *Changing Your Job After Thirty-Five* (Kogan Page, 1985) provides a well-thought-through self-assessment programme (pages 52–73). This enables you via a self-applied questionnaire to draw up a personal profile reflecting your academic, professional and leadership attainments; your basic aptitudes (are they verbal, numerical, practical, creative, methodical, pupil-orientated?); your interests and hobbies; and your personality (to what extent are you sociable, phlegmatic, tough, conforming, self-contained, excitable, sensitive, independent?). It then attempts to match personal characteristics with career types characterised as: executive/decision-making, administrators, altruistic, artistic, literary, persuasive, practical, scientific, technical/technological.

This book – and there are similar ones available on the market – also give you advice on planning a job strategy, using contacts, answering job adverts effectively, using consultancies and agencies, drawing up *curriculum vitaes* and performing well in job interviews. If you have assiduously studied your way through this course you will be in a much stronger position to benefit from this kind of advice and to apply your skills to good effect.

Training and retraining
Your personal stocktaking may suggest occupational areas to which you are suited but for which your qualifications, or training are inadequate. In these circumstances you will need to identify the providing agencies and the location of appropriate courses. Some of the major career training options are given below.

1 *Occupations requiring a degree* This relates to a wide range of professional occupations: for example, management, journalism or the civil service. Often the subject studied is irrelevant; employers merely wish to see evidence of degree-level attainments. If you wish to enter this kind of profession then clearly you first need a degree and the foregoing section on entry into higher education is relevant. Your age will obviously be a factor here: entering university and acquiring a degree may take 4–5 years and most employers are looking for young rather than older graduates.

2 *Occupations requiring specialised postgraduate qualifications*   The most obvious example here is teaching, which requires a post-graduate certificate. Obviously, you need to apply for such courses during your degree course. Usually such qualifications are studied full time but it is also possible to study part-time in some circumstances.

3 *Vocational courses*
   (i) *Business and Technician Education Council* (B/TEC)   BTEC courses coordinate a wide range of pre-vocational and post-experience courses. They operate at four levels: a general diploma or certificate intended for students at 16+ with few academic attainments; a national diploma or certificate for those with some basic qualifications; a higher national diploma or certificate for those over 18 with attainments up to A level; and post-experience courses intended for people already at work. BTEC qualifications can be studied full or part-time (often on a day-release basis) and are provided at polytechnics an colleges of FE).
   (ii) *City and Guilds of London Institute*   This body offers qualifications for industry in over 200 technical subjects. These courses are normally available at FE colleges.
   (iii) *Royal Society of Arts*   This examination board offers qualifications mainly in the secretarial and business studies area.
   (iv) *Professional   Industrial   and   Commercial   Updating (PICKUP)*   The government has been funding this programme, comprising short self-contained courses often not carrying a qualification, for some years. Providers can be found in universities, polytechnics and FE colleges.
   (v) *The Open Tech*   This is an MSC-funded initiative in the field of distance learning materials for vocational courses. In 1985 over 50,000 people were acquiring their training in this way. Often these schemes are paid for by employers.

4 *Professional orientated degree courses*   These are the degree courses which in effect constitute professional training. They include medicine, law, architecture, and town and country planning. In many cases further professional qualifications need to be acquired after completion of degree. These courses are amongst the most prestigious in higher education and are often difficult to gain access to.

5 *Professional qualifications*   There are a number of professions for instance accountancy, or banking, which you can train for when in post. These qualifications are graduated according to difficulty and can be studied either on a day-release basis or, quite typically, a purely private-study basis.

6 *Employment Training (ET)*. This is a huge training programme, again funded by the MSC. You can acquire skills in just about any occupation: typing, setting up your own business, welding, engineering. These courses vary in length and

are free. Part-time courses do not provide a maintenance allowance but full-time courses do. Courses are held at skill centres and in LEA institutions. You can find out more about these courses from your local job centre, career or employment office.

7 *Work-based training* Technology is changing so rapidly in some areas that employers find it best to set up their own in-house training programmes – some of them up to a very high level. These can be studied in a variety of ways; some companies are experimenting currently with distance learning techniques. Discussions are taking place at present to establish some form of wider recognition for such courses of study.

8 *Trade union education* Certain trade union representatives, for example safety officers, have a legal right to paid time off work for relevant training. The Trade Union Congress (TUC) offers a wide range of specialised training for its ten million or so members. 30,000–40,000 people attend such courses each year run for the TUC by institutions like the WEA, extramural departments, polytechnics and FE colleges.

9 *Self-employment* There are over three million self-employed people in Britain, many of them working in their own small companies or just for themselves. Special courses in entrepreneurial skills, establishing your own business and so forth are run by the MSC, but a number of private agencies also operate in this field.

10 *Private-sector training organisations* You can acquire specific skills from a number of private bodies which operate on a profit-making basis. These organisations are particularly present in the 'New Technology' areas like computer training. A word of warning here: check the credentials of the organisation very carefully and compare their charges with similar courses offered in the public sector, e.g., FE colleges and polytechnics.

11 *Training for voluntary work* Britain has a rich tradition in voluntary work with thousands of charitable agencies seeking to help people in all kinds of ways. For those of you wishing to develop a new interest, perhaps at a pre or post-retirement activity, or just to fill up available time in a worthwhile fashion, training opportunities do exist. The best way of finding out is through the local Councils of Voluntary Service.

12 *Training for the unemployed* A number of the opportunities mentioned above apply, naturally, to those people who are not in employment but special programmes for the unemployed exist, most of them funded by the MSC. They operate under a variety of different acronyms – most of them now fairly familiar to us: YTS, ET, RESTART, etc. These schemes were much criticised when they first appeared but many have

now settled down and offer an effective service to the unemployed. Job centres or employment offices are the best sources of information for such courses.

If you wish to find out more about training opportunities then I would recommend the book by A. Pates and M. Good, *Second Chances*, published by the National Extension College. This is an annual guide and contains much useful advice together with names and addresses of the places where you can acquire more detailed information (see further reading section).

Concluding comment

Thi, brings us to the end of *Making the Grade*. If you have studied assiduously, completing all the assignments, we calculate you have put in 150–250 hours. Such practice cannot fail to have increased your competence as a student by a significant amount. *Making the Grade*, of course, is skills-based: it isolates individual skills, explains their nature and apparent mysteries and provides practice in using them in a variety of subjects. The idea behind this approach – based upon much teaching experience – is that adults find it an easier way to re-enter the world of study than conventional subject based courses. In our experience learning *how* to study builds up confidence rapidly; few adults received such special tution in school and it is reassuring for them to discover that most study skills are simply applied common-sense plus practice.

We hope that the course has enabled you to:

1   Increase your confidence – the vital prerequisite for effective study.

2 Assess your own strengths and identify your weaknesses.

3 Enjoy the process of study and generate interest in a number of subject areas.

4 Lay the foundation for future endeavours in training or further/higher education.

We have concentrated upon written work – mainly because we believe good written work draws together the widest possible range of study techniques. All the skills in this course, however, have relevance beyond the world of study: efficient use of time, well-organised, clear-thinking and fluent literate written expression are required in all professional occupations and many other walks of life. We very much hope that studying *Making the Grade* has helped you to grow and find fuller confidence.

Further reading   6

Courses

Boehm, K., Wellings, N. & Behr, C. (eds), *The Student Book: The Applicant's Guide to UK Colleges, Polytechnics and Universities*, Macmillan (annual). Comprehensive listings of all degree courses throughout the higher education system and elsewhere.

British Council, *How to Live in Britain*, Evans Brothers. For overseas students.

CDP, *Polytechnic Courses Handbook*, 309 Regent Street, London WIR 7PE (free).

CNAS, *Directory of First Degree Courses and Opportunities in Higher Education for Mature Students*, 344/345 Gray's Inn Road, London WC1X 8BP (free).

CNAA, *Directory of First Degree and Diploma of Higher Education Courses*, 344–345 Gray's Inn Road, London WC1X 8BP (free).

Councils & Education Press Ltd (annual), *Education Year Book*. Comprehensive address list of all educational organisations and bureaucracies.

CRAC, *Directory of Further Education: The Comprehensive Guide to Courses in UK Polytechnics and Colleges*, Hobsons Press (annual). Useful listings of degree and non-degree courses in further and higher education together with details of how they can be studied, e.g., full-time, part-time, flexi, distance.

DES, *Grants to Students*, Department of Education & Science, York Road, London SE1 7PH.

DES, *Guide to Grants: Designated Courses*, Room 2/11, Elizabeth House, York Road, London SE1 7PH.

ECCTIS, *The Directory of Educational Guidance Service for Adults*, PO Box 88, Sherwood House, Sherwood Drive, Bletchley MK3 6DL (free).

Educational Broadcasting Information (30/FE), Residential Courses Based on BBC Series, BBC, London W1AA 1AA.

Heap, B. *Degree Course Offers*, Careers Consultants (annual). This is a guide to the selection and admissions procedures at British universities, polytechnics and colleges. Concentrates on things like admissions tutor advice, what A level grades are required, and what subjects are on offer. Essential reading for those wishing to enter higher education.

Hutchinson, E. & E., *Learning Later*, Routledge & Kegan Paul.

Joint Matriculation Board (JMB), *21 Returning to Learning*, JMB,

Manchester M15 6EU (free). Opportunities of mature students at the five JMB universities.

London & South Eastern Regional Advisory Council for Further Education, *A Compendium of Advanced Courses in Colleges of Further and Higher Education*, Tavistock House, Tavistock Square, London WC1H 9LR. Useful listings of degree and diploma courses outside universities.

Longman, *Higher Education in the UK: A Handbook for Students and the Advisers*. Aimed at overseas students and produced by the British Council and the Association of Commonwealth Universities.

National Institute of Continuing Education (NIACE), *The Year Book of Adult Continuing Education* (annual).

New Opportunity Press, *Guide to Postgraduate Study: Directory of Opportunities for Graduates*.

Pates, A. & Good, M., *Second Chances: The Annual Guide to Adult Education and Training Opportunities*, National Extension College (annual). This is a comprehensive guide to all the possibilities available in adult education. Well organised and easy to use.

PCAS, *Guide to Applicants*, PO Box 67, Cheltenham, Glos. GL50 3AP (free).

Priestley, B., *British Qualifications*, Kogan Page (annual). Lists qualifications available in Britain and names of awarding bodies.

Sheed & Ward, *The Compendium of University Entrance Requirements*, 2 Creechurch Lane, London EC34 5AQ.

UCCA, *How to Apply for Admission to a University*, PO Box 28, Cheltenham, Glos. GL 50 1HY (free).

Wilby, P., *The Sunday Times Good University Guide*, Collins (annual). This describes universities, polytechnics, and colleges and gives details of what they offer the prospective student – from library opening hours to the number of washbasins in the halls of residence.

Careers
Brown, *Good Retirement Guide 1987*, Gerald Duckworth & Co. Ltd, The Old Piano Factory, 43 Gloucester Crescent, London NW1.

Careers Consultants, *Directory of Independent Training & Tutorial Organisation*. Lists private-sector training providers.

COIC, *Annual Careers Guide: Opportunities in the Professions, Industry, Commerce and the Public Service*, Room M1101, Moorfoot, Sheffield S1 4PQ.

Councils & Education Press (annual), *Social Services Year Book.*

Danncey, G., *The Unemployment Handbook*, NEC, 18 Brooklands Avenue, Cambridge.

Golzen, G. & Plumbley, P. R. *Changing Your Job After 35*, Kogan Page. A reference book which also concentrates upon marketing yourself. Useful appendices of handy information.

Miller, R., & Alston, A., *Equal Opportunities: A Careers Guide for Women and Men*, Penguin.

MSC, *Sponsorship offered to students by employers and professional bodies for first degrees, BTEC, SCOTBEC and Scotec Higher Awards.*

Segal, A., *Careers Encyclopaedia*, Cassell (annual).

Syrett, M., *Goodbye 9–5*, New Opportunity Press.

Wilby, P., *The Sunday Times Good Careers Guide*, Granada.

Useful addresses

Business & Technician
 Education Council (BTEC)
Central House
Upper Woburn Place
London WC1H 0HH

Central Bureau for Educational
 Visits & Exchanges
Seymour House
Seymour Mews
London W1H 9PE

Community Service
 Volunteers
237 Pentonville Road
London N1 9NJ

Coordinating Committee for
 Distance Learning Schemes
 for Vocational Further
 Education
22 Great King Street
Edinburgh EH3 6QH

National Extension College
18 Brooklands Avenue
Cambridge CB2 2KN

Open College of South London
Manor House
58 Clapham Common,
North Side
London SW4 9RZ

Open University Students
 Association
Sherwood House
Sherwood Drive
Bletchley
Milton Keynes MK3 6HL

Pickup Programme
DES
Elizabeth House
York Road
London SE1 7PH

Ecctis
PO Box 88
Sherwood House
Sherwood Drive
Bletchley MK3 6DL

Educational Centres Association
Chequer Centre
Chequer Street
Bunhill Row
London EC1Y 8PL

National Adult School
 Organisation
Norfolk House
Smallbrook, Queensway
Birmingham B5 4JL

National Advisory Centre on
Careers for Women
Drayton House
30 Garden Street
London WC1H 0AX

National Housewives Register
245 Warwick Road
Solihull
West Midlands B92 7AH

The British Council
10 Spring Gardens
London SW1A 2BN

The Executive Secretary
The University of the Third Age
6 Parkside Gardens
London SW19 5EY

The Administrator for Women's
Courses
The Industrial Society
Robert Hyde House
48 Bryanston Square
London W1H 7LN

The Manchester Open College
Federation
All Saints Building
Manchester Polytechnic
Manchester M15 6BH

The Open Tech Unit
MSC
Moorfoot
Sheffield S1 4PQ

The Open University
Walton Hall
Milton Keynes MK7 6AA

The University of Buckingham
Hunter Street
Buckingham MK18 1EG

The WEA National Office
9 Upper Berkeley Street
London W1H 8BY

The UK Council for Overseas
Student Affairs
60 Westbourne Grove
London W2 5PG

TUC Postal Courses Office
Tillicoultry
FK13 6BK

Universities Central Council on
Admissions
PO Box 28
Cheltenham
Glos. GL50 1HY

Pre-Retirement Association of
Great Britain
19 Undine Street
Tooting
London SW17 8PP

Scottish Universities Council of
Entrance
Kinnesburn
Kennedy Gardens
St Andrews
Fife KY16 9DR

Scottish Business Education
Council (SCOTBEC)
22 Great King Street
Edinburgh EH3 6QH

Start Up Your Own Business
OU Business School
Sherwood House
Bletchley
Milton Keynes MK3 6HW

The Advisor for Disabled Students
The Open University
Walton Hall
Milton Keynes MK7 6AA

National Union of Students
461 Holloway Road
London N7
(Scotland: 12 Dublin Street,
Edinburgh EH1 3PP)
Wales: 107 Walter Road, Swansea
SA1 5QQ)

Secondary Examination Council
Newcombe House
Notting Hill Gate
London W11 3JB

Polytechnic Central Admissions
System (PCAS)
PO Box 47
Cheltenham
Glos. CL50 3AP

The Graduate Teacher Training
Registry
3 Crawford Place
London

The General Teaching Council for
Scotland
5 Royal Terrace
Edinburgh EH7 5AF

The Department of Education &
Science
Elisbeth House
York Road
London SE1
(Scotland: Haymarket House,
Clifton Terrace, Edinburgh EH12
5D)
(N. Ireland: Rathgael House,
Balloo Road, Bangor, Co. Down,
Northern Ireland)

GCE examining boards
England and Wales
Associated Examining Board
Wellington House
Aldershot
Hants GU11 1BQ
Tel: (0252) 25551

University of Cambridge Local
Examinations Syndicate
Syndicate Buildings
17 Harvey Road
Cambridge CB1 2EU
Tel: (0223) 61111

Joint Matriculation Board
Manchester M15 2EU
Tel: 061-273 2565

Oxford & Cambridge Schools
Examination Board
Brook House
10 Trumpington Street
Cambridge CB2 1QB
Tel: (0223) 64326
and Elsfield Way
Oxford OX2 8EP
Tel: (0865) 54421

Oxford Delegacy of local
Examinations
Ewert Place
Summertown
Oxford OX2 7BZ
Tel: (0865) 54291

Southern Universities Joint Board
for School Examinations
Coatham Road
Bristol BS6 6DD
Tel: (0272) 36042

Universities Entrance and School
Examinations Council
University of London
66–72 Gower Street
London WC1E 6EE
Tel: 01-636 8000

Welsh Joint Education Committee
245 Western Avenue
Cardiff CF5 2YX
Tel: (02220 561231

Scotland
Scottish Examination Board
Ironmills Road
Dalkeith
Midlothian EH22 1LE
Tel: 031-663 6601

Northern Ireland
Northern Ireland Schools
Examination Council
Examination Office
Beechill House
42 Beechill Road
Belfast BT8 4RS
Tel: (0232) 647261

**Residential adult education
colleges**
Coleg Harlech
Harlech
Merioneth LL46 2PU

Newbattle Abbey College
Dalkeith
Midlothian EH22 3LL

Northern College
Wentworth Castle
Stainborough
Barnsley
South Yorkshire S75 3ET

Plater College
Pullens Lane
Oxford OX3 0DT

Ruskin College
Oxford OX1 2HE

Co-operative College
Stanford Hall
Loughborough LE12 5QR

Hillcroft College
Surbiton
Surrey KT6 6DF

Woodbrook College
1046 Bristol Road
Selly Oak
Birmingham B29 6LJ

Bibliography

There are several study-skills books available on the market. Some of the more useful ones are listed below. All are available, in paperback.

T. Buzan, *Speed Reading*, David & Charles.
—— *Speed Memory*, David & Charles
—— *Use Your Head*, BBC Books
—— *Use Your Memory*, BBC Books
Careers and Occupational Information Centre, *Effective Writing at Work*
—— *Communications at Work*
F. Casey, *How to Study*, Macmillan
G. E. Christ, *The Nuttall Dictionary of English Synonyms and Antonyms*, Frederick Warne
R. Freeman, *How to Study Effectively*, National Extension College, Cambridge
—— *Mastering Study Skills*, Macmillan Master Series
G. Gibbs, *Learning to Study*, National Extension College, Cambridge
Sir E. Gowers, *The Complete Plain Words*, HMSO
K. Howard & J. A. Sharp, *The Management of a Student Research Project*, Gower
J. Inglis & R. Lewis, *Clear Thinking*, National Extension College, Cambridge
M. & E. De Leeuw, *Read Better: Read Faster*, David & Charles
R. Lewis, *How to Write Essays*, National Extension College, Cambridge
—— & M. Pugmire, *How to Use Your Dictionary*, Pelican
H. Maddox, *How to Study*, Pan
A. L. A. Marshall & F. Rowland, *A Guide to Learning Independently*, Open University Press
C. Moor, *Answer the Question*, National Extension College, Cambridge
R. Palmer & A. Pope, *Brain Train*, E. & F. N. Spon
C. Parsons, *How to Study Effectively*, Arrow
E. Partgridge, *A Guide to Good English*, Hamish Hamilton
—— *Usage and Abusage*, Hamish Hamilton
J. Perkin, *It's Never Too Late*, Impact Books

R. Pratley, *Spelling it Out*, BBC Books
D. Rowntree, *Learn How to Study*, Macdonald
T. Sullivan, *Grammar*, National Extension College, Cambridge
——   *Reading and Understanding*, National Extension College, Cambridge
——   *Studying*, National Extension College, Cambridge
——   *Writing*, National Extension College, Cambridge
——   *Writing Essays in Social Sciences*, National Extension College, Cambridge
G. E. Sutcliffe, *Effective Learning for Effective Management*, Prentice-Hall
M. Temple, *Get it Right*, John Murray
R. H. Thouless, *Straight and Crooked Thinking*, Pan

7 Answers to course review exercise

1 (a) Understanding the principal issue or concept behind it.
(b) Spotting the key terms.
(c) Recognising the instruction terms.
2 (a) Answering the wrong question.
(b) Misunderstanding the point of what is being asked for.
(c) Failing to see the emphasis of the question.
(d) Misreading the instructions.
3 (a) Compare: look for similarities and differences between two or more things.
(b) Contrast: deliberately single out and emphasise the differences between two or more things.
(c) Discuss: investigate and examine by argument. Explore implications. Debate the case and possibly consider alternatives.
(d) Outline: give the main features or general principles of a subject, omitting minor details and emphasising structure or arrangement.
4 (a) Introduction.
(b) Points *for* the statement.
(c) Points *against* the statement.
(d) Conclusion.
5 The points of argument, both for and against, are gathered together and discussed in separate *categories*.
6 Any five out of
(a) The descriptive essay.
(b) The 'for and against' essay.
(c) The 'compare and contrast' essay.

     (d)   The analytic essay.
     (e)   The literary appreciation essay.
     (f)   The report of an experiment or investigation.
     (g)   The essay of philosphic analysis.
     (h)   The polemical essay.
     (i)   The 'classical' essay.

7   Induction and deduction.

8   Any four from
     (a)   Begging the question.
     (b)   ‚False dilemma.
     (c)   False analogy.
     (d)   *Post hoc ergo propter hoc.*
     (e)   Thin end of the wedge.
     (f)   Selecting evidence.
     (g)   Demanding impossible proof.

9   The comma, semi-colon, colon, and full stop.

10 (a)   To indicate emphasis.
     (b)   To indicate book or play titles.

11   Any four out of
     (a)   At the beginning of a sentence.
     (b)   For the first person pronoun 'I'.
     (c)   For months and days.
     (d)   For adjectives derived from proper nouns.
     (e)   For first and main words in titles.

12   Subject-verb-object

13   They should all relate to the same theme, topic, or controlling idea.

14 (a)   A controlling idea.
     (b)   Topic sentence.
     (c)   Support sentence(s).
     (d)   Concluding sentence.

15 (a)   Understanding the title or question.
     (b)   Generation of ideas.
     (c)   Preliminary essay plan
     (d)   Assembly of sources.
     (e)   Reading.
     (f)   Note-taking.
     (g)   Detailed essay plan
     (h)   First draft.
     (i)   Second draft.
     (j)   Final reading.

16   That it should be appropriate for the context in which it is being used.

17 (a)   An adjective describes a noun (a *tall* boy).
     (b)   An adverb modifies a verb (he ran *quickly*) or an adjective (an *unusually* tall boy).

18 (a)   Metaphor – a comparison of two things in which we say that one thing *is* the other.

   (b) Simile – a comparison of two things in which we say that one thing is *like* the other.

   (c) Syntax – the arrangement and grammatical relation of words in a sentence.

   (d) Irony – a statement made with humorous or satirical intent which implies the opposite of what it means.

19 Any four out of

   (a) Assessing progress.

   (b) Motivating students.

   (c) Grading students.

   (d) Protecting standards.

   (e) Offering a fair and objective test.

20 (a) Copies of course outline, syllabus, and reading list.

   (b) Textbooks.

   (c) Your lecture and class notes.

   (d) Essays and exercises you have completed.

Review exercise – results

I don't think it is necessary to be mathematical or too finely detailed about the results here. Assuming that you have been reasonably strict with yourself (after all, there is no point in 'cheating' if you want to know how well you have performed), I would suggest that you could grade yourself as follows:

Number of correct answers (64 possible maximum approx)	Comment
50 and over	Clearly this represents a highly successful study experience. The chances are that you should have little problem with any aspect of further study.
40–50	A good result. You can say you have successfully completed the course.
30–40	Fair-to-Good. You need to keep working. Refer back to earlier chapters and brush up any areas of weakness.
20–30	A not very reassuring result. Perhaps you should work through the course again more slowly.
Less than 20	Don't despair. Either take the course again, more carefully or maybe try another type of course with more classroom contact and personal supervision from a tutor.

8 *Guidance notes*

Chapter 1

Exercise 1
1 What are questions *for*?
2 The principal issue or concept behind the question
3 Key terms
4 Instruction terms
5 Common problems or mistakes

Exercise 2

Question 1
(a) The principal idea here is the legal prohibitions of hare-cour-sing, fox-hunting, cock-fighting, and other such activities in which animals are hunted, tormented, maimed, or killed for the sake of entertainment.
(b) The key terms are 'blood sports' and 'banned'.
(c) The instruction is 'discuss' – in other words write about the proposition in an intelligent manner, exploring its impli-cations and considering arguments for and against. You can agree with it, disagree, or just present the arguments with-out offering any opinion of your own.
(d) You would need to limit yourself to *blood* sports. It would be no good including greyhound racing even if you thought this exploited dogs – but you might consider including boar-hunting. You should consider the moral arguments for and against such a ban, and consider the practicality of imple-menting it.
Paraphrase
'Sports which cause pain and death to animals should be legally prohibited. Consider this idea.'

Question 2
(a) The principal idea here is free transport in cities – with the obvious implication that it is proposed in order to relieve traffic congestion.
(b) There are two key terms – 'free' and 'public transport', with 'cities' as an important third which is part key term, part qualifier.
(c) The instruction is to consider *both* the case for *and* the case against. Any answer which left out one of these could only gain half marks at maximum.
(d) You would need to consider all the advantages of such an idea (less traffic congestion, less pollution, less accidents, more convenience, etc.) and the disadvantages (costly, less

convenient, unfair to rural taxpayers, peripheral car parks required, etc.) Again, you are not being asked to come to a conclusion, though you might state your opinion. This, however, would be less important than your coverage of both advantages *and* disadvantages.

Paraphrase
'Consider the arguments in favour of and against free urban public transport.'

Question 3
(a) The principal idea here is that women ought to be limited merely to a domestic role in society.
(b) The key terms are 'woman's place' and 'home'. 'Place' *doesn't* mean a woman should never leave the house – it refers to her position in relation to society and 'home' is obviously meant to represent family life in general.
(c) The instruction asks you to consider this obviously old-fashioned notion in the light of contemporary society and its values. Some possible conflict is implied.
(d) You would need to show that you knew what the quotation originally implied, and then depending upon your opinion in response to it, show how such notions operated today. For instance you could disagree, saying that it would put too great a limitation on women today, when possibilities for independent jobs and careers were open to them and the sharing of household tasks and child-rearing was common. Or you could agree, claiming that in a society which paid men more, it was an *advantage* for a woman to be free of 'wage-slavery' and at liberty to enjoy the fulfilment of close contact with her family.
     In a question of this type you would get extra marks for showing that you could fully understand both sides of the argument and lose marks if it were obvious that you could not.

Paraphrase
' "A woman's role is best limited to the domestic realm." Is this still valid in contemporary society?'

Question 4
(a) The principal issue here is capital punishment and the arguments for and against it.
(b) The key term is 'death penalty'.
(c) The instruction asks you to defend the arguments ('justify the case') in favour of *keeping* capital punishment. That is, it only wishes you to deal with one side of the question.
(d) There are several common arguments in favour of capital punishment – as vengeance or retribution for some crime, as an example to deter others, as a 'necessity' commanded by

some religious code, and so on. You would need to deal with as many of these as possible. But you might also deal with the associated question of which crimes could be punishable by death (premeditated? or multiple murder?). It would be wrong here to consider the arguments *against* its retention, even if they formed the basis of your own beliefs.

I should add here that questions of this type are not designed to search for the truth but to give you exercise in disciplined argument, including discussing opinions which you don't personally hold.

Paraphrase
'Defend the arguments in favour of keeping capital punishment.'

Question 5

(a) The principal issue here is 'abortion on demand' – that is, free access to it as a matter of personal choice.

(b) The key term is 'abortion on demand', but 'right' is an important qualifier, and you should even keep 'woman' in mind (it excludes the idea of a *man* having this right).

(c) The instruction gives you the chance to agree, disagree, or just generally discuss the idea before arriving at some conclusion.

(d) Whether you agree or not, you need to show that you can discuss the moral issues involved – a woman's right to control her own body, unwanted children, free contraception, dangerous pregnancies, the age at which a foetus is considered human, back-street or DIY abortions, abortion itself as a form of birth control, and so on. The more carefully you can think through and express these arguments, the better your answer will be, no matter what your opinion on the matter.

Paraphrase
'Females should have access to termination of pregnancy as a matter of their own choice.'

Question 6

(a) The principal issue here is 'euthanasia', which can be either 'putting someone out of their misery' ('mercy-killing') or sometimes a form of murder condoned by the victim ('put me out of my misery when there is no longer any chance of recovery').

(b) The key term is 'euthanasia' – and since this is an unusual and complex term, you might need to say a few words about it by way of defining the issue.

(c) The instruction is in the form of a double negative – 'refute the case against' – which means that you must overthrow those arguments which would prohibit the practice of euthanasia. Note that this is not *necessarily* the same thing as the arguments in favour of it.

(d) The arguments against might be on grounds which were religious, practical, ethical, etc. (you should get used to considering most questions in terms of these large social and philosophical categories). Your refutations could be based on arguments of: agreement of the victim, cost and pointlessness of keeping alive a non-sentient person, pity and mercy for extreme pain during inevitable death and so on. Obviously, you would have to be careful here and build safeguards against abuse into your answer.

Paraphrase
'Disprove the arguments which would prohibit the practice of 'mercy-killing'.

Question 7
(a) The principal issue here is an individual's right to do what he chooses balanced against another's notions of what is good for him. But the answer will also have to make value judgements about the quality of television programmes.

(b) The key term is 'too much'. It implies a criticism. The statement you must take at face value.

(c) The instruction asks you to discuss television-viewing and consider if it should be controlled or limited.

(d) Your answer would take into account the content and quality of television programmes; how much free time the average person has per week; the individual's right to spend that time as he chooses; the possible effects of so much viewing; the alternative activities such viewing precludes; who that individual *is* (child, infirm pensioner, etc.). The question also raises possible issues such as indoctrination, puritan values, and political control.

Paraphrase
In this case a paraphrase does not seem appropriate.

Exercise 3
Some of the synonyms you might have had are as follows:
(a) meticulous, exacting, particular, scrupulous
(b) vacant, insignificant, insane, trivial
(c) increase, supplement, appendage, addition
(d) famous, celebrated, infamous, disreputable
(e) poverty, indigence, destitution, privation
(f) sanctuary, retreat, hiding place, prison
(g) savoury, toothsome, appetising, palatable
(h) flashy, tasteless, rude, indelicate

Chapter 2

Exercise 1
1 The importance of writing essays.
2 Getting your points into perspective.
3 The 'for and against' essay – Strategy I.
4 Strategy II essays.
5 The comparative 'for and against' essay.
6 Introductions and conclusions.

Exercise 2
We are offering a sample essay plan just, for example, number 4 –
'It is in no way justifiable to use animals in scientific research.' If
you chose one of the other questions, try to check that you have at
least three or four substantial arguments both 'for' and 'against',
make sure that you have some illustrative examples where possible, and that you haven't got any of your points in the wrong
category, and if at all possible check your results with a tutor.

'It is in no way justifiable to use animals in scientific research.'

Introduction	– strong emotional and humanitarian arguments *for*
	– strong practical arguments *against*.
For	– unnecessary suffering in animals (smoking beagles)
	– research often for human vanity (cosmetics)
	– results of tests on animals may be invalid on humans (Thalidomide)
	– 'information' can be obtained by other means
	– human volunteers could be used for testing
Against	– many cures for disease have been found and tested
	– necessary to determine lethal doses somehow
	– human volunteers for testing dangerous viruses and chemicals unlikely
	– genetic transmission rates can be quickly determined on fast breeding species
Conclusion	– arguments are evenly balanced, but information could be shared to prevent unnecessary repe- tition of experiments, and human volunteers could be used for less harmful materials, and cosmetics could be made from natural materials.

Exercise 3
No comment applicable. Consult your tutor.

Exercise 4
Here are some examples of sentences against which you may
compare your own.

218

1 She stopped eating meat, and this abnegation eased her conscience regarding the slaughter of animals.
2 He jumped out of the plane, felt a visceral thrill of fear, and pulled the ripcord in a panic.
3 Either (a) Replacing the door fittings, he screwed a new escutcheon over the keyhole;

   or   (b) The knight's motto was blazoned across the family escutcheon.
4 Shutting the door after the horse has bolted is an otiose gesture.
5 Four more lengthy paragraphs dwelling on exactly the same point were the most prolix part of the essay.
6 Nosey-parkers often take a prurient interest in the private lives of their neighours.
7 He was so infuriated that he rained a rabid degree of animosity on to his antagonist.
8 Fresh air, warm weather, and sunny days are salubrious for all of us.
9 He repaid the money, and with this expiation of his early wrongdoing, began to feel less guilty.
10 The hothouse was redolent of the scent of exotic flowers.
11 She stepped gingerly into the sepulchral gloom of the vault.
12 Flat, warm beer is vapid fare on a hot day.

Chapter 3

Exercise 1
1 The descriptive essay.
2 The 'for and against' essay.
3 The 'compare and contrast' essay.
4 The analytic essay.
5 The literary appreciation essay.
6 The report of an experiment or investigation.
7 The essay in philosophic analysis.
8 The polemical essay.
9 The 'classical' essay.

Exercise 2
We produce below a student's essay plan for example 2, 'Consider the case for and against vegetarianism.'

Introduction	– case 'for' vastly outweighs 'against', yet difficult to change national habits
Case 'for'	– meat-eating to current extent unhealthy (fats)
	– cruel to kill animals, especially in 'factories'
	– more costly to produce meat than other foods
	– all nutrients available in vegetables and cereals

	– Western meat-eating deplets 3rd World economies
Case 'against'	– difficult to change personal and national habits
	– farmers and meat producers would go bankrupt
	– in natural food chain 'big' species eat 'smaller'
	– reduction and moderation could answer the case 'for'
Conclusion	– much stronger case 'for', but change difficult. However, like smoking, habits could change

Exercise 3
No comment applicable. Consult your tutor.

Exercise 4
No comment applicable. Consult your tutor.

Exercise 5
No comment applicable. Consult your tutor.

Chapter 4

Exercise 1
1 The importance of clarity in the use of language.
2 The importance of the validity of arguments.
3 Abuses of language
   – may not express any idea at all
   – may *seem* to express more than it does
   – may stand for a very imprecise idea
   – may be ambiguous or stand for more than one idea
   – may express an attitude rather than an idea
4 Logic
   – two kinds of reasoning: induction and deduction
   – the validity of arguments
5 Common fallacies
   – begging the question
   – false dilemma
   – false analogy
   – *post hoc ergo propter hoc*
   – thin end of the wedge
   – selecting evidence
   – demanding impossible proof

Exercise 2
Some of the points you might have noted are:
(a) 'modern': vague – when does 'modern' begin? 1960? 1970? 1980?

(b) 'modern' is also an emotive word: its conventional opposite is 'old-fashioned', which is *not* a good thing to be!

(c) 'home' is an emotive word too: think of the difference if it were replaced here by 'house'.

(d) 'it' is technically ambiguous here: it could mean the furniture or the home or the maintenance, although most people will read it as referring to the first of these.

(e) 'dull': another ambiguity: it can mean either 'not reflecting light' or 'over-familiar, boring'. The first sense is intended here, but there is perhaps more than a hint of the second also.

(f) 'lifeless': have you ever seen furniture that looks 'alive'? The word is virtually meaningless in this context.

(g) 'a liberal application . . . will be beneficial': a pompous way of saying 'plenty . . . will do it good'. The next sentence begins pompously, too.

(h) 'too much . . . will be excessive': this is to say 'too much will be too much'. The statement has no significant meaning.

(i) 'deep and lustrous sheen': emotive language again: think of the difference if it were replaced by 'nice, bright shine'.

Exercise 3

A The Conservative Party

(a) 'Britain has recovered her self-confidence and self-respect'
This is first of all an over-generalisation. Did the millions of unemployed people feel like this? Very unlikely. And then it is almost impossible to prove. How would you measure the self-respect of an entire nation?

(b) 'We have regained the . . . admiration of other nations'
An emotive claim which, again, would be almost impossible to prove.

(c) 'integrity, resolve, and the will to succeed'
More emotive language. What Mrs Thatcher is hinting at here is Britain's victory in the Falklands war the previous year – but some aspects of military success are being attributed to society as a whole.

(d) 'our second term'
The Manifesto spells out the Party's policy *if* it wins the election, but the use of 'our' here makes it sound as the election has already been won.

(e) 'The choice before the nation is stark'
There follows here a classic 'false dilemma' – either *this* or *that*, with no other possibilities even considered. And the two possibilities are themselves sorts of begged questions.
'. . . to continue our steadfast progress towards recovery': not everyone would agree that a recovery had been made. And the policies of the Opposition are described as 'more

damaging' before they have been put into effect. (You could argue *'would be* more damaging' – but even this small change introduces an element of doubt.)

(f)   'We face three challenges'
Only three? But if she had said 'three *main* challenges' this would have admitted that there were others, and that the problem was more complex and therefore more difficult to deal with.

(g)   'the defence of our country'
Very emotive terms. Apart from the Falklands conflict, 'our country' had not been attacked by anybody for the previous forty years – yet here is 'defence' being elevated to our first priority!

(h)   'the employment of our people'
This manifesto was published at a time when the number of *un*employed people in Britain was almost three million. This is an example of manipulation via changed emphasis – rather like a newspaper headline which reads 'REVOLUTION IN FRANCE – feared by authorities'.

(i)   'the prosperity of the economy'
Language used to express a rather imprecise idea. If "the economy' is the generation of wealth, then that process cannot *itself* be 'prosperous': only *people* can – particularly those people who own and control the process. But it is unlikely that she would wish to draw attention to that distinction.

B   The Liberal/SDP Alliance

(a)   'watershed'
An emotive term (even though a cliché). It suggests that everything in terms of political development will hinge on the events of a single day. But history is a far more subtle and complex matter than that.

(b)   'depression . . . hopelessness . . . decline'
These are all very vague terms because they are not attributed to anyone. It is very unlikely that banks, growing industries, and prosperous people felt any of these things at all. And 'the slide of post-war years' is vaguest of all. What is it that has been 'sliding'?

(c)   'It may be . . . Alternatively it may be'
Another form of false dilemma. As subsequent events proved, neither of these possibilities proved to be the case.

(d)   'the people of this country'
Both an emotive term and an over-generalisation. General elections are often won with majorities as little as a third of the electorate: hardly 'the people'.

(e)   'at the eleventh hour'
Very emotive. It conjures up the moment before a possible

execution – which is not in any way similar to the complex and often quite slow manner in which political change takes place.

(f) 'dogma and bitterness . . . partnership and progress'
Emotive terms – the first two very negative, the second both positive and very 'reasonable'. And of course, it's another false dilemma.

C. *The Labour Party*

(a) 'crying out'
Obviously an emotive term – partly because it is a figure of speech ('anthropomorphism').

(b) 'our country'
Emotive for a different reason. It could just as easily have been '*the* country', but 'our' suggests a bond between the Labour Party and the reader which may not actually exist.

(c) 'To get Britain back to work'
This is rather vague. Quite apart from being grammatically incomplete, it suggests that the whole of Britain has stopped working.

(d) 'rebuild our shattered industries'
Both emotive and vague. It uses the metaphor of buildings having been knocked down: but which were they?

(e) 'To correct . . . Our National Health Service'
Vague. What on earth does this mean?

(f) 'great social services'
The 'great' here is emphatically emotive and approving.

(g) 'what Labour is determined to do'
A sort of 'begging the question'. It is what Labour *would like to do* – if elected.

Exercise 4

1 Factual – we can ask Fred if this is true.
2 Value judgement – it is an opinion. No proof is possible.
3 Factual – it *has* been proven.
4 Value judgement – it is an opinion (it might be possible to have a small and quite limited war using nuclear weapons, for instance).
5 Fact – it would be possible to check if this were true or not. (*Note:* this is not to say that it *is* true.)
6 Value judgement – the 'should' makes it an opinion.
7 Value judgement – the 'deserve' here is a matter of opinion.
8 Value judgement – even if we agree with the sentiment, the 'should' makes it a belief, not a 'fact'.
9 Value judgement – the term 'murdering' is being used meta-phorically here. This is an opinion.
10 Factual – it would be possible to verify this claim.
11 Factual – it could be verified (perhaps with some difficulty).
12 Value judgement – it is an opinion.

Chapter 5

Exercise 1
1 The basic elements of punctuation
  – the comma
  – the semi-colon
  – the colon
  – the full stop
2 Miscellaneous punctuation
  – the exclamation mark
  – the question mark
  – the dash
  – brackets
  – abbreviations
  – italics
  – the apostrophe
  – inverted commas
  – the hyphen
  – capital letters
3 Clear writing
4 Common problems
  – the sentence that goes on too long
  – too much punctuation
  – the missing item
  – the conversational tone
  – participle phrases
  – subject–verb separation
  – case agreement
  – bad starts
5 How to use quotations
  – accurate references
  – how much to quote
  – quotations in a literary essay
  – incorporating the quotation
  – using emphasis

Exercise 2
1 I ran down the beach to the water's edge; the waves lapped over my toes.
2 I ordered drinks for us all: a pint for Roy, a dry Martini for Heather, a whiskey for Philip, and an orange juice for myself.
3 He stared in amazement: he had never seen anything like it before.
4 He turned to go: there was no more to be said.
5 She leapt in the air for joy: she felt on top of the world.
6 The reasons for his behaviour were complex: he had never liked Stephenson, an excitable, difficult person at the best of times; he had woken up with a nagging hangover which got

worse as the day progressed; Davis had hinted that Bolton might well be favoured for the planned promotion, despite his youth and inexperience; and perhaps the most important reasons, Rosemary had told him that very morning that she planned to move in with Frank.

Exercise 3
(a) The false assumption here is that only clouds can obscure our view of the sun. It could have been night-time.
(b) A false assumption that there is a necessary connection between orphans and bad behaviour. Not all orphans are badly behaved, and people may be badly behaved without being orphans.
(c) A false connection between socialism and the USSR. Irrespective of one's political opinions, the government of the USSR may not be operating true socialism, and moreover socialism *may* be operating successfully in some *other* country.
(d) A false assumption that all Chinese people look alike. They may appear so to Europeans, who have not see many of them, but they are no more alike than any other races or nationalities.
(e) The common and false assumption that all women are bad drivers. Many *men* are bad drivers, so the conclusion drawn was not valid.

Exercise 4
1 Once the student has embarked upon the course, having confidence in his (or her) own abilities can be a problem.
2 Many of us feel inadequate, and fear that we can not hope to compete with, say, young students who have just finished their A levels.
3 For many people, studying after work all day is not the best way to achieve good results.
4 There will almost certainly be some gain for these others. For to study is to become a more alert and interesting companion; it is to become more human, because to learn is to develop; and there is ultimately perhaps an additional gain in income and prestige.
5 She was born in the East End of London between the two wars. Although she was part of a loving family, they had no luxuries, and the author describes the cold, bleak rooms they lived in as well as the pub across the way.
6 The book describes their relationships and society's rather difficult demands which they find it impossible to fulfil.
7 One problem is knowing one's own needs. Another is knowing if one's ability is great enough.

Chapter 6

Exercise 1
1 The importance of sentence construction: subject–verb–object.
2 Main and dependant or subordinate clauses.
3 The function of the paragraph.
4 The topic sentence and its development.
5 Linking paragraphs.

Exercise 2
(a) The first sentence is obviously a 'topic sentence' here. It is
     followed by two sentences which develop the topic and give
     examples of women's activity in the war which strengthened
     the suffragettes' argument. The paragraph then ends with a
     sentence which takes the basic topic one stage further.
     The next paragraph follows the same basic structure. First a
     statement (which is linked back to the preceeding sentence);
     then a sentence which gives illustrative examples; and finally
     a sentence which rounds off the argument by pointing to the
     conclusion of the process (the fight for women's suffrage).
(b) First a topic sentence – of a provocative nature. Then a
     statement containing commonplace opinions on the topic.
     Then a new apparent paradox on it.
     The next paragraph explains one half of the notion – that
     there *are* days of sunshine in Britain, but only up to the end of
     August. This is followed by a paragraph outlining the other
     half – that good weather continues longer in the Mediter-
     ranean. It then adds other reasons for the argument and
     ends on a new twist which puts the topic in another light (by
     contrasting autumnal sunshine with winter).
(c) The opening sentence here is obviously designed to set up a
     mystery (how can a politician also be a cricketer?) and to
     open the way for some nostalgic reflection. The sentences
     which follow deal playfully with a combination of remini-
     scence and the connections between cricket and Yorkshire.
     The next paragraph takes the same topic (last week's test
     match) and begins a dramatic report of it. Then it concludes
     with a partial explanation of the mystery – that is, a link back
     to the opening sentence of the first paragraph.
     The third paragraph then completes the explanation: one
     sentence to situate the fantasy, and then another giving a
     dramatic 'voice' to it.

Exercise 3
Here we offer you a student's attempt at example number 8.
The M1 was littered with wreckage. There were cars and lorries
strewn across all three lanes of the southbound carriageway, and
even one or two which had been smashed across the hard

shoulder into the banking. One small delivery van had its wheels in the air like a dead animal lying on its back. It was impossible to see what had caused the pile-up, but in the centre of all the wreckage was a huge pantechnicon lying on its side. There was broken glass everywhere. Ugly lumps of twisted and crushed metal had spun off like meteorites into the grass verge. Cars all around us were screeching to a stop, and as I heard the sound of a wailing siren approaching in the distance I realised that we were due to be trapped for some time in what would be a gigantic hold-up.

Exercise 4
1 This was a unique occasion.
2 Two girls' cycles that had been left leaning against lamp-posts were badly damaged.
3 Whether the shell of an egg is white or brown depends solely on the breed of the bird. Generally speaking, a brown hen will lay a brown egg and a white hen a white one.
4 You can order our rings by post. State size, or enclose string which has been tied round the finger.
5 She is the cleverer of the two.
6 This new pot-pourri bowl should be kept in a dark cupboard of the living room and taken out with the lid removed when the room is occupied.

Chapter 7

Exercise 1
1 Understanding the title or question.
2 Generation of ideas.
3 Preliminary essay plan.
4 Assemble sources.
5 Reading.
6 Note-making.
7 Detailed essay plan.
8 First draft.
9 Second draft.
10 Final reading.

Exercise 2
Compare your own story with this tightly planned and clearly expressed effort by former student, Heather Leach.

Heather Leach

'Television does more harm than good.' Discuss
More than ninety-five per cent of households in Britain have
television, and the majority of people under thirty-five have
never known a world without it. On the bus, in the pub, at work,
people will discuss last night's programme with enthusiasm.
Even those intellectuals who disdain to watch have a lot to say
about it. Television, it appears, cannot be ignored. It exists, and,
to borrow George Bernard Shaw's famous retort, we had better
accept it.

Accepting the reality of television is one thing, judging its impact,
harmful or beneficial, is another. Over the pasty fifty years,
television has become so pervasive a part of our society that its
particular effect on individual and cultural life can never be fully
assessed. Yet there are many who claim to perceive a decline in
educational and intellectual standards, a loss of community life,
and a deterioration of morals, all attributable, say these critics, at
least in part, to television.

There are others who point to the value of television as a liberating and educative medium, bringing culture and information to
many, as well as comfort and simple pleasure to the old and
lonely.

The examination of these attitudes can never lead us to a final
vindication or condemnation of television, but the process of
exploration may help to illuminate not only the medium itself,
but also the society it both reflects and creates.

One of the major criticisms of television is that it is damaging to
family and community life. Instead of talking to each other, it is
argued, people spend their evenings staring at a flickering screen
in semi-darkness. Instead of sharing in the life of the community,
meeting their neighbours, developing their creativity, the
majority of the population, it is said, spend their time vicariously
watching, no longer active, but passive. The image is that of the
mindless masses, lulled and quieted by the new opium.
There is no doubt that television has profoundly changed
people's leisure habits, but whether this change is for the better
or for the worse really depends on how people passed their time
before television appeared. Those who argue that television produces a cultural vacuum often conjure up the image of the family
gathered around the piano and the hearth, singing, playing and
even praying together. The paterfamilias sits in his armchair,
reading a worthy tome, the womenfolk sew and embroider, the
children pursue a quiet game of snakes and ladders on the carpet.
It becomes obvious, as we look more closely at this restful scene,
that this is a middle-class family, a literary creation, relentlessly

idealistic, and probably as far from the real experience of the majority, as the family depicted in today's television advertisements.

It was only a relatively few years before the advent of television that most people were able to do anything very much at all after darkness fell, and it is likely that the combination of long hours of labour and the lack of light, meant that the majority went to bed early, and had neither the means, nor the energy, even if they had the inclination, to engage in these worthy pursuits.

A further development of the 'cultural wasteland' thesis is that of the decline of community spirit, that most elusive of notions, dear to the hearts of inner-city sociologists. It is argued that people no longer get together in shared activity, that church attendance has been decimated, that the music hall is dead, and no one knows their neighbour. It is certainly true, that the growth of the cities and the consequent depopulation of the countryside over the last two centuries, has fundamentally changed the nature of communal life, and that this change has often caused alienation and a loss of neighbourhood and village identity. Television can surely be seen only as a product of the industrialised society, rather than a cause of all its ills. This is not to suggest that watching television for hours at a time is therefore to be applauded, but that criticisms of television as the destroyer of family and community life have doubtful value if they are based on nostalgic regrets for a nonexistent golden age. Raymond Williams has argued that this kind of thinking is based on cultural pessimism '. . . on a conviction that there is nothing but the past to be won. This is because, for other reasons, there is a determined refusal of any genuinely alternative social and cultural order.'[1]

The nostalgia for a lost and peaceful past also underpins the argument that television portrays excessive sex and violence. Many people are offended by scenes of explicit sexual activity, and it is argued that this is not only immoral and disturbing, but also that children, young people and unbalanced adults may be encouraged to experiment and at the very worst, to copy sadistic acts after seeing them on television. There have been a number of recent court cases where this defence has been used: 'I saw it on TV, m'Lud, so I thought it must be allright!' The television companies record far fewer complaints about violence on television, and yet numerous observers have pointed out that hardly an hour passes without somebody being beaten up or killed on screen. It appears that we are more frightened of sex than we are of being gunned down in the street.

Nevertheless, it is generally argued that society is more immoral and violent today than it was in the past, and that television encourages and condones this deterioration of standards. The problem with this kind of assertion is that it is impossible to prove or disprove. The great majority of people have never personally experienced a real crime of violence, yet the increase of rapid communication, particularly through television itself, can create the impression that we are all about to be raped or murdered in our beds. The more vulnerable members of society, the elderly and isolated, must always have been afraid to venture out at night, and surely the poorly-lit streets of Victorian Britain can have been no less dangerous than are most city streets today. The claim that television encourages immorality depends, of course, on which particular set of values you happen to believe in, and there is obvious conflict between those who defend chastity and the Christian marriage, and those who take a broader view.

What we are discussing here is the *content* of television rather than the particular medium. The point is that television is a far more *effective* form of communication than has ever been experienced before, but it is doubtful whether what is being communicated is any more wicked or liberating than the news-papers, the cinema, or the music halls and the penny dreadfuls of the last century.

It has been argued, however, that television may have a particularly harmful effect on children. A recent study carried out by the Institute for Social Research at Michigan University found that children aged 3–5 years spent 13 hours a week watching television, and that 11–12 year-olds spent 26 hours.[2] Many children watch without supervision and parents and child experts have expressed concern that the continuous diet of cops and robbers, etc., with accompanying fist and gun fights, is conditioning children to the idea that such behaviour is not only normal but acceptable. Indeed, if the (possibly apocryphal) story, that I heard recently, of the child, who, when told of her grandmother's death, asked, 'Who shot her?', is true, then such fears may be justified! Television has also been accused of the exploitation of women, and there has been particular anxiety over the depiction of rapes and sexual violence. These accusations have occasionally involved an interesting but uneasy alliance between the feminists and the Christian moralists. It is impossible to prove directly that television harms children, women, or indeed any of us, but what is clear is that there is a great deal of concern. What is surely needed, is to translate this concern into influence, to enable all of us to have a great deal more say in the management, quality and content of television.

Whether television as a medium is a good or a bad thing, is at this stage of the game, an irrelevant question. Television is an artefact, a tool, and like most new phenomenon, has had to take its share of criticism. The printing press, the bicycle and the steam engine have all, in their turn, been viewed with suspicion and fear before being finally accepted as facts of life.

The real issue is one of control. Television is largely in the hands of a white, male, upper and middle-class establishment, predominantly based in the capital. Local television is poorly resourced and the space given for feedback from viewers is pathetically small. It is therefore not surprising that the content and style of programmes is often far from the real needs, feelings, and aspirations of the majority of the population.

Television is undoubtedly here to stay, and the question for the future, as Raymond Williams has indicated, is that of the kind of television that we might create in a world where the media is, 'an organ of true democracy', working for the benefit and well-being of all the people.

1 Raymond Williams, *The Long Revolution*, 1961.
2 'Psychology Today', 1986.

Exercise 3
No comment applicable. Consult your tutor.

Exercise 4
1 My dog only wags its tail when it's raining.
2 The girls' bicycles were painted in their favourite colours.
3 Many days before Princess Marina's visit we practised marching for hours, trying to get each step right.
4 The groom had been married before: his was one of those marriages that never got off the ground.
5 What a marvellous selection there was: mixers, sheet sets, towel sets, pans, crockery and cutlery.
6 The apartment overlooked a quiet sandy bay, which was an ideal and peaceful setting.
7 'It's Only a Paper Moon' was my mother's favourite melody.

Chapter 8

Exercise 1
We started from the most important point regarding good style that it *must* be appropriate to both the subject and the occasion. It is no use writing in an ornate and decorative style if all you are doing is leaving a note for the milkman. Conversely, it would be

bad style to produce an academic essay which was written like a terse note or a letter to a friend. These are extremes of course, but if you keep the principle in mind it will help you generate the most appropriate tone and manner, which are the essential elements of style.

Then to illustrate this point I presented you with writing from a number of different sources. All of us are so used to different types of writing in everyday life (the terseness of a traffic sign, the persuasiveness of advertising) that we hardly notice them as examples of 'style', but this second section was offered both to alert you to the matter of style and then lead on to the question of how it is produced.

In the next stages I was trying to suggest what would be necessary for the sort of analysis required. This boils down to reading much more carefully, closely, and *actively* than you might do normally – reading with pencil in hand, and being prepared to inspect the language and grammar of a passage in detail.

It was for this reason that the next section offered you a brief reminder of the technical terms of grammar and language in general. We don't expect all students to become experts in matters of linguistic analysis, but we *do* believe that familiarity with this technical language will help sensitise you to the question of good style.

We finished with my offering 'appreciations' of good style in passages from writers justly famous for their control and use of language. This is where we strayed into the realms of literary criticism, but we did so for the deliberate purpose of 'seeing what was possible' in language skills and showing you examples of that 'language sensitivity' being applied to prose analysis.

Exercise 2

Extract A
 1 Tabloid journalism.
 2 Fairly simple vocabulary. Much use of emotive terms ('blazed', 'blitzkrieg', 'establishment').
 3 Short clauses and sentences built up to produce 'breathless' rush.
 4 Simple punctuation – but with higher-than-average use of exclamation, question mark, and contraction ('the lot of 'em').
 5 Short sentences with internal rhythms built out of matching constructions ('Boris "boom-boom" Becker' . . . 'Ivan "stone-face" Lendl').
 6 Much use of cliché ('blazed his way . . . brilliant victory . . .

grinning with delight'). Imagery drawn from the Second World War ('blazed . . . victory . . . blitzkrieg').

7 Extensive use of alliteration ('Boris "boom-boom" Becker'), repetition ('I played great, etc.') but rhetorical question ('when will . . .?').

8 The tone is slovenly and coy.

9 It sets out to inform and entertain.

10 It gives very little information and is composed entirely of tabloid journalese – that is, writing composed at a low imaginative level. However, since almost all tabloid journalism is very deliberately written in this manner (and since such newspapers sell millions of copies), it *could* be argued that it achieves the objectives it sets itself.

Extract B

1 It seems to be a government or company regulation.

2 Much use of the terms of officialdom ('Personnel . . . department . . . statutory allowance').

3 Long list of clauses strung together (without punctuation) to form presumably unambiguous legal ruling.

4 No punctuation within sentences. Complex and 'hidden' syntax which makes normal comprehension difficult.

5 One very long sentence followed by one very short. No evidence of any attempt at variety for the reader's benefit.

6 No imagery or figures of speech at all.

7 No use of any literary devices.

8 Tone is purely neutral or factual.

9 It sets out to record the details of a regulation.

10 'Quality' in writing like this is purely a matter of being factually correct. No attempt is made at any literary value – though we can observe that any normal human being would find writing like this extremely difficult to understand.

Extract C

1 Poetry.

2 Wide range of sources. The practical world ('barge . . . poop sails') classical reference ('Venus . . . Cupid') and 'literary' ('amorous . . . person . . . nature').

3 A mixture of short and long phrases in rather complex relation to each other.

4 Punctuation is conventional. Syntax complex because of the use of so many literary devices.

5 The rhythm is that of black verse – that is, iambic pentameter or five stresses to the line.

6 Dense use of imagery ('like a burnish'd throne') original coinings coupled with classical reference ('O'erpicturing that Venus').

7 Dense use of literary devices. Elision ('Purple the sails'),

assonance ('the tune of flutes'), noun-used-as-verb ('glow'), syntactical displacement coupled with paradox ('what they undid did').

8 The tone is serious, poetic, and sensuous.

9 The intention of the speech is to dramatise Cleopatra's appearance, and of the poetry itself to entertain, intellectually stimulate, and to edify.

10 It seems to do all those things successfully – though we should say that for the average reader quite a lot of work or practice in reading Shakespeare will probably be necessary to fully appreciate writing like this.

Extract D

1 Prose fiction.

2 A mixture. Many proper nouns ('London'/'Lord Chancellor'/'Megalosaurus'/'Holborn'); the vocabulary of law ('Michaelmas term'/'Lincoln's Inn Hall') of the urban world ('streets'/'chimney pots'/'umbrellas'/'street-corners') and the animal world ('Elephantine lizard'/'dogs'/'horses'/'foot passengers').

3 From simple to complex – but general tendency towards the long string of subordinate clauses.

4 Punctuation conventional. Syntax less so – with some sentences grammatically 'incomplete' (the first three).

5 Extreme variety in length – from one to forty-three. No regular rhythms.

6 Very rich in imagery (the Megalosaurus on a primeval Holborn Hill, the soot like snowflakes in mourning). Drawn from the world of nature and (in the last sentence) the world of finance.

7 Occasional alliteration ('elephantine lizard up Holborn Hill') and puns (mud 'deposits . . . accumulating at compound interest').

8 The tone is both witty and serious.

9 To entertain, edify, amuse, and to dramatise a murky and muddy day.

10 This is imaginative fiction generally considered to be of the highest quality.

Exercise 3

1 It seems to be socially acceptable now to obtain a divorce. Perhaps couples do not work hard enough at repairing breakdowns in their relationships.

2 Various ethnic and religious groups also view divorce and how the home is affected in different lights.

3 People should have a responsible attitude towards marriage, and this should be mirrored in their attempts to seek solutions to problems which arise from it to affect the home.

4 Situations develop to hurt and upset the children of divorced parents which neither they nor the parent left to cope can prevent. There may be questions from other children at school, for instance – a situation in which everyone else except them has two parents – just everyday little things which never let them forget that they are different.

5 However, two people do not usually become entirely dis-enchanted with each other at the same time, and an over-hasty decision can lead to a long period of regret. This may be both for the one who is left, or the other who cannot rebuild their life because of the residue of misery left behind.

6 Marriage, although not taken quite so seriously today, is still widely accepted as the social norm. But attitudes to divorce have become much more relaxed in the modern world.

Exercise 4
Comment not applicable. Consult your tutor.

Chapter 9

Exercise 1
1 The reasons why we have examinations in our educational system and some of the arguments used against this form of assessment.
2 The different kinds of examinations you may be faced with during your years as a student.
3 The need to think about examinations as an integral part of your course and the need to make examination preparation a normal ongoing aspect of your day-to-day study.
4 The need for a special revision regime in the period immediately prior to the examination and some of the disciplines and techniques you may find helpful during this period.
5 How to handle the examination itself and bring to fruition all the hard work you have put into your course.

Exercise 2
1 *Major errors*
(a) The title has been copied out incorrectly.
(b) There is no proper introduction which either
       – places the question in context
       – discusses the question.
(c) There is far too much slipshod and biased thinking.
(d) Too many unsupported generalisations.
(e) Too much irrelevant material.
(f) The question is not being answered.
(g) There is no sign of any clear structure.

2 Minor (but important) errors

(a) The first sentence immediately abbreviates the question and offers a very feeble response.

(b) The second poses a rhetorical question – instead of answering the one set.

(c) It goes on to make a link between trade unions and the Japanese and Germans which is not at all clear.

(d) The next sentence begins with a cliché whose tone is quite inapropriate.

(e) It slides into bad grammar: 'introducing' should be 'to introduce' and 'the competitors' should be 'the competition'.

(f) The next sentence is grammatically incomplete: it has no active verb.

(g) The next sentence links trade unions and Marxism without saying why.

(h) The next sentence offers a *non sequitur* by making an irrelevant link between trade unions and Stalin.

(i) The next paragraph begins with another cliché, and it is not clear who 'their' refers to.

(j) The next sentence does not have a question mark.

(k) 'Ends' should be 'demise'.

(l) The last sentence assumes that cars and 'fast food' are 'advantages'.

Exercise 3
What follows is a much better example of how the early stages of an answer to this question were handled:

'The New Technology will transform society more radically than any set of political ideas.' Discuss.

If correct this statement has a depressing message for politicians all over the world. In essence it argues that the impact of the New Technology (NT) – computers, robot factories, advanced information technology – will be more far reaching than changes caused by political ideas. To answer this question it will be necessary to identify and assess the social changes which NT will cause – I propose to focus on the structure and location of employment, education and forms of communication – and compare them with the potential for change contained within certain well known political creeds.
But before addressing these matters it is necessary to explain the different ways in which these two agents of change operate. There are an infinite variety of political ideas – communism, socialism, anarchism, conservatism, fascism – which are constantly seeking to influence or control societies. In dictatorships there is one official set of beliefs and usually several rivals operating underground. In democracies there is much more of a 'free

market' in ideas, all jostling for support. It usually takes decades for a system of ideas to develop and become implemented. For example, socialism in Britain began as a collection of contrasting (and competing) ideas in the nineteenth century; the Labour Party was set up in 1900 and won majority power in 1945.

Technology, however, operates in a more subtle but no less dramatic way. The advance of science and the invention of new products and processes are all relatively unpolitical: they proceed on a day to day basis – but over time their impact on our lives can be immense.

The 'Old Technology' transformed northern towns in Britain within three or four decades. Since then, over similar timescales, developments in production techniques have made and ruined individuals, classes of people and whole regions. The New Technology has telescoped this timescale so that 'revolutions' can occur within a decade, a few years or even months . . .

Exercise 4
1 Make every sentence relevant to a *direct answer* to the question.
2 Offer a clear, straightforward *structure*.
3 Write in a clear, readable, grammatically correct *style*.
4 Support all your major points of argument with *evidence*.
5 Provide evidence of *clear thinking*.
6 Show that you are familiar with the *literature* of the subject.
7 Strive for legible *presentation*.

Exercise 5
No comment applicable. Consult your tutor.

Notes for tutors and organisers 9

Organising distance learning courses

These notes are intended to assist tutors and organisers setting up distance learning courses. They are based upon the author's experience in running such courses from the Extra-Mural Department of Manchester University but we would never claim that we have mastered all the difficulties involved. However, for those relatively new to the field of open and distance learning these notes might prove useful.

Marketing the course
Where is the potential market for a distance learning course? Most educational institution mailing lists comprise past students

on conventional courses but whilst publicity for a distance learn-ing course might attract some enrolments from such a mailing list, clearly more precise targeting is required. The kind of people who are likely to be interested in such a course are: people living a considerable distance away from your institution; people in work who cannot manage to attend day and evening courses; house-wives with heavy family commitments; disabled people who cannot travel easily; and people (a small minority) who prefer to study on their own rather than in groups. How can one direct one's publicity to reach such target groups?

(a) Door-to-door mailing, which many adult education institu-tions undertake, can be useful here, but such distributions are normally local in character and the potential distance learning student beyond the locality is thereby lost.

(b) Organisational routes might prove fruitful, e.g. organisa-tions helping the disabled, the National Women's Register, etc. Often these organisations are unwilling to issue mailing lists and one may have to offer inserts into newsletters and other circulars and pay a fee.

(c) Feature articles in the local press can arouse interest but these are usually only possible on a 'one-off' basis – the goodwill of editors cannot be extended indefinitely.

(d) Special leaflets distributed around public places like libra-ries, dentists' waiting rooms, etc. Experience suggests that this is an expensive approach; publicity on Manchester EMD's pilot course was widely distributed to libraries and the enquiries stimulated were almost negligible.

(e) Selected advertisements in the local press. Small 'box' adverts are one approach; short inserts in the personal columns provide another. Of all the advertising approaches suggested these are probably the most effective. Especially productive for us was the small featured advert in the *Man-chester Evening News's* Education page. This produced fifty or sixty responses and several eventual enrolments.

It is important to respond to enquiries with some further informa-tion which explains the nature of the course, gives samples of study materials, etc. Time also has to be allocated for advising and counselling members of the public on the telephone.

Running a distance learning course
The main advantages of distance learning are its flexibility and potential for individual study. Its principle disadvantage is the isolation of the student and the consequent erosion of morale which takes place. Most of the available evidence from the Open University and from foreign experience suggests that the most effective distance learning courses are those which are supple-mented by regular seminars and reinforcing counselling ses-sions. Our experience thoroughly reinforces the latter view.

Evaluation reports at the end of the course revealed that the Saturday meetings had helped to put the materials into a proper perspective and to reinforce motivation substantially.

The pilot course was offered as a 20-Unit Distance Learning Course to be studied over approximately six months. Our experience suggests that this is too 'indigestible' an amount to take at one time. Consequently, we decided to divide the course into two modules, each comprising ten units – hence the two volumes in the present format. Below is a possible blurb for a distance learning version of *Making the grade.*

Making the grade: a distance learning course for adults
This course will prove particularly attractive for people who either prefer to study on their own or who, through circumstances (e.g. work or family commitments) find it impracticable to study on orthodox courses.

Most of the studying will be done at home by students in regular telephone and postal contact with their tutor at the university or college centre. Assignments will be completed and mailed to tutors who will then mark them and return them with comments. Students will be able to fit in their study hours when most convenient for them.

In addition there will be a series of Saturday meetings throughout the year in which course members can meet fellow students and practice specific study skills. There will also be an optional examination which course members can take at the end of their studies.

The course is divided into two modules.

Making the grade I: listening and learning
The first module comprises: Introduction to the course, 1. Being an adult student. 2 Organising and planning your time. 3. Concentration and memory. 4. Studying in groups. 5 Verbal communication. 6. Efficient reading. 7. Making good notes. 8. Generating ideas. 9. What makes a good essay?

This module comprises 50–80 hours' study time and should take 2½ months to complete (assuming average study time).
Making the grade II: Thinking and writing
The second module comprises chapters on: 1. Understanding the question. 2. Planning essays – I for and against. 3. Planning essays II. 4. Thinking clearly. 5. Sentences and paragraphs. 6. Grammar and punctuation. 7. Appreciation of written style. 8. Writing essays from A–Z. 9. Examinations. 10. Taking stock

and opportunities for further study.

This module is more advanced, represents 80–120 hours of study and should take 3½ months to complete.

This course can be studied in two ways:

Method I entails joining the course before the first Saturday meeting. This enables students to study more as a group throughout the courses.

Method II enables anyone to start the course at any time and to complete it when they choose.

The course requires no other books or equipment and represents a saving in normal travel costs.

It will be observed that the course is offered in two basic forms: Method I and Method II. Method I involves a common starting point and specified Saturday meetings. People enrolling for Method I therefore join a group and proceeed through the course together. Method II, on the other hand, is a 'roll on, roll off' approach; it is more flexible and suited to independent study but it does not provide the stimulation and morale reinforcement of Method I. However, it is always possible to organise occasional or even regular personal tutorials for Method II students: this will clearly be a function of staff resources and financial parameters in most cases. Below some notes are offered on various aspects of running a distance learning course.

Meetings
At these meetings a number of activities can be undertaken.
(a) *Introductions.* Experience suggests that the best way of approaching this is to divide the group into twos and invite them to interview each other – say five minutes for each interview. Everyone is then asked to introduce not themselves but the person they have interviewed. This usually works as a useful ice-breaker and produces much interesting biographical information.
(b) *Social Integration Exercises.* There are a number of useful activities here which can be undertaken, e.g., 'problem-exchanging'. The group is asked to divide again into twos and to rank in order of importance the five major problems facing adult students. The group is then merged into groups of four and asked to agree a reduced list of three major problems. The process helps to stimulate discussion and integration whilst also ventilating common problems. The emphasis of study day meetings should always be upon

participation and verbal expression rather than written exercises – although the latter should not be excluded entirely as most study days require a quieter reflective period.

(c) *Practice in study skills*. In this respect the Saturday meetings resemble any study skills or return to study course. Skills like effective reading, note-taking, essay-planning, generation of ideas, verbal expression and so forth need to be practiced and discussed. Clearly the skills chosen for practice need to relate approximately to the chapter recently studied or about to be studied.

(d) *Verbal expression*. Special emphasis needs to be given to verbal expression as, obviously, it does not feature to any great extent in independent learning. A common feature of the Manchester Saturday study days was a final 30-minute 'open forum' in which a topic was chosen for general discussion and debate. This part of the day never failed to go well.

Counselling

This can take place in a number of ways.

(a) *In advance of the course;* students may require advice either on the telephone or in person.

(b) *During the course by telephone*. This can be a problem for many adult education institutions as few wish to provide 'open-ended' telephone counselling services. In Manchester we invited students to ring up tutors during specified times at their own expense. In practice such counselling was minimal – when pressed students did not blame the expense of telephone but the feeling that such telephone calls would 'disturb the tutor unnecessarily'. Clearly, many adult students feel something of a mental block on this subject.

(c) *Towards the end of the course*. As the course begins to approach the end students require personal feedback as to how they have progressed and some more detailed advice as to future opportunities. Chapter 10, Volume II is addressed to this topic but further discussion and explanation is required by many adult students.

Attempts were made in Manchester to encourage 'self-help' groups. All students were given lists of everyone's address and telephone number and they were encouraged to make contact, organise discussion groups or to work through units collectively. In practice, a fair amount of telephone contact took place but no regular self-help meetings. OU experience suggests that such organisation has to be stimulated by tutors for it to be successful.

Assignments

As you have seen, *Making the Grade* begins very straightforwardly with 'free writing' biographical assignments, but moves rapidly into more demanding analytical pieces of work. The guidance notes sections at the end of each volume provide considerable help but many assignments have been set on the assumption that distance-learning tutors will provide the necessary assessment. Below are a few (fairly obvious) guidelines on marking.

1 Adopt encouraging tone: *always* find positive elements even in poor work.
2 Try to criticise constructively by advising 'more effort on designing a clear structure', or whatever. Avoid listing shortcomings in early assignments.
3 Avoid sarcasm, vagueness, sharpness.
4 Correct grammar – spelling, punctuation, syntax – but don't be too pedantic or expect every infinitive not to be split!
5 Question unclear thinking; indicate where argument goes astray; correct misconceptions.

The aim throughout is to be positive, to perceive something good in every piece of work and to offer criticism only indirectly through suggesting how work could be further improved. This point is obvious to any experienced return to study tutor but it certainly needs to be emphasised. One of the basic fears of adults is that they are going to be found wanting and criticised by their tutor – perhaps in the way they were criticised by teachers in school. All our students have commented warmly on the value of constructive criticism they recieved throughout the distance-learning courses run.

Examination and certification

At the end of our courses a Saturday meeting was usually devoted to examinations. The morning dealt with revision and examination technique whilst the afternoon comprised a 2¼-hour general paper. Scripts were marked and grades given as follows:

A— Well-organised, competent work with some flashes of insight. Well up to an undergraduate standard.

B – Competent work, expression clear, answers question effectively. Indicates that student is able to cope with undergraduate work.

C – Basically competent work but with flaws in relation to answering the question, clarity and fluency of expression, structure.

D – Basic ability to answer questions and organise information but development needed in terms of: answering the question, structure, grammar, clarity of expression.

E – Ability on or below GCE O level. Progress required on all aspects of study skills.

F – Work not yet up to O-level pass mark.

Gone are the days when adult students study only for the love of it. An increasing percentage require certificate or evidence that they have studied and submitted work to a required standard. At Manchester an overall grade is offered for performance in course assignments and a grade given for the examination as well as a certificate of completion.

Finance
At Manchester concessions are given for those likely to encounter difficulty in paying the full fee. In practice, some 20% of the fee goes on course materials, 40% on marking, 10–15% on marketing, and 25–30% on administration. Distance learning courses are not cheap to run – in fact they probably work out as marginally more expensive than conventional courses as the tutor/student ratio tends to be quite low. Institutions will need to consider their own resources and pricing policies when setting a course fee.

Administration
Another factor making distance learning courses relatively expensive is the higher than usual administrative requirements. It is essential for one competent person to be in charge of the administration. In Manchester this task was ably performed by one of our best secretaries. She undertook most of the marketing, correspondence to students, handled enrolments, mailed units to students, did all the typing and had a great deal of telephone contact with course participants. In one sense, this kind of distance learning course is as good as its course administrator.

The tutorial staff for a *Making the grade* distance learning course needs to be committed and aware of the requirements of distance learning. The skills required are relatively easy to pick up but experience in the field is obviously a useful advantage. A student load of 15 per tutor in practice is not too onerous. Some students produce very little by way of assignment work whilst others send in reams and reams of material to be marked.

If you require any further advice on any aspect of the package, wish to comment upon its efficacy or make suggested improvements, please contact either of the authors:

Dr Bill Jones
Director, Department of
    Extra-Mural Studies
University of Manchester
Manchester M13 9PL
(Tel: 061-275 3282)

Dr Roy Johnson
Workers' Educational
    Association
Crawford House
University Precinct
Manchester M13 9GH
(Tel: 061-273 7652)

Index